HITCHCOCK
AND TWENTIETH-CENTURY CINEMA

HITCHCOCK
AND TWENTIETH-CENTURY CINEMA

John Orr

 WALLFLOWER PRESS LONDON & NEW YORK

First published in Great Britain in 2005 by
Wallflower Press
6a Middleton Place, Langham Street, London W1W 7TE
www.wallflowerpress.co.uk

A catalogue for this book is available from the British Library.

ISBN 1-904764-55-X (pbk)
ISBN 1-904764-56-8 (hbk)

Book design by Elsa Mathern

Cover images:
Nosferatu, eine Symphonie des Grauens (1922)
L'amour a vingt ans (1962)
Repulsion (1965)
Blue Velvet (1986)

Printed in Great Britain by Antony Rowe Ltd, Chippenham, Wiltshire

CONTENTS

PREFACE

This is, I hope, a new way of looking at Alfred Hitchcock. Rather than ransacking his films or his life yet again, this book tries to place him as a matrix-figure in the great forward surge of twentieth-century cinema. Hitchcock today is a global figure from a time still close to us in its texture and its sensibility. He remains a living presence and many directors are still under his spell. Among all great film artists he was one of the most prolific and also one of the most commercially successful. His box-office appeal has never been in doubt. Like many great directors he has a talent for making film a medium of the senses that also engages our understanding of the world: he makes us watch, feel and think at the same time. In our response to his greatest pictures these three processes are all intertwined. They are, in fact, inseparable. Writing this book has not only been a pleasure, but also a privilege – a privilege of witnessing (and re-witnessing) in the live medium of the moving image the creative force of one of cinema's true greats.

I would like to offer a special thanks to Martine Beugnet and Duncan Petrie for their encouragement and their invaluable response to this project, and to my publisher, Yoram Allon, for his friendly, informed cooperation.

John Orr
Edinburgh
September 2005

chapter 1

HITCH AS MATRIX-FIGURE: HITCHCOCK AND TWENTIETH-CENTURY CINEMA

This book is being written adjacent to a framed Hitchcock image that hangs at a right angle to the desktop, on the far wall of the room. His thriller set in a Manhattan apartment, *Rope* (1948), inspires the image. It displays a coiled rope, double-knotted, looping down level with a diagonal fold in a scarlet curtain. Suspended between the two knots is another loop in the centre of the frame that looks like a hangman's noose. It is not a specific image from the film but an image keyed in by the strangulation that begins it so shockingly; an image conveying the feel and menace of the Hitchcock narrative, not only in this film but also throughout his long career. It signifies, at the very least, killing and retribution, crime and punishment, guilt and judgement. Yet the image is no abstract signifier: it is concrete and immediate as Hitchcock's images are. It sends a direct signal to the senses. Hitchcock once said that his films were intended to create goose bumps on the neck of the spectator. Glancing across at this image is a clear and present reminder of his intent.

The motif is a screen print by Sam Ainslie, who displayed it in an exhibition at the Glasgow Print Studio in Autumn 2003 called simply *HITCH*. Other Scottish artists, among them Steven Campbell, Peter Howson, Ray Richardson and Adrian Wiszniewski also created images triggered by other famous films: *Spellbound* (1945), *Strangers on a Train* (1951), *Vertigo* (1958), *North by Northwest* (1959), *Psycho* (1960), *The Birds* (1963), *Torn Curtain* (1966). The media varied, from screen and digital print to photopolymer and oil or acrylic on canvas. All were images that departed from the photographic still, as signs of Hitchcock's cinema taken over into other visual forms. Yet this translation is testament to the enduring power of his moving images. There are few film directors in the world, past or present, who could prompt such a testament. And this exhibition, modest in scale but marvellous in execution, is only one indication of what can be done. It was not the first nor will it be the last 'translation' of Hitchcock out of cinema. Hitch has been inspiration to a number of multi-media and installation events, the best known perhaps being Douglas Gordon's *24-Hour Psycho* at the London Hayward Exhibition *Spellbound* in 1996, which slowed Hitchcock's film down to a speed of two frames per second (see Mulvey 2000). Three years later the

MOMA Oxford Exhibition with contributions from filmmakers and other visual artists marked the Hitchcock centenary in the UK. Not to be outdone, a Francophone exhibition premiered in Montreal in 2000 was then displayed at the Pompidou Centre in Paris, with Hitchcock film excerpts, storyboards and publicity stills set alongside work from many great visual artists of the twentieth century.

Legacies

If he is transferable in this way across visual forms, Hitchcock is more trans-ferable *within* the form where homage and pastiche abound. This periodic transfer started in a big way while he was still alive, no more so than in the French New Wave where François Truffaut, who wrote on Hitchcock and did a series of famous interviews with him, also made a quartet of homage films – *Fahrenheit 451* (1966), *The Bride Wore Black* (1967), *Mississippi Mermaid* (1969) and *Finally Sunday!* (1983). The authors of the best Hitchcock study ever, Eric Rohmer and Claude Chabrol, went on to use his themes and motifs just as closely in their own films. As if to announce future intent, Chabrol had early on paid mock homage to Hitchcock (who of course tried to appear in each of his pictures), by advertising his book on Hitchcock in his 1959 film, *Les Cousins*; the sad provincial hero (Gérard Blain) can be seen at one point in a bookshop browsing a copy of the Rohmer-Chabrol tribute! Elsewhere in Paris documentary filmmaker Chris Marker who worked mostly on social and political themes, paid a succinct double-homage to *Vertigo*, first with the memory-haunting sequences of his short film *La Jetée* (1962) and then twenty years later with the San Francisco sequence of the *Vertigo* tour in his compelling documentary *Sans Soleil* (1985).

But Hitchcock made an even stronger impact on the future of box-office cinema. The creation of the James Bond series in the 1960s, for example, was only made possible by the dynamism and drive of his earlier spy thrillers from *The 39 Steps* (1935) right through to *North by Northwest*, the immediate inspiration. American directors also paid their respects. In 1958 Stanley Donen reunited Cary Grant and Ingrid Bergman for *Indiscreet*, a film that echoed their dazzling roles in Hitchcock's *Notorious* (1946), and followed it in 1963 with *Charade* with Grant playing opposite Audrey Hepburn in clear echoes of *To Catch a Thief* (1955). At the start of the 1960s *Psycho* reinvigorated the Hollywood horror genre and cleared the way for the 1970s sensation narratives of Brian De Palma, George A. Romero and John Carpenter. In terms of its attention to place and detail and its powers of horror, it found a much worthier successor in William Friedkin's Washington-based fable, *The Exorcist* (1973). Meanwhile *The Birds* was a key source for many spectacle-disaster movies premised on special effects that lit up Hollywood in the late 1970s and have been big box-office ever since. Filmed on location in San Francisco *Vertigo*, Hitchcock's great study of erotic obsession, became the unwitting Ur-text for wilder things in the work of Brian De Palma: in his lurid incest drama *Obsession* (1976) and his pseudo-erotic shocker *Body Double* (1984), which also cannibalised *Rear Window* (1954). It also surfaces through the dubious homage of Paul Verhoeven's bombastic, soft-core *Basic Instinct* (1992), sadly box-office gold and also filmed on San Francisco locations. More San Francisco homage duly came from other glossy pictures, the smart suspenseful *Jagged Edge* (1987) with Glenn Close and Jeff Bridges reprising the roles (with genders reversed) of defence lawyer and defendant in *The Paradine Case* (1947), and soon after the nonsensical *Final Analysis* (1992) with Richard Gere and Kim Basinger.

After Hitchcock's death in 1980 we might have expected his work to become unfashionable and fade away. But since then, as we have seen, the impact has intensified. Hollywood, in effect, has commodified his memory and homage has become obsessive. There were two sequels to *Psycho*, the first with Anthony Perkins in a 1983 reprise of his role as Norman Bates, the second in 1986 where Perkins was not only Bates again but also directed and shot at the start a strange homage to the bell-tower scene that ends *Vertigo*. As if not to be outdone, there has been a 1999 remake of the original *Psycho* by Gus Van Sant that copies it with some key variations but also films it, inexplicably, in colour. (It could be argued that Van Sant's real attempt to recapture the sheer horror of the Hitchcock film comes in his 2003 meditation on the Columbine High School massacre, *Elephant*.) Earlier *Psycho*'s horror lineage had spread into the 1960s renaissance of European cinema with powerful repercussions. Its narrative momentum seems essential to Roman Polanski's South Kensington chamber-drama *Repulsion* (1965) filmed just five years later. Elsewhere, its Gothic reanimation of the dead Mother whose skull is super-imposed on the face of the hapless Norman sitting in his prison cell, has been seen as a source of the identity-superimpositions in Ingmar Bergman's more abstract and enigmatic *Persona* (1966) (see Ness 2003: 181–2). We could also make the case that Bergman's late German psychodrama *From the Life of the Marionettes* (1980), with its deranged businessman who murders a prostitute whom he mistakes for his hated spouse, is a key link between the Hitchcock classic and David Lynch's disturbing, psychogenic *Lost Highway* (1996).

Elsewhere Canadian directors who generally cast a quizzical Northern eye over the genre habits of their American neighbours have produced ingenious variations. Set in Toronto, David Cronenberg's car fetish film *Crash* (1996), with its destructive pairing of Eros and technology, is one of the most powerful renderings of North American apocalypse since *The Birds*. In Francophone Canada *Le Confessionnal* (1995) by Robert Lepage exposes as false the division between homage and originality. His film was not only a conscious sequel to the Québec thriller *I Confess* (1952) but alternates dramatically between then and now (1989) in its time-sequence to intimate much darker secrets than the ones Hitchcock had uncovered. Daringly, it also integrates shots from the Hitchcock original with an invented story around the making of the film in which Hitchcock is treated as a fictional character. Not to be outdone, his fellow Canadian Atom Egoyan, strongly influenced by Hitchcock in his memory films *Exotica* (1994) and *The Sweet Hereafter* (1997), then adapted a Jack Trevor story of an Irish girl in Birmingham, *Felicia's Journey* (1999), where he has a stout reclusive killer from a past age called Hilditch (Bob Hoskins), smother-loved as a child by his mother and reared on her strange cooking lessons, a figure who seems a slyly affectionate portrait of a gastronomic Hitchcock transformed into one of his own villains. In Egoyan's perverse equation Hilditch, we might speculate, equals Hitch.

Meanwhile back in Hollywood the third screen remake of John Buchan's *The Thirty-Nine Steps* is currently slated for production with Robert Towne directing (the first, of course, being Hitchcock's 1935 adaptation). Of course there had been an unofficial one in 1990 by the talented Australian, Peter Weir. Weir had used the handcuff motif of Hitchcock's film – where the fugitive couple are literally stuck with one another – as metaphoric inspiration for *Green Card* (1990), a smart romantic comedy about a furtive French migrant and his American 'wife' in New York trapped by their planned marriage of convenience. Subsequently Weir culled the major themes of fear and trauma from *Spellbound* and *Vertigo* to make his haunting story of a plane crash survivor (Jeff Bridges) in *Fearless* (1993) again with homage sequences in San Francisco using special effects. Another haunting reprise came in 1988 with Roman Polanski's *Frantic*, where American doctor (Harrison Ford), speaking no French, arrives with his wife (Betty Buckley) at dawn in an eerie unsettling Paris for a conference-cum-holiday. He enjoys neither as his wife disappears as soon as they have unpacked in their hotel. The sudden kidnapping with its political agenda echoes Hitchcock's colour remake of his *The Man Who Knew Too Much* (1956) with like family kidnapping and like American doctor, James Stewart this time, in Marrakech. Ford's tenacious paranoia and key perception-lapses mirror those of his famous predecessor though Polanski of course has his own ingenious variations. At the cruder end of the market, Andrew Davis, who made his blockbuster *The Fugitive* (1993) by hyping up all the elements of the Hitchcock chase into manic proportions for (again) Harrison Ford, then went on to remake *Dial 'M' for Murder* (1950) by changing the title to *A Perfect Murder* (1998), changing locations from London to New York and casting Gwyneth Paltrow as a dead ringer for Grace Kelly. If anything the film shows us just how much Paltrow and Michael Douglas pale by comparison with Kelly and Ray Milland in the original.

Not to be outdone, the French have come up with more subtle variations. Veteran Eric Rohmer's *L'Anglaise et le Duc* (*The Lady & the Duke*, 2001), based on a Scottish noblewoman's diary of danger in the French Revolution, strongly echoes Hitchcock's only major costume film, the star vehicle for Ingrid Bergman, *Under Capricorn* (1949), set in nineteenth-century Australia and shot in a London studio. As if to pay homage to that artifice Rohmer, the great realist, changes tack and gives us a studio movie for the digital age with painted scenery and computer-generated images. In 1998, Nicole Garcia's ambitious *Place Vendôme* updates the Hitchcock thriller to the shadowy world of European diamond merchants, and also remakes *Vertigo* in Paris by focussing on the female figures of Hitchcock's plot, reworking in French terms an imaginary rivalry between a real Madeleine Elster (whom we see in *Vertigo* only as a corpse) and her young rival-imitator, Judy Barton (Kim Novak). On one reading Garcia's film, recycling Bernard Herrmann's *Vertigo* music for its vertiginous sequences, is a conscious reversal of Hitchcock's tragic ending, a fable of female redemption in which Marianne (Catherine Deneuve) rescues both herself and her young impostor, Nathalie (Emmanuelle Seigner) from a double betrayal (see Kline 2003: 36–9). We add another reference point. The substance of Deneuve's central performance as an abject, betrayed alcoholic who finds renewed hope, seems to owe much to the commanding figure of Bergman in *Under Capricorn* and *Notorious*, who of course had found similar redemption in impossible circumstance. Finally Gilles Mimouni's elegant thriller *L'Appartement* (1997) pays simultaneous homage to Hitchcock *and* Truffaut by subjecting Hitchcock's doubling and voyeur motifs, and his *mise-en-scène*, to hyperactive Truffaut-like camerawork. The dazzling result is an eclectic style-mix that crosses *Rear Window* and *Vertigo* with Truffaut's *La Peau douce* (1964).

Other names and titles could be added to the list at the turn of the century. In East Asia, we could cite Chinese filmmakers like Wong Kar-Wai, who used *Notorious* as a model for his poetic memory film *In the Mood for Love* (2000), or Lou Ye, who made *Suzhou River* in the same year and set it in contemporary Shanghai as a conscious homage to *Vertigo*. An even stronger link can be found in the disturbing Japanese shocker, Takashi Miike's *Audition* (2000), which integrates elements of *Psycho* and *Vertigo* with aspects of the Japanese ghost narrative perfected by Kenji Mizoguchi's classic *Ugetsu Monogatari* (1953). A composed table of pure terror, Takashi's film shows us a film producer obsessed with auditioning an unknown for a new film at the same time as for the role of his new wife. The chosen one – slim, beautiful, modest, deferential and dressed in virginal all-white – is not, however, what she seems. As the object of the producer's constant obsession she echoes the role of Madeleine Elster in *Vertigo*, a contemporary Japanese version of a beautiful ghost. Yet the climactic violence comes from a different Hitchcock tradition. True, it has its portents early in the film but when it erupts it is still as shocking, as unexpected, as psychically disturbing as the killings in *Psycho*. In both his late films Hitchcock plays in different ways on the elusive relationship of appearance and reality and Takashi's film blends their legacy with a chilling composure.

The salient point here is not the formation of any one Hitchcock school of filmmaking, but the enduring power of his themes and images everywhere. At the turn of the century Hitchcock is ubiquitous. As we shall see, the 1990s revival of film noir, or neo-noir, could well be called post-Hitchcock noir, a crossover genre that blends noir and Hitchcock motifs that in the 1940s had stood in opposition to one another. In Joel and Ethan Coen's black-and-white pastiche movie *The Man Who Wasn't There* (2001), set in post-war California, noir themes of adultery and murder echoing Billy Wilder's classic *Double Indemnity* (1944) are shot on location in Santa Rosa, the small town north of San Francisco that had been the famous site of Hitchcock's *Shadow of a Doubt* (1943). And Hitchcock's film had in turn been an inspiration to the location shooting in Californian Noir used from 1944 onwards by Wilder, Robert Siodmak and Otto Preminger. Preminger's cynical smalltown melodrama, *Fallen Angel* (1945), is a prime and triumphant case in point.

We can see here, witnessing this immense overload, that Hitchcock's legacy has become a mixed blessing. There have been many inspirational movies, and many new directions fired up by his supreme example. On the other hand, homage often shades into imitation or pastiche into repetition, both a temptation for directors to bump up their credentials when they are seeking an easy way out. There is always the thrill of mystery at the centre of Hitchcock's work and the lure in a less censored age governed by speed and information of opening out the Hitchcock narrative, making it faster and more explicit, stepping up the suspense, cranking up the violence, but equally junking the well-made story, the articulate dialogue, the nuances of editing, the formalisms of *mise-en-scène*. Generally the effect is the opposite of what is intended. What shows through instead with this contagion of imitation is a time-illusion of 'progressive cinema', of moving things one stage on for a new age and a new generation, an illusion of progress that masks a compulsion to repeat, a compulsion indeed that is often threadbare, an easy addiction in which 'inspiration' is too easily an excuse for lacking vision. As opposed to the illusion of the step forward, however, there lies perspicacity in the shift sideward, the incorporation of Hitchcock into a strong existing auteurist vision. Notable here is a sharing of key qualities, the use of the camera to replicate fundamentals of human vision in the exploration of cinematic space and of narrative to replicate fundamental rhythms of everyday life; the attention to detail in *mise-en-scène*, and respect for the power of the spoken word as well as the image. It is out of these qualities that the essential Hitchcock elements of the extra-ordinary flow – mystery, memory, suspense, ambivalence, terror.

In this respect we can note a precise *translation of vision* among some directors who take Hitchcock in their own direction. Several figures stand out: Chabrol, Rohmer, Resnais, Polanski, Lynch and Weir. They are all successors to him precisely because they are all *unlike* him. That is to say, they absorb him into the world of their *own* vision, because they all have a starting point that is independent of his. At a glance, therefore, we can easily compare Hitchcock's films to theirs. Yet once we have made surface comparisons, we will soon find depth and complexity to keep us guessing. For, critically speaking, we are always in parallel worlds. The same sensation occurs when taking Hitchcock *backward*. Rolling back in time, he had a big legacy to inherit and would have been nothing without it, a legacy unusual for an Anglo-American director of his time that sprang from his early cinephile enthusiasms in 1920s London. It was indeed varied: the surrealist impulse of Luis Buñuel and Salvador Dalí countered by the montage aesthetics of Lev Kuleshov and Sergei Eisenstein, and then the key inheritance of Weimar cinema, especially the work of Friedrich Wilhelm Murnau and Fritz Lang, that lasted throughout his professional life. Surrealism, Soviet montage, expressionism: great moments of early modernism and all blended seamlessly into the Hitchcock oeuvre.

At the same time his contemporaries have always loomed large. It is easy to imagine Hitchcock and Buñuel looking closely at each other's films throughout their dazzling careers and then duly taking note. Truffaut has pointed to *Shadow of a Doubt* as inspiration for Buñuel's Mexican murder drama *The Criminal Life of Archibaldo de la Cruz* (1955) (Truffaut 1994: 266). Towards the end of his career Hitchcock professed great admiration for *Tristana* (1968) and *That Obscure Object of Desire* (1977). Elsewhere, the steely eroticisms of American film noir ran in counterpoint to the erotic romance of American Hitchcock while Hitchcock duly donated his flight motifs to successors in post-war British film before his departure for American shores. In the capable hands of directors like Carol Reed and Alberto Cavalcanti they flourished without him. Likewise you could say that on the British front Hitchcock continually traded motifs and images with Michael Powell, and on the American front with Orson Welles. Like him both had absorbed the vision of German expressionism and then went on to develop distinctive films of their own out of its broad legacy. Yet it was Hitchcock who hogged the limelight as Welles was pilloried for *The Lady from Shanghai* (1948) and Powell attacked at the end of the next decade for *Peeping Tom* (1960). Most critics today would value both films highly but that would have been no consolation to Powell or to Welles back then. By contrast Hitchcock always knew how to play safe when in doubt without compromising his vision. He was shrewd enough and lucky enough to escape opprobrium for his controlled provocations. Yet provocations they were. To challenge the conventions and the censorship of the time, cinematic and social, yet always communicate directly with a mass audience: such a working mandate linked Hitchcock to another Hollywood contemporary of European origin he greatly admired, Billy Wilder. Both were determined to test the edges of Hollywood censorship while challenging their audiences, but always doing so through well constructed, emotionally absorbing films. If Hitchcock has a rival in this sense it is not Welles or Lang who experienced mixed fortunes in Hollywood. It was the writer/director of *Double Indemnity, The Lost Weekend* (1945) and *Sunset Boulevard* (1950). Working within the studio system Hitchcock, like Wilder, used its strength and money astutely to keep a grip on his mass audience. If he flopped at the box-office when he went back to post-war London to make the ambitious *Under Capricorn,* Hitchcock knew how to bounce back on returning to Hollywood with *Strangers on a Train.* If *Vertigo* proved too obscure for audiences in 1958, *North by Northwest* and *Psycho* would soon have them on the edge of their seats.

This intermingled history sets up our main metaphor. In discussing *Rear Window,* Rohmer and Chabrol called James Stewart as L. B. Jeffries the photographer with prying eyes, a 'matrix-figure' whose gaze dominates the enclosed space of the Greenwich Village courtyard where the spectacle of murder unfolds (Rohmer & Chabrol 1979: 124). It is a brilliant metaphor, but perhaps does not go far enough. For in the history of Western cinema Hitchcock himself became something of a matrix-figure. Indeed, the lean figure of Stewart as the tall, wheelchair-bound photographer is a mirror image of his short, portly director seated in the director's chair, orchestrating the space and spectacle of his vision. The image is enduring: Hitchcock not only at the centre of his own cinema but of cinema as such. Through his work so much of the entire life of Western cinema has been nurtured and dispersed. So much shock, so much suspense, so much montage, so much mystery, so much watching, so much doubling, so much disaster, so much redemption: it all goes back to him. Or rather, because it also precedes him, it all goes through him. That enables us to look at this special link between Hitch and his fellow-filmmakers as a form of fate that ties in through echo and repetition down the years. In the last century the fate of Hitchcock and cinema were inextricable. In this century the odds are that they will continue to be so.

The other Hitchcock connection lies in the way he refashioned the relationship between auteur and genre. The Hitchcock 'thriller' or 'romance' had an authorial mark that was unmistakeable. As a towering figure in mid-century Hitchcock thus mediates the future, between a system of cinephile authorship and a Hollywood genre system reworking plots and narratives from written sources in fiction or drama that brighten the faces of studio producers. From 1940 he worked within popular genre to turn it around but from *Rear Window* onward to *Marnie* (1964) he effectively transcended it. Though he had begun to produce his own films successfully after his break with David O. Selznick in 1947, he was never a financially independent director and during the crisis afflicting the twilight of his career after *Marnie* he made no attempt to move in that direction. Indeed he had little conceptual relationship to New American Cinema of the 1970s, though the inspired acting of Karen Black, Barbara Harris and Bruce Dern in *Family Plot* (1976) shows clear dramatic crossover. Indeed the ageing Hitchcock had taken a tumble as New American Cinema began to prosper. Production delays in 1963 had meant the ambitious *Marnie* was largely confined to studio sound stages, much to its detriment, and its US box-office failure meant difficulties in funding later projects. He then turned back to previous British concerns, including a wish to film John's Buchan's 1924 thriller *The Three Hostages*. One of his great, unrealised ambitions late in life was to film J. M. Barrie's ghost play *Mary Rose* (1920). It seems in retrospect to have been a nostalgic gesture and it was blocked by MCA-Universal when he intended it as a follow-up to *Marnie* (Krohn 2000: 278). In an era that seemed to be slipping away from him he filmed mundane Cold War thrillers like *Torn Curtain* and *Topaz* (1969) before returning to London to film one of his powerful British pictures – *Frenzy* (1972).

Yet the prehistory of *Frenzy* as a different (and aborted) project to be shot in New Jersey and New York City – *Kaleidoscope* – suggests that after the drearily orthodox *Torn Curtain*, Hitchcock *did* want to update his filmic style, late in life, to absorb the European modernisms of the 1960s. The bold experiments in form by Michelangelo Antonioni and Jean-Luc Godard that he watched avidly in the mid-1960s were a special inspiration. A serial-killer story like the later *Frenzy* (and inspired by the life of British murderer Neville Heath), this was to be a location shoot with sequences featuring male and female nudity, natural light, experimental colour and handheld camera (see Auiler 2001: 443–5, 547–8). Horrified by the explicit nature of the material and the unorthodox means of shooting, MCA executives including Lew Wassermann redirected Hitchcock away from this cutting-edge innovation to the banal disasters of *Topaz* and away from his quest to prove to himself and his audience that he was the equal of the new European innovators. Fragments of a draft screenplay written by Hitchcock himself suggest a fascinating scenario (Auiler 2001: 279–89). Yet the irony was that with *Vertigo*, *Psycho* and *The Birds*, Hitchcock had already proved his modernist credentials without fully realising it. As we shall see, *The Birds* equals any film anywhere of its decade in its artistic confrontation with the risks of nature and the perils of modernity. In truth, Hitchcock had already made his point. At the same time the studio knock-back on the *Kaleidoscope* project, for which in 1967 Hitchcock had already done initial filming, was a heavy blow both to personal morale and artistic freedom. By shooting *Frenzy* in London he was able to escape the studio's prying eyes, but also reverted to shooting narrative for a less experimental kind of film. Ironically, he also reclaimed his full auteurism by strengthening his position as a stockholder in MCA, too late to prevent the jettisoning of *Kaleidoscope* or *Mary Rose*, but salvaging without a doubt his twilight contribution to 1970s cinema.

Though he seldom took a screenwriting credit Hitchcock was also a matrix-figure in another sense – at the centre of everything he filmed, at the centre of a product he nurtured into existence on all levels – adaptation, treatment, storyboarding, costuming, screenplay, shooting script, design, *mise-en-scène* and editing. His preparation was meticulous and, for some, too mechanical. True, his time with hands-on producers Michael Balcon at British-Gaumont and then with Selznick in Hollywood had sometimes constrained his options. Yet he would still try, creatively speaking, to flesh out his role as director to the full: to orchestrate everything in minute and precise detail using his main actors, writers and his many brilliant collaborators. In America Hitchcock found such lasting and creative collaborators in art director Robert Boyle, music composer Bernard Herrmann, costume designer Edith Head, cinematographer Robert Burks and editor George Tomasini. All were treated as creative colleagues and as instruments of his cinematic design, all as invaluable specialists bringing texture and detail to his vision. Between these two roles, instrument and collaborator, his collective work ethic ensured there was never a lasting contradiction. In the intense American period between 1940 and 1963, filmmaking became a continuous process achieved without any significant break. To this end, he would almost always overlap his films, starting work on *North by Northwest*, for example, when *Vertigo* was still in post-production or discussing *Marnie* with screenwriter Evan Hunter on set while filming *The Birds* (even though Hunter was fated not to last the course with his adaptation of Winston Graham's novel). Naturally Hitchcock was not 'original', if we demand a writer-director who uses original material with few literary sources and still carves a dynamic career out of modest budgets. He was, for sure, no John Cassavetes or Ingmar Bergman. He was the product of a studio system, which he then manipulated triumphantly to his own ends. That in itself was no mean achievement. The question of originality can never produce open and shut answers. We must remember that Shakespeare had pillaged history chronicles, the Renaissance, the classics and the plays of fellow dramatists to forge the greatest theatre ever written in the English language. Everything, as Hitchcock knew, came from somewhere else, but you could always imprint it with your own signature.

Hitchcock and modernity

In the course of his career we can take the easy divide, 1939, between British and American Hitchcock as a watershed, as the start of something more profound. In the British phase of the 1930s there had been a penchant for suspense, smart spy stories and a passing, often quirky commentary on the English class system. In the American phase he gets serious. Suspense modulates into psychodrama as the complexities of crisis-situation deepen. Here his narratives rotate around a recurring theme – the internal violation of bourgeois order. It is a violation that has a variety of sources, a multitude of causes. Three overlapping forms stand out in the American period. The first is the threat from without (political) that becomes a threat within (social); the second is the threat from within (individual) that highlights the failure of social order; the third lies in the failures of the law itself. The first form works through the anti-Nazi phase of the 1940s from *Foreign Correspondent* (1940) to *Notorious*, where Hitchcock's traitors are bourgeois renegades, closet Nazis who have retained their charm and social manners but have lost all sense of humanity. The second profiles the psychotic killers of *Shadow of a Doubt, Spellbound, Rope* and *Strangers on a Train,* whose motives are purely individual but whose action also springs from a proto-Nazi contempt for humanity, killers who feel the masses are inferior beings and that they, in contrast, are exceptional ones who rise above such mediocrity. The third phase shows the law as either inept or corrupt or indifferent, or a combination of all three: such variations run through *Saboteur* (1942), *Shadow of a Doubt, The Paradine Case, I Confess, Dial 'M' for Murder, Rear Window, The Man Who Knew Too Much* and *The Wrong Man* (1956). More oblique signs of ineptness are also present in *Vertigo, North by Northwest, Psycho* and *The Birds.* The trend has a long history. In *Dial 'M' for Murder* Chief Inspector Hubbard (John Williams) not only rescues Margot (Grace Kelly) from the gallows at the last minute, he is also rescuing the law, which includes himself, from near-fatal stupidity. In *Frenzy,* twenty years later, Inspector Oxford (Alec McCowen) more or less pulls the same last-minute rabbit out of the hat, trapping cheery cockney Bob Rusk (Barry Foster), the serial killer and rapist for whom his grumpy double, Richard Blaney (Jon Finch) had been stupidly mistaken, but only after Blaney has escaped from prison hospital to take his revenge.

While Orson Welles was a more dynamic and forceful critic of the cupidity of the law, in films like *Touch of Evil* (1958) and *The Trial* (1962), Hitchcock was not far behind, working through understatement or humour rather than confrontation. In the era of the studio code he had little choice. But as the code started to fray at the edges in the late 1950s, the limitations of the law loom larger in his films: in *The Man Who Knew Too Much* the official indifference to the kidnapping, in *The Wrong Man* the cheap corner-cutting and false accusation that leads to quick prosecution, in *Vertigo* the post-mortem on Madeleine's 'death' that never considers foul play, in *North by Northwest* the cynicism of Cold War espionage in which individuals are dispensable, in *Psycho* the official complacency that has never investigated the darker side of Norman Bates, in *The Birds* the police failure to recognise impending catastrophe. Hitchcock was not only fascinated by the failures of the law. The law was a flawed mediator, in his vision, between the public and the intimate spheres of the modern world. Even if it proves itself absolutely right which is not all that often, Hitchcock calls into question its procedures, its judgement, its powers. Yet this vision is slow-burning, something in fact that precedes American Hitchcock. It starts back on the streets in London with his silent film *The Lodger* (1926) and a basic pattern emerges that informs many of the early pictures.

In *The Lodger* Ivor Novello is very nearly the victim of mob justice before he reveals he is an aristocrat seeking the serial killer for whom he is mistaken, the monster who has numbered the lodger's sister amongst his many victims. Hitchcock then comes in closer to confront the shortfall of the law. In the stunning volte-face that ends *The Manxman* (1928), the lawyer-become-judge takes charge of the case of his ex-lover who has tried to commit suicide (a crime at the time) after being left with his illegitimate child. He then acknowledges his part in the build-up to the attempted 'crime' and proceeds to peel off his wig and stand down in front of an astonished court to seek conciliation with the accused wife and her bemused husband. If this is the law court as pure theatre, then Hitchcock repeats it in *Murder!* (1930) where the ambivalent and effeminate Sir John, an upper-class enforcer who finally reverses a wrong-woman murder sentence, does so only because he had earlier capitulated in the jury room to the guilty verdict of his fellow-jurors. Pursuit of the real murderer, Handel Fane (a cross-dressing actor and trapeze artist), then becomes a form of dubious atonement. Hitchcock also produces more secretive scenarios. In *Blackmail* (1929) and *Sabotage* (1936) his detectives may not be smart enough to prevent wrongdoing but they are shrewd enough to cover up the killings by the wronged women whom they covet, getting them off the hook in order to hook them. In *Young and Innocent* (1937), by contrast, the police are quintessential clueless coppers: not only do they allow the man they wrongly suspect of murder to escape, they also allow him to be aided by the daughter of the Chief Constable who never believes his offspring capable of such complicity. Hitchcock's police detectives have never been too bright but, equally, some have a hidden agenda and others are devious. Standard cop thrillers with solid enforcer-heroes are a world away from his vision. Investigation, official or otherwise, is ever undermined by the investigator's blemished vision. And lawyers come off no better: in *The Paradine Case* defence lawyer Anthony Keane (Gregory Peck) makes a public fool of himself by falling in love with his client Maddelena Paradine (Alida Valli), believing her innocent of murder when she is in fact guilty. He then disintegrates in court as Valli dramatically confesses, under his fool-hardy interrogation, to the crime of which she stands accused.

Hitchcock's world of the law is generally one of shortfall investigators sometimes finding the guilty innocent or more often finding the innocent guilty. In any event the relationship between law and justice is wickedly dys-functional, and as his career progresses the vision gets darker. Yet Hitchcock never makes the mistake of treating the error of misidentification as all too obvious. He makes sure misperception is a mistake his audience could easily make themselves, one that *anybody* could make, even when they have the ad-vantage his narration gives them at critical moments over toiling investiga-tors. And when he has a successful investigator, like Jeffries in *Rear Window*, Hitchcock ensures that his hero is blemished in other ways. The intersection of an intimate life and a public life, the point where for better or worse the law intervenes is the means by which Hitchcock's vision forges a wide link-age – that of modernity to its destiny or fate. The intimate life of the modern is a flawed and fragile thing open to the ebb and flow of a dangerous life, never set in stone. Here Hitchcock works in two key areas where his vision overrules convention and produces some startling results – sexuality and the family.

At the centre of Hitchcock's vision of sexuality are variations on hetero-sexual romance, which take pride of place in his work. Romance can be hectic (*The 39 Steps*), therapeutic (*Spellbound*), redemptive (*Notorious*), erotic (*North by Northwest*) or tragic (*Vertigo*). All work within the boundaries of the Studio code and official censorship, though often at their very edge. There is a dy-namism and depth here in Hitchcock intimacies that go way beyond standard forms of melodrama or romantic comedy. All are richly subtle, unexpected variations on the expected. But Hitchcock also goes further in his use of sub-text, which augments the more obvious forms of romance through sexual variation. Although, for example, the steamy hotel-room scene that opens *Psycho* involves a single woman and divorced man, the sweaty secrecy of the assignation implies a liaison between a single woman and a *married* man, that is to say, the scene as evidence of adultery. In understated ways Hitchcock always tries to extend the range of what is possible. (At the end of *North by Northwest* when he was not allowed to show Cary Grant and Eva Marie Saint climbing into their Pullman berth and kissing horizontally unless they were finally married, he retaliated with the closing shot of their train rushing into a tunnel at the moment of embrace.) By the time of *Frenzy* made for Univer-sal in 1972 when the Hollywood studio code had collapsed into a more liberal ratings system, the rape-murder sequence at the core of the picture is much more graphic and disturbing than anything Hitchcock had previously shown

Fig. 1 Clutching Norman's double: Janet Leigh and John Gavin in *Psycho*

onscreen. But that is also because the romance motif in his work had by this time also gone out the window. Nearing the end of his career, he became truly (and briefly) explicit. *Psycho*, made only twelve years earlier, seemed the height of discretion by comparison.

Yet for Hitchcock Eros is usually inseparable from love. The opening of *Psycho* may be steamy but there is also deadness in the knowing solitude of its lovers, an excess of familiarity where love and Eros are dying simultaneously. Hitchcock was more in his element in showing the *first* encounter of romance, an encounter that is also a feature of motion, circulation and the speed of modernity. In his sound features the romance of the first romance narrative, *The 39 Steps*, takes place under the duress of hectic flight, a motif repeated Stateside in the wartime *Saboteur* and then more powerfully in the Chicago-bound train of *North by Northwest* where his erotic couple consummate their discreet one-night stand. Elsewhere the first encounter of Grant and Ingrid Bergman in *Notorious* at a late night party only gains its full resonance from the drunken car ride afterwards while the infatuation of James Stewart with Kim Novak in *Vertigo* is inseparable from his car stalking and furtive following through the streets of San Francisco. And the fugitive romance of Bergman and Gregory Peck in *Spellbound* is enhanced by their train escape from New York. In all five films, love and Eros fuse *only* through the auto-motion of the modern machine, the intimate stillness of the lovers at times set against the recurrent movement surrounding them. By contrast, in the narratives of enclosed mansions or rooms, in the Manderley of *Rebecca* (1940) or the prison encounters of *The Paradine Case*, in the apartments of *Rope, Dial 'M' for Murder* and *Rear Window*, love is rendered sterile, entropic, dissipated. Eros is either stillborn or else it is seen as a lingering menace, not a salvation. With the truly romantic couple, only some defining instance of modernity's motion tips the balance into Eros. It traverses a no-man's-land of uncertainty, of bodily and psychic tension that has its own adrenalin rush; which Cary Grant and Eva Marie Saint convey to its full in their train encounter to end all train encounters, a *mise-en-scène* so sensual and yet so effortless it is often copied but never repeated.

Elsewhere there is a grey area in Hitchcock's vision that goes beyond heterosexual romance. It is not strictly homosexual but rather a template for a *triangulation of desire* or love-triangle that works uneasily, or not at all, within heterosexual format. The term 'bisexual' barely does justice to it. Its first explicit appearance is in his last silent film *The Manxman*. On the face of it this is a romantic drama in which two close friends on the Isle of Man, Philip (Malcolm Keen), a lawyer, and Pete (Carl Brisson), a fisherman, are both attracted to the same girl, Kate (Anny Ondra), with damaging consequences. Yet embedded in the film is a subterranean sense that its close male friendship is more than meets the eye. The lawyer's wordless, furtive gaze signifies clear attraction to his handsome fisherman pal who seems too naïve to notice the difference between friendship and desire, and in turn is attracted to Kate, whom he later marries. Yet during their courtship the girl *has* noticed her suitor's 'closeness' with the lawyer and the lawyer's covert jealousy. When Pete goes off to sea, Phil takes his place as rival for the girl, whom he seduces, transferring affection from male to female. When false news arrives of Pete's death at sea, Kate exclaims, 'At last we're free!' (It is an ambiguous cry of relief echoed in two later films, *The Paradine Case* when Alida Valli confesses to her husband's killing as a ploy intended to 'free' the love of Louis Jourdan, and in the like words of Anne Baxter to Montgomery Clift after Villette's death at the start of *I Confess*.) In all three films, the same motif is broached: sexually ambiguous elimination of 'the rival'. In *The Manxman* the gestural language of silent film makes this more visually explicit. The naïve handsome fisherman is a dual object of desire, the object of a *dual gaze*, who does not understand desire: the fullness of *their* knowledge, however, makes of his best friend and girlfriend (both desiring him) partners in a complicity of looks and signs that goes beyond narrative's official meaning. For the girl, inciting the lawyer's transfer of affection from Pete (where it is something unspoken) to her (where it is openly displayed) means the elimination of a rival sexuality *even if* it is at the expense of a naïve first lover. It is a pure, ambiguous exchange (also an exchange of class from proletarian to bourgeois signifying her social ambition). For Hitchcock it is a prototype for much to come. The knowing couple trade their love rivalry for the hapless Pete into a love for each other in his absence, where he becomes the excluded other. And there is no road back. Yet when he does come back (since the report of his death was false) he continues to 'love' Kate as his wife and 'love' Philip as a friend. The result: impasse.

The Manxman's love-triangle sets up many of American Hitchcock's dramas of torn loyalty, in *Rebecca* (must the new Mrs de Winter, in taking on the role of Rebecca, take on her sexuality too?), *Rope, Strangers on a Train* or, more obliquely, *The Paradine Case* and *I Confess*. In *The Paradine Case* with its post-war English setting, official disclosure at the murder trial reveals a husband jealous of his young wife's affair with his valet. Subtext hints suggest that Maddalena Paradine may have poisoned her rich husband to free his handsome valet, Latour, from sexual domination by his master. In subtext, and subtext only, the condemned woman has killed the man she married so as to 'liberate' her reluctant lover from a very different sexual identity. There are minor traces too in the Tippi Hedren films, *The Birds* and *Marnie*, subtle shadings where, as Melanie and Marnie, Hedren not only inspires jealousy in other women close to the men with whom she is involved but also, one suspects, a sneaking affection for her bold intimacy with men they once desired. In *The Birds* the framing together of the rival women in Annie's house where Melanie stays while visiting Mitch has a tense intimacy that is only resolved by Annie's horrific death in the bird-attack. Suzanne Pleshette as Annie and Diane Baker as cousin Lil in *Marnie* are both dark-haired women full of face and body with strong jaw-lines, in contrast to Hedren – blonde, thin-faced, slim-bodied. If they physically resemble one another in that contrast, Hitchcock lets the ambiguity linger. Have they passed in their affection from the man each has given up on, to the beautiful woman – Hedren – who has taken their place? Or are they hopelessly undecided? As Lil's face is pressed in long shot to an upstairs window of the family home, gazing in quiet desperation at the departing Mark and Marnie, we might ask which of the two she will miss the most. It is of course subtext, a back-story that stays incomplete, something unspoken. But in Hitchcock you feel it is palpably there, adding yet another tangled layer to unresolved questions of jealousy. In his unrealised 1967 *Kaleidoscope* Hitchcock appears to continue with the drama of torn loyalty but set it out explicitly. His vision of the charming psychopath killer Willie, so attractive to women, was also intended to deepen the subtle homosexual profiling he had developed for Bruno in *Strangers on a Train*.

If Hitchcock cues the multiple sexualities of our age from within the studio code his later work also comments on the frailties of that most revered of institutions, the family. The 1950s and 1960s were – in official discourse at least – the golden age of the nuclear family, the married couple with (usually) two children, advertised as the ideal model for a modernising capitalist society. It has long since become an ideal clouded by extreme scepticism, and is now a minority preference in many Western societies at the start of the new century. In mid-century the nuclear family had been seen by social commentators as the key to a stable life in a rapidly modernising world. By the turn of the century it has become a domestic arrangement in free-fall. If Hitchcock displays it under extreme duress, showing external pressures that threaten to bring it down – the kidnapping in *The Man Who Knew Too Much* or the unjust arrest in *The Wrong Man* – you feel it also because he has a sense of its inherent fragility. *The Birds* brings such brittleness to fruition in the attack on the Brenner home, where, under total strain, the 'family' without a male head (the dead father's portrait hangs on the wall) has reconstituted itself with Melanie as its ambiguous fourth element. At times she seems like a long-lost daughter to Lydia Brenner but also like a long-lost mother to Lydia's young daughter, Cathy: she seems at times like a sister to Mitch but also at times, like his lover. In crisis, there is no fixity of definition. There is an echo of this alarming lack almost immediately in *Marnie* when Mark takes his new wife back to her old home in Baltimore, where she becomes once more her mother's daughter to replace the young surrogate (neighbour's) daughter who has replaced her in her absence. There is the same quartet effect in the framing – females of three generations and the male as outsider, an effect reinforced by Marnie's flashback scenes of the sailor who had attacked her mother when she was a child.

In all these films Hitchcock stresses the horrific vulnerability of children, avoiding standard Hollywood cuteness or sentimentality in the power of his images. The attempted murder of the girl-child, niece Charlie in *Shadow of a Doubt*, the ruthless kidnap of the McKennas' son in *The Man Who Knew Too Much*, the blank incomprehension of the Balestrero children in *The Wrong Man* as their family life falls apart, the childhood toys in the attic of *Psycho*'s child-like killer Norman Bates, the horrific attacks on the schoolchildren in *The Birds* and the terrified witnessing of the Brenner daughter Cathy, the trauma of the childhood flashback scene that ends *Marnie*; Hitchcock does not spare the weak and the innocent. Conversely, he reserves his most acid observations for matrimony and the childless household. Here the final icing on the cake (or arsenic in the coffee cup) is the loveless marriage in *Frenzy*. It is a fate the wrong man accused of murder and the police inspector who hounds him both share, while the actual killer who searches out 'relationships' through a marriage bureau is incapable of any intimacy bar torture and killing. The wrong man's marriage has failed miserably and he is childless. The inspector's domestic life, equally childless, is a bizarre round of culinary experiences orchestrated by his dotty wife. But the horror of the rape/killing by Rusk in the marriage bureau of Brenda Blaney is intensified by dark dramatic irony. Brenda is working professionally to prop up an institution – marriage – that has failed her personally: for her pains she is faced by the nightmare client who will rape and strangle her. And her ex-husband will be accused of the killing. The symbolic site of restoration (marriage matching) becomes a crime scene of utter spoliation. Brenda's devotion to a faltering cause is the cause of her own death, a bleak vision in a dark film to round out a deepening pessimism about modern life. It was a relief that Hitchcock could end his career with a sharp comedy, *Family Plot*, in which intimacy did work, but only because its couples were loving partners in crime.

Modernity and catastrophe: *The Birds*

The Birds is a late summation of many great things in Hitchcock – above all his cinematic style, his deep knowledge of film and his dark vision of modernity. It is a film in which all of these come to fruition, and come together. He displays his use of style at its strongest where it prompts multiple readings of narration through a designed interplay of artifice and reality. At the same time he blends together the historical high points of modernist filmmaking – the silent cinema of the 1920s that produced surrealism, expressionism and montage with the abstract, ambiguous intimacies of European film circa 1960, particularly the work of Bergman, Resnais and Antonioni that he had seen prior to the making of *The Birds*. He thus shoots a film on location in California's Bodega Bay that is contemporary in every sense of the word and convinces us of its setting as a small fishing town, which naturalises its characters, its topography and its sense of place. Yet it is also a *constructed* film that switches in the same sequence from exterior shots to studio shots with rear projection, from the actual town centre to its replication in a studio back lot, from naturalistic landscapes to multiple matte compositions that atmospherically resemble them. Its terrifying vision of the birds as a force of nature unleashed on the human world is only made possible through the use of special effects. In short it makes us aware, just as much as *Rear Window* or *Vertigo*, that it is pure cinema.

The story, of course, is not his and came from the pen of Daphne du Maurier in 1951. Hitchcock claimed to Truffaut that he could hardly remember the original but her short narrative, set in a remote Cornwall village, has many of his incidents that fired his visual imagination – the besieged family in their farmhouse with birds stabbing with their beaks at the front door and swarming down the chimney, and a neighbouring farmer brutally pecked to death. Yet in Evan Hunter's screenplay his American family is a different kind of family: more prosperous, more sophisticated and the central characters are the film's own. If the Brenner family – Lydia (Jessica Tandy), Mitch (Rod Taylor) and Cathy (Veronica Cartwright) – are the film's very own, then so is its sophisticated intruder, Melanie Daniels. More-over, the coastal setting and its abstract *mise-en-scène* seem to come less from anything du Maurier wrote than from recent films Hitchcock had seen by Antonioni – *L'avventura* (1960), *La notte* (1961) – and Bergman – *The Seventh Seal* (1958) and *Through a Glass Darkly* (1960). In both his films Bergman had used Swedish coastal settings. *The Seventh Seal* with its allegorical story of medieval plague and divine judgment was remembered by many for the game of chess Bergman's crusading knight plays and loses with the figure of Death on the seashore. Like *The Birds* it was apocalyptic yet psychologi-cally complex. In Hitchcock's film we get a different kind of duel with Death played out by the seashore, in the world of the present where the enemy is not the plague but the attack of the birds. To make it contemporary we can think of Bergman's other film, *Through a Glass Darkly*, which despite its biblical title, is a contemporary story of madness within a close-knit family at their summerhouse on a remote island. Karin (Harriet Andersson) is a young married woman who undergoes complete breakdown and then seduc-es her teenage brother, to the consternation of her ineffectual husband and hypocritical father. In the cracks of the wall in an attic room to which Karin retreats, she claims to hear God's voice speaking to her, a voice that triggers her madness. In the attic room of Brenner's home that Melanie Daniels en-igmatically visits the morning after the bird attack, she is confronted by the avian creatures, which have infiltrated the cracks and fissures of the roof. They all but destroy her. Karin's traumatic collapse at the end of Bergman's film is mirrored in Melanie's traumatic collapse at the end of *The Birds*. And after several days of enduring live birds being thrown at her for the montage of the attack sequence, Tippi Hedren had collapsed as much as her character, Melanie. For the scenes in long shot where she is carried down-stairs from the attic by Mitch her rescuer and revived on the living-room couch Hedren was no longer there, away recuperating and replaced on set by a double.

Antonioni's *L'avventura* provides a different angle of inspiration not only through its coastal landscapes of Sicily and the Lipari islands but also through its use of Monica Vitta as Claudia, a young Roman sophisticate out of her depth and out of sorts in a remote world that was not her own. Her uncertain affair with Sandro (Gabriele Ferzetti), fiancé of her disappearing best friend, seems a model for the drained, edgy relationship of Melanie with Mitch, though not the one Evan Hunter had envisaged when he referred to the couple in his screenplay as 'screwball lovers'. Though the film starts out in San Francisco mining the familiar vein of romantic comedy, Hitchcock gradually turns it after her arrival in Bodega Bay into something different, cooler and more fragmented, with uncertain emotions. The picnic sequence on the cliff that Hitchcock wrote into the final script, much to Hunter's dismay, with its couple framed together through high-angle shots of the coastline echoes in its framing the tense ambiguous relationship of Vitti and Ferzetti in *L'avventura* as they scour remote cliffs in search of Anna. In his next film, *La notte*, Antonioni experimented with the novelty of electronic music on his soundtrack. Hitchcock decided to do the same with great success on his picture, creating artificial bird screeches and dispensing with a musical score. Yet this malaise of the emotions that Hitchcock takes from Antonioni and Bergman is only a prelude to a wider catastrophe, that of the massed avian attack. Both the European filmmakers then went on to make oblique studies of failed intimacy within the shadow of the nuclear age – Antonioni in *L'eclisse* (1962), Bergman in *The Silence* (1963) – but their coolly apocalyptic fables here are in complete contrast to Hitchcock's visceral and sensuous vision of a universal terror. In preparing and executing this, he goes back to earlier inspirations at the start of his life in cinema.

Before we turn to this, let us remark on the figural similarities of Vitti and Hedren, beautiful and sophisticated, incongruously overdressed and framed by rock, coastline and water. In the location shooting there is a strong naturalistic element to Antonioni's abstract and painterly design, showing his origins in Italian neo-realism. For the outboard motor sequence in *The Birds*, however, where Melanie rents a boat and speeds across the bay to take Mitch by surprise and deliver the caged lovebirds to his house as his sister's birthday present, there is a distinctly artificial feel amid the natural setting, something uncanny. Hedren looks like an A-list model straight off the catwalk. (The incongruity recalls Tallulah Bankhead in Hitch's wartime drama *Lifeboat*, as survivor of a U-boat attack adrift in the Atlantic in á mink coat and looking as if she had just come from a Broadway first night; by the end of both films, of course, the clothes of Hedren and Bankhead are in tatters.) In the boat sequences across the bay and back, the alternation within sequence between long-shot location-takes and medium or close shots of Melanie with studio back projection, sets up a strange counterpoint. The latter were visually enhanced at the time by a transition from a blue- to a new yellow-screen technology using sodium lamps for superior back projection, an innovation that cut out colour seepage and gave greater clarity and definition to composite images. Its effect here is to give to Hedren's screen image, her image of arrival in Bodega Bay – swept-up honey-blonde hair, unlikely fur coat and pale-green suit – a luminous quality that is not shared by any of the locals. In fact she fits the description given earlier to Madeleine Elster in *Vertigo*, that of a 'beautiful ghost'. Who is she, exactly? Where has she really come from? Is she really earthed, truly grounded? Or is she another San Francisco ghost like the one Hitchcock had manufactured for his earlier picture? Another way to put it is this. Is it the bird attacks that finally make her human, and the creatures of the sky that bring her down to earth? Or more

Fig. 2 Desolation row: Tippi Hedren and Rod Taylor in *The Birds*

precisely, does the first gull that swoops down on the boat and draws blood from her forehead prove to us literally that she is flesh and blood?

Hitchcock's interest in the existential modernisms of Antonioni results in the blending of two key techniques in the making of *The Birds*. It becomes one of his most improvised films with many last-minute changes and Hitchcock eliminates all the rational or allegorical explanations, or hints of them, for the bird Blitzkriegs that are present in the different drafts of Evan Hunter's screenplay (Krohn 2000: 238–43). The film was shot in the autumn (1962) of one of the century's gravest political crises, the Cuban Missile affair, which many commentators at the time feared could result in nuclear war between the United States and the Soviet Union. Though this would certainly have charged the atmosphere of Hitchcock's filmmaking in Northern California, the final cut shows no direct sign of it. Hitchcock eliminated politics just as he eliminated science fiction. The attacks for him were ineffable terror, the sum of all catastrophes in the modern age emanating here from a natural source, unpredictable and possibly without end. It is why in the age of global terror networks and the misplaced responses they elicit – both adding dangers at the start of this century to the existing threat of nuclear war – his film will continue to have such a steely resonance. For it intimates the detail of terror on a local scale but makes its import universal. It is something that happens here (Bodega Bay) but it could also happen anywhere, and may well go on to do so. As fellow-creatures the attacking birds remind us of the powers of human destruction, but as the winged creatures of nature, the even greater power of natural catastrophe. Of course the two are often conjoined. In the age of man-made climate change where our energy excesses intimate disaster for us in different forms – pollution, heat, drought, fire, floods, tempests, hurricanes – there is no clear divide between nature and culture in the realm of catastrophe. In Hitchcock's masterpiece the situation is likewise. His film may be based on barely plausible assumptions about birds, despite the growing incidence of isolated attacks on humans, but it continues to resonate as a masterwork that contains the sum of all our fears.

This is a horror film about plausible horrors, and there is an upending of the natural order that is truly Shakespearean in its effect. It is understandable, therefore, that new modernist aesthetics bringing in the 1960s were necessary but not sufficient for the film's ambition. Hitchcock also went back to his cinematic roots. His artifice-location counterpoint that drives one off against the other links him back more firmly to the film aesthetics of an earlier age: to expressionist art and, conversely, the technical power of editing. Edvard Munch's famous painting, *The Scream*, textured much of the art design of Robert Boyle, and was then transferred to storyboards plotting in detail the human reaction to bird attack. The diving swoop of a single gull, whose beak slashes Melanie's forehead as she brings her boat back round the bay to harbour, is a quick, precise image. It recalls in its surreal power of shock the famous shot of a razor slitting the eyeball at the start of *Un Chien Andalou* (1929), the sharp incisive motion that produces the shock incision. The use of quick-fire montage in the attack sequences recalls Eisenstein's editing in his silent classic, *Battleship Potemkin* (1925). In the schoolhouse attack we could say that Hitchcock restages and transforms the Odessa Steps massacre into a mass attack where, miraculously, all the victims survive their wounds. Later, for the attic attack on Melanie the scissors in the cutting room are out again, and this time working overtime.

In *Battleship Potemkin* Eisenstein uses quick orchestrated montage to indicate the different phases of revolt, where there are two staged and starred contrasts, the first the mutiny that starts below decks on the battleship with the saga of maggot-filled meat, the second the counter-attack on shore by armed Cossacks, a phalanx moving mechanically in step who drive the panicking crowd before them down the steep city steps. It is a source of the Hitchcock 'open and shut' contrast, the mutiny at first interior within the crews' quarters, but the shore massacre exterior, in the open public places of the city by the shore of the Black Sea. (In his open schoolhouse sequence, Hitchcock pays homage to *Battleship Potemkin* by transforming the shattered lens of the woman's fallen pince-nez on the Steps, a famous image, into the shattered, fallen glasses of a besieged girl as she runs into town.)

The sense of live terror in both films is quite remarkable. Just as Hedren suffered trauma for her live acting, so Eisenstein's shooting on the real location is rumoured to have created casualties among his stampeding extras. (In Hitchcock's flight sequence, of course, the birds are shot separately and matted on during editing.) The double montage in *The Birds* goes in the opposite direction, spatially, from *Battleship Potemkin*: from the open space of the road descending into town to the enclosed attic of the Brenner home to which Melanie ascends in anticipation of her fate. If Eisenstein's progression is closed to open, Hitchcock's is open to closed. As opposed to rapid alternation between long and close shots in the schoolhouse flight, the enclosed sequence of the attic attack is done through the quick-fire matching of close shots as Melanie is pinned against the door; fragments of her body under attack, swift cutting between head and feet, or between the arm arcing the torch in desperate defence and reverse POV shots as the birds strike. (Here the shower-scene in *Psycho* is echoed by Melanie's gradual fall under stabbing beaks whose sharp movement resembles the striking knife of Marion Crane's killer.) In *Marnie* Hitchcock would soon repeat this double montage with Hedren through an open-to-closed chronology that gives us the open, exterior montage of the hunt – fragmenting the tragic fall of her beloved Forio as it hits a fence and falls beneath her – to the closed interior montage of the childhood flashback, memories of being trapped in a room with her mother and her mother's sailor client. This is cutting in rhythmic repetition, in which the first foreshadows the second and the second echoes the first, the flashing fragmentation of distorted bodies in conflicting motion: in the first sequence horse and rider, in the second child, mother and sailor. Both end in tragic death.

The *mise-en-scène* of the schoolhouse attack also shows us exactly what defines Hitchcock's method of filming, the switch back and forth between objective and subjective shots. The jungle gym scene is a key prelude to the sequence: Melanie sits outside the school smoking on a bench, waiting for Annie's class to finish, her back to the fence enclosing the gym behind her. Hitchcock sets up ambiguous montage: he cuts back and forth from medium-close ups of the waiting Melanie to the scattered arrival of birds on the climbing frame behind her. Here the audience is privileged at first by shots of what happens behind her back without her knowledge. Melanie's face is clouded by a growing anxiety but since she never turns round it is never clear at what point she first senses what we are seeing. Is the anxious look a sign of what she currently sees or what she remembers from the picnic attacks on the previous day? We only know for sure when she finally sees the creatures above through a special eye-line match. She glances up and left of screen. The match cut shows a panning shot of a single bird flying left to right behind her. Her eyes follow its flight. The bird alights on the frame where hundreds are now perched. Turned around in the reverse angle cut, she is now standing in horror. Her shock is mirrored in ours, and this is the point at which Hitchcock clearly sutures her point-of-view and that of his audience. She may have missed the first feathered arrivals we have clearly seen but we have also missed during the camera's focus on her, the mass arrival that makes the left-to-right pan end in shock revelation for her and for us.

Even in these sequences, where Hedren is the focus of our attention, there is always a steely objective element in Hitchcock's camera. She may dominate the early part of the film but even then she is a figure of mystery. We never see her at work or at home, with family or with friends and we are encouraged to see her as object, to try and figure her out, never to feel fully familiar with her. Later of course her stark individuality is drowned in collective events and collective trauma. At key junctures the major moments of catastrophe are seen from afar. The bird attack that starts outside the schoolhouse ends with the explosion at the gas station whose deadly consequence Hitchcock's camera shows from a high-angle God-like point of view, in the sky above the town. Elsewhere Melanie is also limited in her role as a filter of the collective gaze. It is Lydia Brenner, not she, who drives out to the Glaiser farmhouse and discovers the farmer's mutilated corpse with its pecked-out eyes. Later the brunt of the practical fight against the birds comes from Mitch who then occupies centre frame and at the end, even when Melanie has recovered consciousness after the attic attack she looks comatose in her bandaged head and shredded clothes, barely alive. As the family act and talk around her, she hardly seems to have a consciousness at all. This constant shifting of focus, even when there is a dominant field of vision, suggests a framing of Hitchcock's method in terms of what some critics have called an aesthetic of 'intrarealist' effect (see Sallitt 1980; Smith 1999). To see this composite blending, technically complex, is to guard against the dangers of seeing in his camera either a purely omniscient gaze or a purely subjective cinema of obsession.

This leads us onto a final point. *The Birds* is a very salient feature about the limits of perception or, more precisely, the unfinished translation of fragmented perceptions into a conceptual ordering of things. In the film no one can give a final answer to explain the unexpected attacks. No one can predict when they will start or when they will end. All this is finally beyond human understanding. The attacks are in no way supernatural – there is no get-out clause here – and yet no convincing reason for them can be given. This is truly tough for Hitchcock's audience; tougher than in any other film because the result of the actions we cannot explain is catastrophe. And here it is collective; it affects us all. This, momentously, is the high point of Hitchcock's art and also the most troubling. Here it is not the ordinary things of daily life that elude both the film's victims and the audience watching them: it is something more powerful. Indeed it is so powerful it shatters the usual irony of limits that Hitchcock's philosophy places on perception. For in general his cinema leads us by varying degrees to the same endpoint. There will always be something new and different in experience to elude us, and yet we (audience and heroes alike) will always try to master it. In most of his films his subjects do eventually succeed, but only at great cost to themselves. Yet in his later films they usually fail and the limitation becomes a source of anguish, to us as well as to them. That anguish is a key to the philosophy of life expressed so powerfully in his art: to its wider implications we must now turn.

chapter 2

LOST IDENTITIES: HITCHCOCK AND DAVID HUME

In looking at the role of Hitchcock in twentieth-century cinema, let us go back to a time when there was no cinema. There is no clear link between the cockney, Catholic director of modern times and the eminent Scottish philosopher who happened to be Edinburgh's greatest thinker at the end of his nation's Calvinist age. David Hume is an unlikely candidate for a book like this. Not only were Hume and Hitchcock divided by nation and religion: one lived through much of the eighteenth century, the other through most of the twentieth. Yet to posit Hume as a forgotten ancestor has intriguing possibilities. Hume was a philosopher by profession, Hitchcock by default. Most philosophers interpret the world: most filmmakers construct an imaginary one. Had Hitchcock ever read Hume? Given his strict Jesuit education, it seems unlikely. Yet in a sense it does not matter. Things impersonal often transmit themselves down the centuries in ways that go beyond stealth or design. An accretion of thinking and feeling percolates through the culture and cannot be nailed by chapter and verse alone. The constant flow of empiricism as a key doctrine in the philosophy of 'The Isles', to use the geographic term of Norman Davies (2000: xxiv–xli), has been taken for granted, though few have taken it wider than philosophy, where empiricism is seen by many culture-critics as old fashioned. At the start of the twenty-first century the concept of experience has been deemed naïve in the fading arena of the 'postmodern' at its most kitsch, where philosophy is often coded complacently as a pastiche or deconstruction of something else. Yet experience does have an impersonal and objective reach beyond the modish domain of sexed-up confessional biography. And this is where Hitchcock's work excels. Experience is a crucial component in his aesthetic of the 'intra-real', where he shifts perspective back and forth between characters, and between character and spectator.

If Hitchcock was a philosopher in the world of film, it is not because of the Jesuits who taught him, or any theological worldview, but rather because he draws on a culture of meaning which originates in the eighteenth century and stresses the primacy of experience as the fragile basis of understanding. Viewed in the long term, Hitchcock's filmic vision was built on the loose empire of the senses Hume had begun to construct in his vision of human nature two hundred years earlier. It is a flawed, imperfect edifice that gives pride of place to the power and logic of the senses, the vagaries of trial and error, the power of the passions over reason, induction over deduction; and it sees in human nature the force-field of belief as ever holding sway over the complexities of knowledge. Its prime text is *A Treatise of Human Nature*, published in 1739–40. 'It appears', Hume wrote in the first book of the *Treatise*, 'that the *belief* or *assent*, which always attends the memory and senses, is nothing but the vivacity of those perceptions they present' (2000: 61). Hitchcock makes the vivacity of those perceptions that induce belief the fount of his moving image just as Hume saw in them the key to the human condition. As Hitchcock is always busy constructing fictions for mass consumption, this leads to a sensuous, visceral cinema. His films always engage *our* sense of the senses. For Hume, however, the dynamics of such perception had led to a paradox: it meant that philosophers had to proceed with caution. 'It is therefore by *experience* only', he continues, 'that we can infer the existence of one object from that of another' (ibid.). Guesswork, inference, the vivacity of sense-impressions, the basing of future expectation on past experience that issues very firmly in a culture of custom – these are all part of the Humean complex that questions all claims to absolute certainty and absolute knowledge. 'All probable reasoning', he wrote, 'is nothing but a species of sensation' (2000: 72). Born into a world of devout Calvinism that had proclaimed its own certainties, Hume ended his life a refined sceptic who had questioned not only the nature of the world but also the nature of selfhood and, without ever being an atheist, the nature of any belief in God. In his eyes all these entities were human fictions of the most creative sort, but still fictions beyond the complete evidence of the senses.

For Hume, life is a jigsaw to be assembled piece by piece and at the centre of the Hitchcock narrative too there is always a quest to resolve a puzzle that rises out of the vexed relations between sense-experience and knowledge – not in terms of the whodunit, which Hitchcock disparaged, but in terms of perception in general, the perceptual shortfall that at some time all his characters will endure. Yet as a filmmaker Hitchcock was not engaged in philosophy *per se*. While Hume had attempted to delineate universal aspects of perception, and through that, of 'human nature', Hitchcock's more modest task involves a perceptual doubling. His film fables are fables about fictional characters whose fate is bound up with the act of perceiving a world in flux, and of translating acts of perception into forms of knowledge. The success of his films, however, is bound up with the spectator's pleasurable act of perceiving their perceiving, of perceiving how perception operates in imaginary others, how it works in situations that are constructed fictions. Thus Hume's 'vivacity of perception' is translated here as a double operation. The first phase relates to how it impacts on characters in a film and the second to how it impacts on the audiences watching character enactment within that film. The disparity between subject-perception and viewer-perception is at its greatest in films like *Frenzy*, where the audience discovers early on that Bob Rusk (Barry Foster) is the necktie strangler, but all those around him are the last to suspect him. Between character and spectator there is always some irreducible difference. This is highlighted in a different way by the character of 'Jeff' Jeffries in *Rear Window*. For a character to be physically immobile for the duration of a film is rare in commercial cinema. Yet that is precisely the fate of the seated spectator watching him on the screen. Hitchcock appears to approve the confluence but then, in a sharp reminder, breaks the frame when the murder suspect pushes Jeff out of the window of his apartment – that is, sends him spinning into motion. For just as viewers are immobile in watching, the technology of film usually does the opposite for the action viewed. It speeds up mobility. Though editing, we jump situations with a dream-like logic so that real time is both fragmented and compressed and viewed selectively. In setting action very often in moving situations, the travel technologies of boats, cars, trains and planes, Hitchcock at times stretches the difference between the position of seated spectators and the spectacle they witness, but also the spatial positioning of his characters and the experience they endure. At the same time by 'drawing us in' – a common way of describing Hitchcock's power by students of his films – we are vicarious witnesses of a fate that is not ours but could well be. It is this double referencing unique to film that makes of Hitchcock a philosopher of the senses in the twentieth century. And the senses, as ever, are not reassuring but problematic.

As an epistemologist Hume had been a radical conservative who had given us the vision of a life in which experience leads to change, in which we constantly have to adjust our perception to the impact on the senses of new situations. The general insight points the way forward to what he could not anticipate – the scientific discoveries in perception that marked Hitchcock's century. We now know this. In the complex nature of seeing, the key relationship of eye and brain reveals to us how perceptions are converted into conceptual knowledge as a feedback effect, through the constant play of trial and error (see Gregory 1997: 250–5). Hume could not anticipate this. Yet for him customs in general – regular ways of seeing, thinking and feeling – were the key antidotes to chaos. As habit, tradition or received wisdom, the mindset of custom always prevailed in fine-tuning that transformation to the new and the unexpected. At best we proceed piece-by-piece and even at the extremities of the new, custom is the sediment that brings things back into line, and orders our perceptions. For Hitchcock too the conservative impulse of custom is strong, and shows itself reflexively in his persistent use of the well-made plot where structure and progression order the puzzles of narrative. But from this foundation his filmic imagination deals in our deep fear of perceptual collapse. In his thriller narratives he dramatises this very predicament, this very fear, but then *takes it further*. What if the force of unexpected experience completely breaks down the power of custom and convention, of our normal ways of seeing? What if the point of crisis, induced from the outside, is so traumatic it threatens to be a point of no return? How do we restore equilibrium? In *North by Northwest* Roger O. Thornhill is an advertising executive mistaken for someone else and kidnapped without warning by Soviet agents in a busy Manhattan hotel lobby. Later, in flight from his captors, he is sent to a bus stop in the Mid-West prairie south of Chicago to wait for a possible contact. The flat landscape of the wheat fields, stretching as far as the eye can see, uninhabited, has no distinguishing qualities. It is a landscape degree zero. Even in flight there is no continuity, for Thornhill is about to start his flight all over again. Any reliance on habit, custom, trust, expectation has evaporated in the midday heat.

Master of the unpredictable, Hitchcock was himself addicted to the predictable – an addict of custom, fully aware of its frailties. A notorious conformist in his personal life, he was conservative by habit and formal in demeanour, a petit-bourgeois product of the British Edwardian era. Two centuries earlier, in a pre-Enlightenment Scotland struggling to find its way after the Act of Union, Hume had associated custom with tradition. But crucially Hitchcock differs: he sees order as a species of social conformity and a feature of modernity. His experience is moulded by the organised industrial era of the early twentieth century – conformity in the office, in public institutions, in the family and marriage, in religion and the habits of everyday life, all in all an abiding sense of the normal. So that in his early films the abnormal nearly always came from the outside, tearing at the social fabric. The psychopathic murderer of the late-Victorian era, Jack the Ripper, whom Hitchcock used as a model for his silent masterpiece *The Lodger* is the figure who on the face of it points up the normality of the rest of us. But in the common desire for vengeance he creates the city crowd seeking rough justice so that the perceived monster can also be a mirror image of popular impulse to destruction. For that very reason he continues to excite our attention. In the post-Edwardian world the other great figure of the outside that excites us through a talent for perfidy is the spy, the personification of external threat, vaguely German in the 1930s pictures then pointedly Nazi in the wartime films. It is this eruption from the outside that overthrows the customary mind-set and tears a hole in the fabric of order, but only because it taps into something within, our own capacity for betrayal. It is also why Hitchcock would confide to Truffaut in the 1970s that a new age of terrorism, where terror could become a normalised occurrence in the experience of civil society, confounded the vital distinction on which his cinema had been based

(Truffaut 1986b: 520). Of course, as an Edwardian East-Ender he had been all too aware of the chaos and unpredictability of the crowd in modern city life, something echoed early on in *The Lodger, The Man Who Knew Too Much* and *Sabotage*. Yet broadly he starts from the template of an ordered world, very British, that contains all such threats. His view of major disorder was that of eruption and invasion, the outside threatening to become the inside by preying on its hidden weaknesses.

His plots always take us to that crucial moment when customary ways of acting and thinking fall apart. In an ordered world, fatal disorders erupt without warning. In *The 39 Steps* Richard Hannay bears witness to the aftermath of a killing in his Portland Square flat for which he is falsely framed and accused. He flees by train to a new world (Scotland) where he can prove his innocence only by incriminating the guilty. Yet this 'wrong man' scenario, embedded here in the dynamics of flight, was a favourite Hitchcock trope, a prime source of suspense all the way from *The Lodger* via his docudrama bearing that name, *The Wrong Man*, to the macabre tale of wrong identity, *Frenzy*. In this sudden limbo where the customary is abrogated, the only identity the central protagonist appears to have is a *mistaken identity*. This is a formula taken to its extreme, as we have seen, at the start of *North by Northwest* when Thornhill is abducted by secret agents because he is mistaken for George Kaplan, a spy who does not even exist, who is in effect a CIA fiction created to fool the other side in the Cold War espionage of bluff and double-bluff. Thornhill is not only the wrong man. He is a non-existent wrong man.

At this point of transition in the Hitchcock film, the only identity is mistaken identity, or no identity. And it can be a 'wrong woman' scenario too. In *Vertigo* Scottie Ferguson (James Stewart) falls in love with the auburn-haired Judy Barton (Kim Novak) without realising she was his previous love in a different incarnation, the blonde Madeline Elster. Yet Judy's eager impersonation of the affluent Madeleine at Scottie's bidding is also a sign of her nonidentity as working girl Barton, just as Tippi Hedren, the man-hating thief of *Marnie* would change hair colour and social security cards, from Marion Holland to Margaret Edgar, in the film's opening sequence to embark upon a new persona and 'new life'. In *To Catch a Thief* ex-jewel robber John Scobie (Cary Grant) is aided in his Riviera quest to catch a deadly imitator by Danielle, the young daughter of a former Resistance friend, played by Brigitte Auber, who turns out to be the very thief he is looking for. Grant repeats such misidentification in *North by Northwest* when he has no idea whether the gorgeous blonde he meets on a Chicago train, Eve Kendall (Eva Marie Saint) is friend or foe or both at the same time, and whether she is there by accident or design. And in *Rebecca* identity even lacks the nominal title of a defining name. For Joan Fontaine is the quintessential 'Girl with No Name', the second 'Mrs de Winter' with no clear sense of self in the world of Manderley, the vast country house still dominated by the name of her predecessor, installed in the film's title and repeated in her presence as if somehow the dead Rebecca were still alive, still lurking in the hidden recesses of the Cornish mansion. For the Girl with No Name the good life becomes unbearable. While everyone utters the name 'Rebecca' no one mentions or seems to know hers at all.

Hitchcock's inspiration in framing the substitute spouse is, at one stage removed, a Humean conceit. She is set up in a world of tradition but has lost her way. In Book One of the *Treatise* Hume concludes by speculating on personal identity but instead of reassuring us about its solidity, denies that we have any. Our different and distant perceptions can never be run into a single composite. Grand metaphysicians, for sure, will falsely fabricate the unity of their mind, yet the rest of us mere mortals 'are nothing but a bundle or collection of different perceptions, which succeed each other with an inconceivable rapidity, and are in a perpetual flux and movement' (2000: 165). The idea of the self, or of a soul, of any kind of inner substance – dismissed by Hume as an 'unintelligible chimera' (2000: 152) – is itself a fiction designed, in his eyes, to disguise the constant variations of perception. If we impose the invariant on the variable, this is not merely a category-error but a constructed fiction to mask the protean nature of our altering existence. What then can save us from total disintegration? It is memory alone that 'does not so much *produce* as *discover* personal identity, by showing us the relation of cause and effect among our different perceptions'. Custom and memory are Hume's failsafe devices, the fallback position. Yet Hitchcock blows a hole in both of them. For the twentieth-century artist that Hitchcock was, custom is always fragile and memory can also be the prison-house of pain from which we seek release, not the guarantor of selfhood. Following Freud, we might say this is the key moment at which Hitchcock deviates from Hume. For memory often discovers the wrong identity, the wrong persona locked into a compulsion to repeat the pain and suffering of the troubled past. Memory does not reassure us. On the contrary, it can lock the door shut.

Hitchcock then is halfway between Hume and Freud, but never stranded. Uncannily, his films absorb Freud into the Humean template. In many of his most poetic narratives the idea of memory is foregrounded as the troubled core of a troubled self: in *Rebecca, Spellbound, Notorious, Under Capricorn, Vertigo* and *Marnie*. If memory is cognitive in Hume's version, it is also emotional in Hitchcock's. If it is not one of Hume's passions, Hitchcock for sure makes it one of his, and at times an open wound. Here both are fascina*
by the association of objects, of those connections with the life-worl*
by Hume the 'secret ties' of which at times we are scarcely con*
foreshadows the Freudian unconscious that turns it around *

could never have envisaged. His secret ties are healing, the ties that bind. Yet in Freud and Hitchcock they are cast asunder. Thus Hitchcock portentously makes play of the 'secret tie' in the association-trauma of parallel lines made by the fork on the white tablecloth in *Spellbound* during Gregory Peck's amnesia. Unknown to Peck these lines trigger the trauma of a killing witnessed on a ski slope, oblique memories of ski tracks in the snow when memory itself is obliterated. In fact, Hitchcock is much better with the open wound of memory where the pain is known, the wound that disfigures the look of the anguished subject; Ingrid Bergman in *Notorious* and *Under Capricorn*, James Stewart in *Vertigo*. In the way that Hitchcock films Bergman, memory is not something repressed but all too present and hurtful, something seared onto the skin. The knowledge of what you were that your memory provides, threatens to tear you apart. At the start of *Notorious* Bergman's drunken delirium is a vain refuge from the disfigurement of her family's Nazi past. As Lady Henrietta in *Under Capricorn*, that same delirium of the look conceals the secret of a deadly exchange, of punishment for guilt. Husband Sam Flusky (Joseph Cotten) has been sentenced and banished to Australia for a crime, the killing of her brother that Bergman has committed and cannot forget. Here memory shades the iconography of the look and imprints itself upon the memorable face. For as Rohmer and Chabrol remind us 'this film, as was already true in *Notorious*, is the story of a face, that of Ingrid Bergman' (1979: 102).

Dramas of transaction

Many critics, overdosing on Freud and Lacan, would take memory and the unconscious as excuses to make the Hitchcock subject a traumatised wreck, a suitable case for treatment, again and again. They ignore the vital factor that Hume's embrace of experience had offered, a stronger solution that ushers in very different circumstances: the key focus of Hitchcock's cinema is on the *dramas of transaction* that changed predicament generates. It lies in the external nature of relations that exist beyond the substance of related entities. As Gilles Deleuze has pointed out, in Hume relations are always external to their terms: human communication thus takes place through external relations and through the mediation of objects. These take priority over identity, not the other way around (2001: 37–8). For this reason the French philosopher sees a succinct connection between these two disparate figures, Hume and Hitchcock, in British life (1986: x). Human nature, if it is anything, is the self's volatile mix of discovering the life-world and being discovered by it in a matrix of object-relations. More accurately the constitution of the self is that process. In Hitchcock meaning and identity are not individual truths of being where you reveal the 'real person' but changing forms of transaction between subjects, characters that are always mediated by object and situation, that have an external fate.

This has a knock-on effect for film narrative. In Hitchcock the dramatic moment is an upheaval that *accelerates* narrative momentum, an upheaval that alters relations with others and with things. By doing so, it also changes the nature of the protean 'self'. In his best work, therefore, his main characters are not constant selves with clear identities in a hostile world but persons rapidly altered by a rapidly altering experience. In *The Wrong Man* the power of the film lies not only in the false accusation and imprisonment of Manny Balestrero (Henry Fonda), the misrecognition that deems him 'a hold-up man'. It lies also in the impact of that false arrest on his devoted wife, Rose

Fig. 3 'false accusation...': Henry Fonda and Vera Miles in *The Wrong Man*

(Vera Miles) who has a breakdown and goes insane. Yet the film does not attempt to psychoanalyse her. Rather, it records the impact on her of changing relations that are beyond her control. Just as we see his transformation from honest citizen to accused prisoner we witness her transformation from sanity into madness. The ceremony of degradation afflicts both: he has a cell in a prison, she a confined room in a home for the mentally ill. Yet if we see her breakdown, and harrowing it is, the film does not try to explain it. That is to say, it does not *explain* how she has become someone else, but it does *show* how she has become someone else. For Hitchcock, changing identity in cinema rests on dramatic moments, on key epiphanies: it is moulded by sudden transformations of circumstance. He was aware of the rarity of such moments but also aware of the power of film to dramatise that rarity.

In this world of change there is often a continuity of resemblance given through a specific set of relations, through opposites attracting and hence through the similarity of the opposed Other. Hitchcock's sensibility adds to Hume's scepticism a later Scottish configuration that comes out of it in the nineteenth century, that of James Hogg and Robert Louis Stevenson, with their disturbing literary fictions of the Double, that demonic figure of resemblance conjured out of a haze of inchoate perception. In his late-romantic gloss upon this romantic connection of identity and resemblance that is filtered through German expressionism, Hitchcock's figure of the double is precisely where resemblance highlights the *weakness* of identity in its claim to autonomous being. As Hume noted we always look out for resemblance to firm up identity in the nature of anything we observe, human or otherwise. To do this on a human plane is then to subtend to our self a primal form of perception. Resemblance not only presents a cracked mirror to the self, as it does in *Vertigo, Strangers on a Train, The Birds* or *Frenzy*, but also to the self's febrile relations with others. In *Rear Window* there is a 'double doubling' as well: the intimate couples at opposite windows (the paired investigators, Jeff and Lisa, and the paired investigated, the troubled Thorwalds) are doubled as inverted *images* of each other; also, while scanning the courtyard windows more widely, *everyone* whom wheelchair photographer Jeffries spies on seems to mirror some aspect of his own predicament. Meanwhile at the end of *Psycho* there is also a doubling of pairs: Marion Crane and Norman Bates, Lila Crane and Sam Loomis. To give them the actors' names, the investigating couple, Janet Leigh's divorced lover John Gavin and Leigh's sister, Vera Miles, who are looking for the murdered Leigh, end up 'finding' her other, involuntary 'partner', killer Anthony Perkins. With its echo of the couple-effect in *Rear Window*, investigators Gavin and Miles are the couple-double, complete with physical likeness, of Perkins and Leigh, the shy stuttering killer and his victim now sunk in a car boot at the bottom of a swamp. Paired investigators, paired investigated, role-reversal and resemblance: symmetrical repetitions with kaleidoscopic variations. Long after the darkness of *Psycho* Hitchcock's film career ends in 1976 with *Family Plot* and a couple-match of comic symmetry. The smart kidnappers, Fran and Adamson (Karen Black and William Devane), wealthy and gloating, are finally outwitted by their cheaper doubles, a pair of money failures and amateur hustlers Blanche and Lumley (Barbara Harris and Bruce Dern): a case of the pot calling the kettle blacker than black.

Doubling and non-identity

Doubling and non-identity are perfectly matched in *Dial 'M' for Murder* where they are a function of tainted exchange. Husband Tony Wendice (Ray Milland) blackmails old college crony Swann (Anthony Dawson) into killing his adulterous spouse Margot (Grace Kelly) in order to inherit her fulsome will. Dawson is an army deserter and confidence trickster with several aliases, a man of no fixed abode or identity. Yet he is well-spoken, well-dressed, and moustachioed with slicked black hair. After Kelly kills him with scissors in desperate self-defence and Milland tries to pin a murder rap on her to conceal his own plot, an inspector calls to unravel the plot before Kelly is executed for her non-existent crime. Inspector Hubbard (John Williams, who also played the role in Frederick Knott's stage play) is well-spoken, well-dressed and moustachioed with slicked black hair. In the realm of visual resemblance it is as if the bourgeois renegade, the criminal con-man, has come back to life as the acceptable face of the Law, humane, decent and cunning. But the resemblance is no arbitrary matter. It is both a function of the protean identity of the trickster and his quest for metaphysical revenge. He metaphorically reincarnates himself as the law-enforcer to get his own back on the blackmailer who has unwittingly sent him to his death. If this sounds far-fetched, let us remember that Anthony Shaffer's play-turned-film by Joseph L. Mankiewicz, *Sleuth* (1972), makes such metaphysics actual. Laurence Olivier cons Michael Caine into a plot to steal his wife's jewellery by putting on a clown's disguise then leaves him for dead. Caine returns literally in the film's second act, disguised as Inspector Doppler, to hound and torment his erstwhile persecutor. With its enclosed theatrical power-games, *Sleuth* could well be *Dial 'M' for Murder*'s sequel. Here the victim returns in disguise to exact revenge: in Hitchcock's more complex film the victim's double who was someone else but uncannily alike, had performed the same function.

Non-identity can also be erotic in its transfers. In flight on the Chicago train because of mistaken identity, Thornhill mistakes Eve for a smart independent businesswoman aiding him because she is captivated by the glamour of his flight, and because, perhaps, he was by this time the great Hollywood star Cary Grant. Later he then mistakes her, as we do, for a Russian agent

Fig. 4 The inscrutable Eve: Eva Marie Saint and Martin Landau in *North by Northwest*

who has betrayed him when in fact she is a double agent enlisted with the task of 'saving' him, though not with seducing him, which is what she has happily done. Thornhill by this time may still not know who she really is and Soviet spy Philip Vandamm (James Mason) whose lover she also is, also does not know who she really is. And until the end the audience does not know who she really is. In classical Hollywood narrative romance is premised on the kiss and the embrace. Yet Hitchcock duly transforms romance into Eros by deepening the contrast between the couple's tactile encounter and their mental relations of *non-identity*. The train scenes actually define Kendall/ Saint for us more clearly when we know not who she is, than do the final scenes where she reveals herself as working for CIA boss Leo G. Carroll. Viscerally, she is who she is not, just as circumstantially Thornhill-as-Kaplan is also who he is not. To find out who she 'really' is, is to limit the openness of possibility. For she is what she has become to us, watching her as the action unfolds.

This leads us to a general point. In Hitchcock identity is redefined through the forming of new relations. Identity does not pre-exist those relations or transcend them. Without them it is nothing, and moreover it is nothing without a world of significant objects that mediate between his characters in its reformation, objects whose power to connect are both material and symbolic in form. They are instrumental in an obvious way: yet they also symbolise key forms of human exchange. Cinematically, such key objects are repeating images that imprint themselves on the spectating brain. Here are just a few of the more memorable – the handcuffs in *The 39 Steps* and in *Saboteur*, the glass of milk in *Suspicion* (1941), the open razor in *Spellbound*, the wine bottle in *Notorious*, the rope in *Rope*, the telephoto lens in *Rear Window*, the front-door key in *Dial 'M' for Murder*, the portrait of Carlotta Valdez – and hair spiral – in *Vertigo*, the caged love-birds in *The Birds*, the safe in *Marnie*, the tiepin in *Frenzy*. Hitchcock's subjects are defined by a crucial relation to precise objects that relate them in turn to those fateful Others who are (for good or ill) defining the nature of their fraught lives. As objects framed by the moving image in varieties of repetition Hitchcock ensures they have for their audiences, to paraphrase Hume, maximum force and vivacity. As they impact upon us, identity is perpetually refined and redefined by external relations. Precise objects objectify the relations of Hitchcock's subjects and bind them together.

Even the device of confession, with its religious source, seen as a secret unveiling of the soul's guilt or sinfulness, exclusive and intimate, is vital to this exteriority. It is a function of transaction more than of selfhood, a relation between the one who listens and the one who speaks, priest and worshipper, analyst and patient. For Hitchcock it is to *whom* you confess that is just as important, or often more so, than *what* you confess. Of course it is both. Yet the soul's secrets only have meaning when said to someone who has equal meaning to the teller: the witness is then bound to the sinner through the transgressive nature of the secret. The confession works best too when there is ambiguity at the heart of its context. It is because John Ballantyne (Gregory Peck) in *Spellbound* has pretended to be her professional superior that analyst Constance Pedersen (Ingrid Bergman) is later moved by his confessions as her traumatised patient. Because aggressive suitor Mark Rutland is erotically attracted – as Bergman was by Peck – to his would-be lover Marnie he finds her confessions riveting. Confession, in short, is a turn-on: confession, romanticised, is the prelude to a kiss, or here beyond romance, to marital rape. But it is also more. It works best when Hitchcock eschews its official conventions. On first sight he is at his weakest when constrained by them, with the technicalities of the priesthood in *I Confess* or the psycho-babble that mars the end of *Spellbound*. (The power of both films, in fact, comes from the complex subtext to a simplistic text.) He is undoubtedly at his strongest when the fixed roles of the confessional – religious (Catholicism) or secular (psychoanalysis) – are broken down. In *Vertigo* James Stewart is a cop-turned-private-investigator-turned-pseudo-analyst trying to 'cure' Kim Novak of her deathly infatuation with mad ancestor Carlotta Valdez.

Hitchcock then turns the film around to show us the destructiveness of his passion. In Joseph Stefano's draft screenplay for *Marnie* – shelved when Grace Kelly became unavailable for the part of Marnie – the roles of shrink and husband were divided. Later, when Hitchcock re-ignited the project and turned to playwright Jay Presson Allen for his final script, the roles become combined triumphantly in the figure of Mark, amateur analyst, ambivalent lover, marital rapist.

Deadly exchanges

The Hitchcock confessional has strong roots in the Catholic doctrine of sin and repentance with which he was all too familiar. Indeed this is where it first becomes a *transaction*, by virtue of two things: first through the confessor's bearing witness that implicates him (as in *I Confess*) and then through the expiation of the sin that brings release to the sinner. Later it had a secular take-up as therapy-science in the age of Freud: psychoanalysis after all inaugurated the cult of the talking cure for the twentieth century, a cult that was a growing movement in the US when Hitchcock reached Hollywood in the 1940s. But in both cases, faith and science, there is a common denominator. Confession is also a form of *exchange*. Moreover forms of exchange, as Rohmer and Chabrol have shown us so clearly, are vital components of the external relation in Hitchcock's work. In the Rohmer-Chabrol formula, there are four basic forms: (1) moral exchange (the transfer of guilt); (2) psychological exchange (suspicion); (3) dramatic exchange (blackmail); and (4) 'concrete' exchange (to-and-fro movement) (1979: ix). Often combinations of the four dovetail as trans-active elements of Hitchcock's film form. We can surely add to this the observation that any one transfer usually embodies some elements of all the others. For how in Hitchcock can you separate them? In suspicion, there are usually elements of guilt, in guilt often elements of blackmail and so on. And we can add something else too. Exchange is a register of shifting power-relations where Hitchcock's protagonists make moves for and against each other in a game that is ever changing and often deadly.

Rohmer and Chabrol also contend that in Hitchcock there is no zero-sum concept of guilt. We might think the innocent would recognise their innocence and the guilty acknowledge their guilt. Yet the opposite is true. The more innocent Hitchcock's subjects are the more they exhibit symptoms of guilt (1979: 44). The more outrageous the accusations levelled by the police against Manny Balestrero in *The Wrong Man*, for example, the more he seems to accept them with an air of numbed fatality. Meanwhile the police detective who incriminates him is suitably unfazed when he realises his big mistake. The guiltier Hitchcock's subjects, the less guilt bothers them. All the way from Joseph Cotten in *Shadow of a Doubt* to Barry Foster in *Frenzy* we have

Fig. 5 Lost in space: Cary Grant and Eva Marie Saint in *North by Northwest*

prime guiltless performances of villainy. And here the transfer of guilt is always a dramatic bonus; Robert Walker blithely transferring guilt to the hapless Farley Granger in *Strangers on a Train*, Cotten deviously transferring guilt to his vulnerable niece Teresa Wright in Hitchcock's smalltown psychodrama, Ray Milland ingeniously transferring guilt to Grace Kelly, his assaulted spouse in *Dial 'M' for Murder, Frenzy*'s Forster happily transferring guilt to Jon Finch, his morose younger double in Covent Garden. Here Hitchcock's interest in guilt cannot be reduced, as he reminded Truffaut, to the question of original sin and it made no sense to regard him as a 'Catholic artist'. For innocence was equally important in questions of secular justice. Conversely, the internalisation of values – our sense of what is just and fair – balances out the law's errors and limitations, which in Hitchcock's flair for irony are manifold.

And finally a word about the 'transfer of guilt' that takes us beyond the Catholic metaphysics of Rohmer and Chabrol to the critical writing of René Girard. One of its sources is in a primal form of symbolic exchange that is religious, not secular, and symbolised in Western civilisation by Christian communion rites. According to Girard, the significance of Christ's Passion was the substitution of self-sacrifice for blood-sacrifice in the historical relationship of violence and the sacred (1979: 39–67). Primal guilt transfer can also be conceived of in a special way, not as an offshoot of moral sin but its substitution by a guilt that cannot, by definition, be assuaged. We are indebted that Christ's self-sacrifice has saved us, but guilty too that we have not prevented that sacrifice from taking place in the first place. But then it could not be otherwise if we are to be 'saved'. Guilt, on this reckoning, is irrational yet built into the devout psyche and Hitchcock's films trade on this in an oblique way, and in mundane and practical settings. In his films the source of the guilt too is transformed: it is no longer in the 'good', or the Son of God, but in the evil of mankind that we are also powerless to prevent. The historic transference is vital. Hitchcock's subjects feel guilty not about the crucifixion but about a current evil they cannot stop. Not only are Hitchcock's wrong men and women falsely accused, they often feel an irrational guilt about an evil emanating from other sources that they could not prevent. If Hitchcock's play on the transfer of guilt works so effectively by making it empirical, not transcendental, a feature of forms of transaction that can affect all of us in our everyday lives, it is also because it is embodied in an epoch that is uneasily half-secular and half-religious, by a 'sacrificial unconscious' (see Orr 1998: 32–68).

Let us return to Hume. 'All kinds of reasoning', he wrote, 'consist in nothing but a *comparison*, and a discovery of those relations, either constant or inconstant, which two or more objects bear to each other' (2000: 52). In watching Hitchcock's films with their exchange aesthetic this is the kind of reasoning the spectator must employ. Yet the spectator's judgement is often fired up by visceral means, by sensation. Hitchcock often induces our response to these relations in two ways, one of *shock* or *terror* when we are in the dark and thus startled by what suddenly happens and the other of *suspense* when we are already on a knife-edge because of what we know, but cannot second-guess the consequences. 'On the screen', he wrote in 1949, 'terror is induced by surprise, suspense by forewarning' (Gottlieb 1997: 118). In both cases spectators are forced to reconstruct the destructive relations between pursuers and pursued, guilty and innocent, asking themselves why and how. This follows in part from a pattern of intelligible narrative we always find in the Hollywood cinema of Hitchcock's time. There is no final cul-de-sac: on the surface most things too in Hitchcock narration are knowable (if not known). Yet Hitchcock does go further. In any key transaction everything is clear and ambiguous *at the same time*. For this reason the geometry of destructive relations is a constant challenge. We always move forward with the plot to find out what happens, through shock or suspense, but then have the trickier task of working out the relationship of innocence and guilt (moral judgment). For Hitchcock is as fascinated by innocence as he is by guilt. In figuring out their ambiguous relations we end up exposing the elegant edifice that is Hitchcock's formal construction and unerring trademark, as something very different – an elaborate house of cards.

Hitchcock then is a philosopher at one stage removed. He is always transferring his experience of experience into a conscious fiction aided by others
in the film community. Often the source of his fiction is written fiction, but
it is his experience of the world and his moulding (with his screenwriters)
of that fiction that counts more. Fiction is an elegant construction, an edifice
for the story. But within its framework chaos ensues. According to Hume,
constructing fictions is something all of us do some of the time, whether
we know it our not, in our daily lives. For the construction of belief out of
experience is itself a form of enduring fiction that nourishes us in the course
of our everyday living, that makes sense of our inchoate worlds even if it
stretches the evidence to breaking-point. It is also an active pursuit. In his
'Book of the Passions' Hume also compares philosophy to hunting (2000:
451), for both match passion to utility, the thrill of the chase to the purpose
of consuming our booty, that is, delivering meaning. In Hitchcock's quest
narratives his subjects turn into philosopher-hunters in a rather different
way. Often they are caught up obsessively in the passion of the perceptual
chase by force of circumstance, either to atone for past failures or because
they themselves are the hunted. The dilemma is often stark: hunt or be hunted, stalk out the truth or become the prey of falsity, chase in order to end the
chaos of their flight.

    Rohmer and Chabrol were right: exchange, in Hitchcock, is the 'sub-
stance', the only substance, of his cinematic form. Dissecting the enigma of
his characters always has resonance but we have to understand that they are
what they are because they are what they become in the duration of his plots.
It is why any flashback to time past (to a time, that is, before the film begins)
is unusual and only rarely works (as it does in *Marnie* or *I Confess*, the great
exceptions to the rule). For Hitchcock is more interested in how the past
works itself out in the present, on what it means now than what it once was.
In this stress on the present the fate of the second Mrs De Winter far over-
shadows the importance of Rebecca's elusive nature. The revelations about
the shipwreck that are part of the dénouement constitute the film's MacGuffin, the necessary disclosure (Maxim absolved of blame, Rebecca a villain) to
seal a neat but empty closure to replace the ending Hitchcock wanted but was
denied. Thus for most viewers the real ending is the enduring image Hitchcock creates (not in the book) of the now insane Mrs Danvers at the upper
window perishing amidst the flames of Manderley. Anyone who watches the
film closely can see the course it charts: the impact on Joan Fontaine of escaping one female nightmare (companion to an overbearing American dowager) through an 'ideal' marriage (rich, handsome but indifferent Maxim de
Winter) only to confront a second nightmare (lesbian housekeeper Danvers).
Flight from constraint is a necessary impulse of the free at heart. But here
choice is a double-edged sword. Fontaine swaps one form of exchange (unde-

sirable) for another (potentially desirable) only to end up involuntarily with a third (impossible) where the roles of the first exchange are completely reversed – Fontaine is now the mistress, Danvers the housekeeper – yet has her new status undermined by the use of knowledge-as-power (Fontaine ever in the dark, Danvers as forbidding keeper of Rebecca's memory). We might note too how memory works here in the threat to identity. Hume had stated that memory is the fallback position of the fragile self but Fontaine wants to forget her own past in her new life at Manderley only to be confronted at every turn by the past of the predecessor she has never met. In a form of deadly exchange she has to trade in her own memories and accept the memorialising of her predecessor, who is also her deadly rival.

We can see here the importance of Hitchcock's formalist approach to character that put him at odds with the Method school of acting emerging from the New York Actor's Studio and transforming American film in the 1950s. In his male actors Hitchcock wanted a strong singular image that could be manufactured and controlled, often fixity to set against the oscillation, equally controlled, of his ambivalent heroines. With few exceptions, he created a cinema of *figures*, not of characters, the creation of icons in which the reaction shot, the close-up and montage are paramount. Here it is the encounter not the self that is paramount: Robert Donat versus Madeleine Carroll, Cary Grant versus Ingrid Bergman, Joseph Cotten versus Teresa Wright, James Stewart versus Kim Novak, Sean Connery versus Tippi Hedren. The 'versus' of adversaries is how we remember them. In contrast, it was Elia Kazan, Fred Zinneman, Nicholas Ray, Arthur Penn and Douglas Sirk who directed the psychodramas of fullness and depth in the 1950s, the search for deep, misunderstood selfhoods. Here the Stanislavskian or Method acting of James Dean, Marlon Brando, Montgomery Clift and Paul Newman sets the later standard for Robert De Niro, Al Pacino, Dustin Hoffman, Meryl Streep, Daniel Day Lewis, Sean Penn and many others. They all try to tease out the reality of character as a thing of moral and physical substance. By contrast the Hitchcock focus is pure and precise: on identities lost and found. In his chase thrillers and his comedies they are recovered after a fashion, always tongue-in-cheek. In his later and darker period, starting with *Rear Window*, they are never truly recovered at all. In *The Wrong Man*, *Vertigo*, *Psycho* and *The Birds* something is lost, and lost forever.

Miracle transitions

Let us now return to yet another dimension of Hume that can be found lurking in *Rear Window*. What Hitchcock does here, in his most powerfully reflexive film, is to meditate on the audio-visual imaging of a fiction that turns out to be 'a truth', a miracle transition if you like, that turns belief into knowledge. As text, it is inductive. Jeff cobbles together, from fragmented evidence and a set of educated guesses, a contention that Thorwald has murdered his wife and dismembered her body. And he is no active investigator but wheelchair-bound and fallible. His impaired physique (the broken bones of a bad accident encased in plaster) seems a metaphorical stand-in for the vulnerable subject of Humean philosophy. His bodily state should be enough to give inductive reasoning a bad name; yet the opposite turns out to be the case. His low sex-drive and excess curiosity imbalance his use of the senses to his advantage – seeing and hearing at the expense of smell and touch. Moreover it is *distant* sight and hearing over anything close at hand. His ears strain to disentangle a multitude of courtyard sounds. Seated by his window, his neck cranes constantly: his eyeballs swivel to the corners of his eyes. Famously he neglects the nearness of the beautiful Grace Kelly in favour of sights and sounds from the far windows of the courtyard. Deficits of smell and touch as senses close to the body are balanced out by a surfeit of distant sense-impressions, the seeing and hearing in which seeing is prolonged staring and hearing is over-hearing or straining to hear what is out of earshot. For Jeff the lure of out there is always greater than the attraction of here. The fact that he can deduce anything from this miasma of perceptual imbalance is a small miracle. But that perhaps is Hitchcock's laconic point.

Here something new enters the equation. Hitchcock well knew from his strict education that curiosity was pronounced a sin under the Catholic moral code (Truffaut 1986b: 490). Staring and overhearing can be sinful occupations since they stray beyond the normal grounds of perception regulated by a proper theology. Hitchcock's cinema is a form of rebellion at one stage removed, where the play on curiosity complements the play on confession. His most fascinating characters explore the world more obsessively than modesty allows. Yet if Hitchcock's cinema is on the rebound from aspects of a Catholic system of belief, as Rohmer and Chabrol assert, then that belief-system must still have an intrinsic importance. It cannot be reduced to a pure geometry of mental images as Deleuze insists it should be, or where exchange is purely a formal, filmic relationship between component parts of the life-process on screen (1986: 202–4). Exchange is still a matter of human fate, not a trans-human process of transacting where objects are seen as having an equal imagistic status to the beings using them.

By ignoring the question of value and reducing exchange-relations to object relations that are in turn reduced to mental images, Deleuze's fertile comments cease to be fertile; he throws the baby out with the bathwater. Hitchcock's characters are then seen not so much as material bodies but as machines. True, Rohmer and Chabrol do exaggerate the importance of Catholic systems in Hitchcock's cinema. They confuse the edifice of narrative as a well-constructed fiction – which Hitchcock sometimes left initially to his screenwriters – with a Platonic Idea, a leitmotif or guiding idea often indicated by the Hitchcock film title that imposes the perfection of form upon a formless world. But many Hitchcock titles were changed during production or added afterwards. They approximate the process we see on the screen and no more: they are not exact signifiers and never can be. Moreover the tight construction of the fiction always plays off against the subjective chaos and misrecognitions of perception. There is a 'via media' we can assert, between the Platonic and the relational. Some form of received belief – Hitchcock remained a devout Catholic all his life – will leave its trace in *relational form* on his filmmaking. And this is important. The transaction of the confession is one key residue. The transformation of sin into guilt in the age of modernity is another. And here's another, as Midge (Barbara Bel Geddes) says to the shrink in *Vertigo*: curiosity killed the cat and in *Rear Window* it nearly kills 'Jeff' Jeffries. But then in Hitchcock curiosity – the sin – is inseparable from the miracle of belief transformed into pure 'knowledge', which is a form of grace whose possibilities never leave Hitchcock's work.

We can again quote Hume – this time on curiosity:

> Beside the love of knowledge, which displays itself in the sciences, there is a certain curiosity implanted in human nature, which is a passion deriv'd from a quite different principle. Some people have an insatiable desire of knowing the actions and circumstances of their neighbours, tho' their interest be in no way concerned with them, and they must entirely depend on others for their information… (2000: 289)

He could well have been prophesying the event that was *Rear Window*. And curiosity *is* a great passion. 'As the vivacity of the idea gives pleasure, so its certainty prevents uneasiness', Hume continues, 'by fixing one particular idea in the mind, and keeping it from wavering in the choice of objects' (ibid.). This could well the motto for L. B. Jeffries: fixity of the idea, sensitivity of the ear, fanaticism of the gaze. Here Hume and Hitchcock converge. For both, curiosity is one of the great passions that underpin reason and all its deductions and that make reason indeed its slave.

If the passion-sin of curiosity plunges Jeff into a new set of transactions, it is not purely because Hitchcock wants to explore the voyeuristic nature of his personality. What he probes more fully is the unbalanced transaction between the wounded hunter and his unknowing objects opposite, but also in conjunction, the redefining of relations between himself and his allies – his lover, housekeeper and local detective who are drawn into the template of the hunt and into a voyeur's curiosity. Denying their accusations of 'idle' curiosity Jeff soon transfers to them the force and vivacity of his own perceptions. That is, he convinces them that a murder has been committed, on the basis of flimsy evidence where he can see through windows but not behind walls. Yet the force and vivacity of selective perceptions, natural (but limited to the eye and the ear) and technical (enhanced through his telephoto lens), are taken up as a persuasive story and reinforced by the others using active means from which Jeff's immobility prevents him. In breaking into the murderer's apartment via the fire escape and then stealing the victim's wedding ring, Lisa (Grace Kelly) is the active agent of his immobile curiosity and her action itself is a source of erotic attraction for him. (He moans 'No! No!' as the pleasure of watching her intrusion engulfs him.) The desire aroused, despite denial, at seeing her violation of male property (a trope repeated with the safe-robbing in *Marnie*) overrides any desire to touch her, a desire her famous slow-motion kiss had earlier failed to generate.

The act of intrusion he watches from across the courtyard is also a form of exchange. Lisa's movements rekindle Jeff's interest in her, which is what she wants, by serving as his active detective, which is what he wants. Yet the erotic and the moral can never be identical. If there has been no murder after all, then her actions and his, acts of voyeuristic intrusion, are criminal, a minor form of complicity enacted by this exchange. In Hitchcock's cine-philosophy, exchange and complicity often tie the knot, and thrust relations into realms of deep ambiguity; no less famously than in *Strangers on a Train* where, as Guy, Farley Granger's failure to keep his side of a murderous bargain with Bruno (Robert Walker) finally helps to exonerate him. Is Guy less guilty because he has refused (but only just) his side of the bargain, namely to kill Bruno's father after Bruno had gone ahead and strangled Guy's wife with sadistic pleasure? Is he less guilty because Bruno has lured him into the spectre of murderous exchange in the first place? Is he exonerated by his change of heart that finally sees him hunt down his wife's blackmailing killer, even though he has secretly desired her murder? Finally the question comes back to another kind of desire: is Guy not made weak in resisting the devil's pact in the first place by a desire that dares not speak its name, a hidden desire for the man who promises to kill his wife?

In structuring narrative Hitchcock knew that a plot objective was vital to generating the transactions he wished to show. The MacGuffin was his name for a narrative device masquerading as a plot objective, like the secret formula that must be found in *The 39 Steps* (Spoto 1983: 145). Its significance is not what it is but *that* it is. The term, coined by Hitchcock in conversation with his Scottish screenwriter Angus MacPhail, designates a formula, a 'something' that must be found, whatever it is, and so provide a neat restoration of equilibrium to relations that are in disequilibria. It is not what is discovered that counts, but *that* it is, a formula that works for thrillers like *The 39 Steps*, *The Lady Vanishes* (1938) and *Foreign Correspondent*. In some cases we realise the MacGuffin is not necessarily a red herring. After all, the uranium ore in *Notorious* that is the cause-of-all-things-suspenseful and which Hitchcock called a MacGuffin was a sharp educated guess on his part, with some hands-on research, about the beginnings of atomic espionage in 1945 (see McGilligan 2003: 370–1). In his best films the MacGuffin can be more, not less, than meets the eye. Even so, if we think too closely about many Hitchcock plots – *Suspicion, Spellbound, Dial 'M' for Murder* or *Vertigo* – we find them so implausible we feel it must be their *filmic* logic that forces us to suspend disbelief. Restoration of equilibrium is something about which Hitchcock usually cares less about than the disequilibria preceding it; it should be seen as a 'miraculous', but tongue-in-cheek, plot closure that poses as the fruit of triumphant logic. But it actually surpasses all logic. The function is elsewhere. Its very weakness means that retrospectively it does give clarity to transactions preceding it. Its disappointment-value, its lack of credibility enhances *their* residual powers. In *Spellbound* you sense that Hitchcock is more interested in the twinned fate of Peck and Bergman than in Peck's implausible confusion over the ski murder he has witnessed and which a 'talking cure' ponderously brings into the light of day. Or rather he is more interested in the dynamics of Bergman initially drawing it out of him – the 'how' that fuses Eros and power overruling the 'what' of the MacGuffin. A revelation is at hand, but really is not. Instead the revelation is Hitchcock's mode of revealing. Here his laconic irony allowed him to meditate on the miracle of the devised ending. Often the MacGuffin is better seen as a 'MacMiracle' and this leads us back to Hume, who did not believe in miracles at all.

Curiously, Hume developed his thoughts on religious miracles while in France after dialogue with Jesuit priests at La Flèche seminary, and Hitchcock had certainly imbibed his own fair share of miracle theology in his Jesuit education. Both unerringly sense what drives the appeal of the miracle as a pure revelation for human nature; Hume called it 'the passion of *surprise* and *wonder*'. As a sceptic, however, the philosopher also warns: 'If the spirit of religion joins itself to the love of wonder, there is an end of common sense.' But Hume notes too the other essential ingredient, the shared nature of the miracle. As witnessing it is 'an agreeable emotion'; thus 'people love to partake of the satisfaction at second-hand or by rebound' (1971: 213). (To challenge miracles was an act of courage for Hume in eighteenth-century Scotland, but he was not so courageous as to endanger his own skin. It was a section he chose to withdraw from the first publication of the *Treatise on Human Nature*.) Yet his description of the miracle still seems appropriate to the way in which the plot 'MacMiracle' of *Rear Window* works. Jeffries enthusiastically relays observations as a way of persuading others of the revelation-at-hand. Of course the revelation, as in any detection plot, is not of God's goodness but of mortal evil. Hitchcock often plays on the ironic disconnection of 'God' and 'good'. Here he explores the irony even further. The detection miracle seems a result of chance observation but it is actually the result of addictive surveillance, which the spouse-murder then 'exonerates'. The power of Jeffries' conviction is matched here by the director's power of deconstruction. As Jeffries convinces his allies, and the audience, of his revelation-at-hand Hitchcock is busy deconstructing the excess curiosity driving him in the first place. This double movement, the subtending of the miracle and its concurrent refusal, is what gives the film its ontological edge.

At the same time, *The Wrong Man* is Hitchcock's clearest challenge to Humean scepticism, by virtue of its documentary truth. For Hitchcock reconstructs an actual court case, where a juror's chance remark and the resulting declaration of a mistrial did save Manny Balestrero from wrongful conviction. Here he poses a different question: perhaps chance is not chance after all. To reinforce the point Hitchcock invents a sequence that pivots on one of the great lap-dissolves of cinema. As the persecuted Manny prays to Christ's portrait, his face is gradually replaced by that of his criminal double, the real hold-up man about to embark on another escapade in which, this time, he gets caught (Brill 1999: 212–13). True miracles will not go away and cannot be wiped out by a knowing irony. Indeed irony here works in their favour, the irony of timing as miraculous intervention. In Hitchcock the question remains open, and the answer to the question ever a mystery. If *Rear Window* or *Spellbound* depend on 'MacMiracles' to sustain Hitchcock's true interest in something very different, here a genuine miracle of chance *is* his true interest and its mystery will not go away. The term 'MacMiracle' is hence too flippant and should be abandoned. For despite all his ironic bracketing, Hitchcock was serious. Our exchange model shows us instead that what we have is a *perverse miracle*, a trade-off where the miraculous event occurs but only at a price: for Balestrero, release as the price of his wife's sanity, for Jeffries, the breaking of both legs as the price of successful sleuthing, for Scottie Ferguson the loss of Madeleine that obviates his unravelling of her true identity and the curing of his vertigo, while for Melanie Daniels a deep bonding with the Brenner family is only made possible by the massed bird assault that nearly takes her life and leaves her devastated.

Hitchcock's 'Scottish' philosopher

Between *Rear Window* and *The Wrong Man* Hitchcock gave us his remake of *The Man Who Knew Too Much*, again with James Stewart in the lead male role, and again posing the question of the detective 'miracle' about which, as a film philosopher, Hitchcock was so ambivalent. Taking Stewart's four Hitchcock pictures, a common pattern of investigation emerges: commonsense-man investigates unlikely events, one of which turns to be a kidnapping and planned assassination, the other three unlikely murders. At one level Stewart is a version of the material American smalltown guy, plain-talking and direct, his feet firmly on the ground. In his life he had been, growing up with Scots-Irish lineage in upstate Pennsylvania. At another level, all four films embroil him in layers of perceptual confusion where at times he takes leave of his senses, somewhat dubiously, in order to solve a mystery. In *The Man Who Knew Too Much* he is cast as Dr Ben McKenna and in *Vertigo* as ex-policeman John 'Scottie' Ferguson', Scottish names that echo the actor's own and indicate a tenacious homespun philosopher. Both films – unlike *Rope* and *Rear Window* – are films of change and motion, yet what singles out the kidnap thriller from the other three is a further dislocation. As Rupert Cadell in *Rope*, then as Jeff and as Scottie, Stewart was cast as a city-dweller on home turf. Here he is abroad and adrift with wife Jo (Doris Day) and son Hank (Christopher Olson) in tow, first in French colonial Morocco and then in London. While the other three films play on our sense of the uncanny, the unfamiliar being played out in familiar places, this is a story of the strange and the unexpected elsewhere, an elsewhere in which Stewart never really gets his bearings at all. Hitchcock, moreover, plays with some irony on our sense of cultural strangeness. We might expect freaky things to happen in Marrakech but once back in London we expect a more readable 'Western' culture to emerge. Of course, it does not. The McKennas find London just as eerie and unpredictable.

The film is thus a quest marked by a series of mis-recognitions, which shift our character sympathies around in no small manner (see Smith 1995: 86–95). Hitchcock ups the ante early on, when the McKenna family take the bus in from the airport to Marrakech. As the bus jolts on a bumpy road Hank accidentally pulls the veil from the face of a Muslim passenger and prompts a near riot. The disbelieving trio learn from a nearby Frenchman, who calms down the passengers with a few words of Arabic, that Hank has just committed a serious offence to local custom and faith. Being naïve insensitive tourists does not augur well for what follows. But then what follows is even more unpredictable. The McKennas accept Frenchman Louis Bernard (Daniel Gelin) as their new friend but Ben gets angry with him for breaking a dinner date and eating elsewhere in the same restaurant with a woman companion. Meanwhile they meet an English couple, the Draytons, who stare at them unduly provoking their unease but then befriend them, putting them fully at their ease. This is a typical Hitchcock transfer: suddenly the friendly guy becomes distant while the hostile couple become friendly. On the low awkward dining couches where Stewart finds nowhere to put his long legs and no willing fingers with which to eat his spiced chicken joints, the English accents of the Draytons are soothing and reassuring. The two couples are framed opposite one another in shot/reverse-shot to stress resemblance, true at the level of language and culture, yet false at another level of which the Mackennas are blithely unaware, that of ideology. For the very English Mr Drayton (Bernard Miles) masquerading as a United Nations aid official is in fact a Soviet spy. Though this is a French colony on the verge of independence, the danger comes not from the locals but from their fellow Westerners, who are anything but what they seem.

McKenna has thus misread two situations, if not a third, since Bernard is also a spy, a French agent on 'our' side who has spotted a possible assassin from the 'other' side. This is sealed by the marketplace sequence the next day where an Arab staggers threateningly towards Stewart (echoing the irate Arab who shouts at him on the bus). Only here we have another role-reversal. The 'Arab' is actually Bernard in blackface, staggering because he has been stabbed in the back, by another 'Arab' in blackface, in fact a European spy. In the commotion Ben and Jo (with Mr Drayton) leave Hank with Mrs Drayton while they visit the police commissioner who tells Ben who Bernard really is. Ben then dispatches the solicitous Drayton to find Hank and his wife, thus unintentionally delivering his son into the arms of his Soviet kidnappers. At every key moment Stewart has reacted like anyone in his Western audience might do, and reacted strongly and wrongly. 'Commonsense' has led him into one mistake after another. He is so grounded that he cannot read the signs: or in other words the customary signs of his own world no longer apply in this one and he is utterly lost.

Hitchcock, however, has not finished with us and plays another shrewd joke on his audience at his hero's expense in the Ambrose Chapel(1) sequences. 'Ambrose Chapel' is the last word of the dying Bernard whispering of a London assassination plot. Stewart/McKenna takes it to be a person, Ambrose Chapell, not a place, and thus sets out on another fool's errand, which lands him at an unlikely taxidermist's where chaos duly reigns, as he demands the return of his son. On her own initiative Jo then visits a different Ambrose Chapel, a Protestant place of worship where Mrs Drayton wields a collection-box and Mr Drayton sports a dog collar to deliver his sermon to a congregation of ageing women. Part of the joke is of course that a taxidermist is no less likely to be a Soviet kidnapper than a Protestant clergyman. But then neither is likely; the movie's choice of one to fill the unlikely role is arbitrary on Hitchcock's part in a very knowing way. In the Hitchcock world of perception there is a narrow line between being stupidly wrong and inspiringly right. That is also his vision of the world as such, the world outside film. His filmic universe thus exaggerates what happens to us all the time.

The two London versions of Ambrose Chapel(1) provide a fascinating mix of continuity and contrast with the Morocco sequences. Cliché would have given us a rainy London to set against a hot, parched North Africa, yet the grimy London streets seem bright with light and baked in a summer heat. The contrast lies in the volume and the fullness of the frame. The Marrakech marketplace is alive with noise, traffic and bustle but the empty London streets along which Ben and Jo stride in uncertain quest are eerily quiet and car-less. In Morocco the McKennas cannot escape from people: in London they are hard put to find them. This is London in the style of a De Chirico painting and a contrast of continents Antonioni was later to echo in *The Passenger* (1975). The separate journeys are filmed in repetition on almost identical streets, but Hitchcock rings the changes on the shooting style. As Ben walks up the empty alleyway to the taxidermists, the camera follows with an eerie POV shot, a trademark version of anticipation and suspense, but metaphorically a version of going up a blind alley. Jo's journey to the Chapel produces the opposite effect. She stops opposite and looks across at the closed chapel door, totally unpromising. But then Hitchcock produces a miracle cut that goes beyond her point-of-view. We are suddenly inside where a service is about to take place. The Draytons' female accomplice is playing at the organ, Mrs Drayton is busy with a collection box and her husband is readying himself for the sacred event of worship. It is indeed a revelation, but framed like a daydream of revelation, of wish-fulfilment. It is the film's version of the Hitchcock Miracle, where the cut is analogous to a leap of faith, which is then exonerated. To the audience who sees it, and to Jo who cannot see it but perhaps imagines it, it seems the one sure image, finally a truth beyond appearances in a film where appearance has been everything.

We can end this speculation on philosopher and cineaste with yet another point of contact – that of the *sublime* and add to it the question of naming. Here there is a fascinating transformation in Stewart's acting from *Rope* and *Rear Window* to the great masterpiece *Vertigo*. He starts off as the acting investigator and ends up as the investigator investigated. In the first two films he is confined to a single room, until the murderer thrusts him down into the courtyard at the end of *Rear Window*. In *The Man Who Knew Too Much* he has to rely on the spouse he regards as an inferior detective to correct his misrecognitions. In *Vertigo* he is largely on own. He treks endlessly though a whole city, San Francisco – whose initials are those of his own name – and beyond, to the sequoias in Big Basin Park and the mission at San Juan Bautista. In this quest-journey as Scottie Ferguson, Stewart's grip on the actual loosens and finally disintegrates. It seems in fact like a passage from tenacious perception to schizoid fantasy, replicating in shorthand the passage in history from the Humean subject of the eighteenth century (mainstay of the Enlightenment) to the disintegrating personas created by James Hogg and Robert Louis Stevenson in the nineteenth (Enlightenment's romantic nemesis). For these are figures who, like Scottie Ferguson, see double and go insane.

Where does the sublime fit into this? Hume speaks of it in passing in the *Treatise* and sets up a paradox. The vivacity of reflection usually diminishes the greater the distance in space and time of the subject from its object, yet the sublime is such that we *elevate* things of great distance – the temples and churches of earlier civilisations, the grandeur of distant mountain ranges (see Noel 1994: 221–3). What is Hume's solution? The awe and admiration of the greatness of landscape transcends distance but only through 'opposition' (2000: 275–6). For its overcoming is a challenge to our imagination that gives us real pleasure. In Hitchcock the sublime, usually spatial, is likewise a challenge to comprehend the grandeur of scale, and 'conquer' vertigo but can lead to terror as much as to pleasure. Here he is on the side of Burke rather than Hume since it was Burke who spoke of the sublime's 'delightful horror'. If we look *up* at the sight of the Statue of Liberty in *Saboteur* or the Presidential faces carved in the rock of Mount Rushmore in *North by Northwest*, the sight is awesome and pleasurable, but also kitsch. For this, knowingly, is the tourist or artificial sublime. If, however, we are suspended in struggle at the tip of either, looking *down* from a great height, the horror is etched into our gaze. The upward gaze that we identify with modernity's triumph, and which the director mocks, is transformed into the downward look where we dare not look, for there lies death and the darkness of void. Hitchcock ensures it engages our sense to the full. The downward stare reaches perfection in the eyes of James Stewart at the start of *Vertigo*: hanging from ripped guttering into the void of space, then the cut to the famous POV vertigo shot down the side of the tall building in which Hitchcock blended a reverse track with a forward zoom. Thereafter San Francisco becomes a true city of heights in Hitchcock's *mise-en-scène* of the car stalking where Scottie tracks Madeleine and nearly all the shots are *downhill* shots, as are the Corniche shots in *To Catch a Thief*, where Cary Grant and Grace Kelly dice with death on hairpin bends or its comically sexy Californian reprise, the 'orgasm descent' endured by Barbara Harris and Bruce Dern in *Family Plot*.

As Noel points out, Hume's take on the sublime involves the key question of aesthetic judgment; it is the impression of distance in the perceiving eye, not distance itself that is crucial (1994: 222). The sublime is in the eye of the beholder and his semi-subjective stance seems to anticipate Kant, whose view of it is much better known. This too seems to be central to Hitchcock's vision. To focus once more on Stewart we find that Scottie's condition, vertigo, is where the sublime becomes agoraphobic. The sequoia trees, the Mission tower, the Golden Gate Bridge are all places that induce the sense of a falling from a great height that is simultaneously the source of attraction and horror. Critically, in the second part of the film Hitchcock adds to Scottie's spatial condition the key afflictions of time. In his disturbed memory the images of the past related to Madeleine become sublime and have to be recaptured. Yet they are all part of a compulsion to repeat that ends in nightmare. They are *too close* in time to be truly sublime since they are still part of the living tissue of memory. Against the odds Scottie urges them to be so, to be images of *an impossible sublime*. The images of the dead Madeleine he sees in every other woman he meets, the re-treading of the same path and the same places, the rotating embrace in the Empire hotel room shot against the back-projection of the stables they had visited at the Mission tower, these are all forms of 'delightful horror' that will end in tragedy.

After the claustrophobia of single rooms in *Rope* and *Rear Window* and their conceit of progressive time, *Vertigo* gives us the opposite: openness of spatial encounter, impossible reversals of time. Remember that in *Rope* the atmosphere is doubly claustrophobic. Not only is it limited to one room: the human object of investigation is a corpse buried in a chest that acts as an impromptu dining table. In *Rear Window* there is, by contrast a residue of the sublime, but it is a form of wheelchair sublime. The courtyard windows stand in for the images of the daring adventure photos that adorn Jeff's apartment walls. *Vertigo* is a release and frees Stewart from the windowed prison of his previous Hitchcock movies. Yet it is a release into a greater horror. The down-to-earth investigator, flawed and complicit, is finally freed to explore his phantasmagoria in open spaces. His quest for the impossible sublime has lift-off. It duly leaves the world of the senses behind and replaces it with one of hallucinated doubles. Here, finally, there are no miracles.

If philosophy is the buried lineage in Hitchcock that gets lost in the endless recycling of psychoanalysis and its modish double, psychobabble, then in order to be resurrected, the lineage has to be linked more firmly to his cinematic heritage. Here we can turn to something that is universally acknowledged but still undervalued, Hitchcock's debt to the great filmmakers of Weimar cinema. As we shall see, Hitchcock was never an expressionist but a master, aesthetically speaking, of the expressive moment in film narrative. Many of the great themes of Weimar film are also his, but reworked in such a way as to be transformed. If Weimar produced great figures who made the journey as Hitchcock did, across the Atlantic, the inspiration he took from them was merely a spur to the creations of his mature cinema, truly original, indelibly his own.

chapter 3

EXPRESSIVE MOMENTS: HITCHCOCK AND WEIMAR CINEMA

In the 1920s Hitchcock had turned into a true British director by being somewhere else – Weimar Germany. Here he encountered an exciting cinema whose key innovators, among others, were Friedrich Wilhelm Murnau and Fritz Lang. In Berlin he not only worked as art director and set designer on *The Blackguard* (1924), a Gainsborough-UFA film overseen by Lang's producer, Erich Pommer, but also visited the set of Lang's *Metropolis* at the vast Neubabelsberg Studio to the west of the city. Kinetic crowd scenes of Lang's spectacle-movie shot in 1924–25 may well have inspired the mob sequences at the end of Hitchcock's great silent thriller, *The Lodger*, made on his return to England. The crowd scenes in Lang's earlier *Dr Mabuse, der Spieler* (*Dr Mabuse, the Gambler*, 1922) almost certainly did. Meanwhile the memorable figure of 'the lodger', Ivor Novello, shrouded in a huge dark cape and staring with fanatic eyes on the doorstep of a lower-middle-class home, cued something bizarrely unsettling: Hitchcock's make-over of an English matinee idol into a London vampire worthy of Murnau's *Nosferatu-eine Symphonie des Grauens* (1922). In Berlin Hitchcock had also watched Murnau filming *Der Letzte Mann* (*The Last Laugh*, 1924) with its daring mobile camera shots. From both directors he discovered the key to silent cinema – the priority of the moving image over the titled word. 'My models were forever after the German filmmakers of 1924 and 1925', he later wrote. 'They were trying very hard to express ideas in purely visual terms' (Spoto 1983: 67–8). Indeed Murnau not only tried hard but triumphed emphatically. *Nosferatu*, *Faust* (1926), *The Last Laugh* and his great Hollywood debut, *Sunrise* (1927), are all landmarks in silent cinema that vindicate the expressionist legacy – pure visual stories that tell themselves. The Murnau legacy shows itself soon after in Hitchcock's last silent feature, *The Manxman*, whose ambiguous romance is told, as noted, almost entirely through images.

Was Hitchcock therefore an expressionist? The answer must be yes and no. He used it, copied it, but also went beyond it in forging an *expressive* cinema – which was both more and less than that of the German films he loved. Weimar style also moved away in the late 1920s from its expressionist origins so that its legacy for Western cinema as a whole, firmed up by the flight of so many gifted filmmakers from Hitler's regime, was a synthetic blending of art opposites that came out of Weimar culture. First we need to set the scene before 1914. With the rise of expressionist poetry, drama and painting, the Naturalism prevalent at the turn of century was replaced by something more apocalyptic, a vision of modernity as artificial and deranged, of technology as militaristic and destructive, of the masses as oppressed and rebellious, of civilisation as out of joint unless redeemed by revolutionary utopia (see Eisner 1969: 23–44). Often the movement's creative fictions are subjects vulnerable to the world's turbulence, who imagine with horror its endless flux – unbalanced, disordered, chaotic – not fully knowing whether such disorder is also an affliction of their soul. Weimar film absorbed all these elements but as it progressed towards the sound era it modified this art style, where the actual world and the subjective vision of its fictional subjects are out of kilter through *Neue Sachlichkeit* (New Objectivity), aesthetics where empathy and distortion are denied, where documentary method and critical distance are at the heart of the modern artwork. New Objectivity was strongly influenced by the new technologies of communication, by the popular press with its newsprint, captions and cartoon serials, by photography, advertising, film and radio. In 1927, the year of the release of *Metropolis* with its grand expressionist vision of a futuristic city, came a poetic and sinewy documentary of a real one, Walter Ruttmann's *Berlin: Symphony of a City*. That year presented a stark choice between two contrasting visions, yet by 1931 Fritz Lang had blended expressionist and New Objectivity aesthetics perfectly for *M*, his dark and disturbing vision of contemporary Berlin. For many contemporary critics it is not only his greatest film but also the greatest German film ever (McGilligan 1997: 480).

By 1930 film's rapid technical development had called the expressionist heritage into question. The stage-set artifice in the fairytale world of *The Cabinet of Dr Caligari*, with its Gothic distortions of perspective, was perfect for post-war cinema but did not work for discursive sound narratives. A metaphysic of derangement found its purest expression in silent pictures. One thinks of the opening and closing sequences of Murnau's *Faust*, with its 'fugues of light', which illustrate at the start 'the clash between the explosive brightness of the archangel and the darkness that surrounds the devil' and at the end 'the gentle sunlight which seems to colour the sky' and 'becomes the counterpoint which brings the promise of redemption' (Eisner 1973: 164). Derangement also lies in the phantasmic figures of the un-organic as technology unbound, the robot, the zombie, the vampire, the sleepwalker, automata that steamroller nature out existence (see Deleuze 1986: 51). The most sentimental resolution of this sickness occurs at the end of *Metropolis*, where Lang and screenwriter Thea von Harbou turn it into a false dilemma falsely resolved. The good Maria tries to project her sweetheart Freder as the new and necessary 'heart' mediating in the Worker's City between the heartless 'brain' of technology that produces modern machines and the mindless 'body' of those workers enslaved to its diurnal rhythms, thus creating a new exalted but dubious social order.

Expressionist stylistics also had its own metaphysic of film space. Sometimes seen as just exaggerated stylisation in look or in movement, it always placed the stylisation of the face or the body, the gaze or the gesture in the context of a spatial frame in its *mise-en-scène*. Rohmer puts this most succinctly: 'Movements and gestures whose meaning seemed contingent are in a sense – by their insertion into a certain spatial universe – grounded in necessity' (1989: 26). For Rohmer, Murnau was the supreme master of this daring form of *mise-en-scène*, Welles its most brilliant translator into American cinema. But it is something we also find in Hitchcock. While *The Manxman* was his powerful early evocation of filmic space, the stronger legacy lay in the special design of the Hitchcock murder. At its most effective it is an event that seems on first sight to be contingent but then convinces us it is grounded in necessity. The murder is a key moment in narration that changes the contingent into the necessary: such expressive moments gained strength as Hitchcock's career progressed. *Psycho* gives us here a brilliant study in spatial contrast with its two killings, one claustrophobic the other agoraphobic, which validate Rohmer's point. The murder of Marion Crane in the famous shower montage sequence is a study in kinetic claustrophobia. Trapped between shower curtain and tile surround in the bath of her motel room, she cannot escape from the knife-wielding figure both she and the audience only see in silhouette. She cannot move anywhere but down, so as her body slides down the tiles her head eventually comes to lie in death where her feet had been in life. A spatial montage of entrapment moulds the gaze of horror imprinted on her face. Later, the killing of Arbogast (Martin Balsam), the private investigator, on the vast open staircase of the Bates mansion is the kinetic opposite. Attacked from above by the knife-wielding killer who remains unseen, the high-angled camera follows his backward movement down the stairs, close in on the victim's astounded face, the eyes seeing in clear daylight what Marion had only glimpsed through curtain, steam and water jet. It is clearly a process shot of the staircase matched in editing to the unbalanced body: but the artifice adds to the impact. The vain retreat is a like an endless failing into void, agoraphobic in its threat, a descent into nothingness. In this spatial pairing of contrast and repetition Hitchcock transcends the shock-effect of the generic horror movie and creates his own vision of destiny. At first the killings seem sudden and arbitrary. In retrospect we feel they could not have happened otherwise.

The naturalist framing of *Psycho*, a landscape created out of the life-style and landmarks of 1950s America where even the Bates mansion draws on the Northern Californian style of Gingerbread Gothic, is a far cry from Weimar film in 1925. This leads us to a deeper contrast. *Faust* and *Metropolis* are both *works* of vision, expressive in their entirety, while Hitchcock's films contains *moments* of vision that are expressive in nature but melded into a narrative that is discursive, a world that is naturalised, that embodies order for the most part only to lose it at key instants. Hitchcock never made films about a mythic past or a menacing future, so while Lang's architectural framings for *Die Nibelungen* (1924) and *Metropolis* would have impressed him – in particular the flair for ornament, design and the movement of crowds – their immediate themes and obsessions were never his. Nor were Lang's grandiose metaphysics of the spirit ever his. Nonetheless, Lang and Murnau's visions would impose upon him the realisation that cinematically speaking the world's loss of equilibrium must lie in the detail. In *The Last Laugh* Murnau uses expressive distortion to great effect in Emil Jannings' drunken delirium at home after his demotion from hotel doorman to washroom attendant. He starts to hallucinate ghost porters failing to lift an enormous trunk which he then balances on one hand, a strange lift gliding up the transparent floors of an imaginary building, the doubled face of a woman neighbour with a coffee pot laughing at his misfortune as he can no longer figure what is part of his dream and what is part of his waking life. Murnau's use of dissolves, wipes, superimpositions and dollying camera creates a montage of multiple phantoms in motion, balanced out by exact chiaroscuro of light and shade. In Hitchcock the dramatic change of fortune can also be hallucinatory. We can think of the animated dream sequence in *Vertigo* after Madeleine's 'death' by falling (designed by abstract expressionist John Ferren) in which the distraught Scottie, feeling helpless and guilty to the point of breakdown, is subject to vertiginous nightmares as Hitchcock repeats in abstract form the vertigo motifs made metonymic in Scottie's stalking of Madeleine through the streets of San Francisco. The subjectivist legacy in expressionist montage – the world taken over into the mind of the disturbed subject – thus offers up to Hitchcock a rich source of visual epiphany and its poetic repetition.

In *Metropolis* another great epiphany forms through hallucination during the factory explosion spectacle in the worker's underground. Amidst smoke and fire, the young Freder, delirious, hallucinates the machine, whose rhythms enslave its workers to the tyranny of mechanical time, as a techno-version of Moloch, false biblical God of Sacrifice. Moloch devours worker-victims through the open orifice of its gigantic mouth. The delirium of the living machine as false God shakes him to the core. Far away from Lang's gigantism, we see in *Marnie* that subjective delirium on a human scale, this time a horror of inoffensive nature, an image visually more direct, but psychologically more complex. For the most part, Marnie's world is stable and natural, far away from the phantasmagoria of Lang's worker-city. Yet her neurotic aversion to red gladioli, sudden and unexpected, is an instance of general aversion to the colour red which then repeats itself at key moments through the film. One thing is for sure. It makes her shake all over. Hitchcock floods the screen with red to signify the Pyrrhic victory of the subjective, the power of the imagination triumphant in the cowering and fearful body. It is a startle-effect, a visual punctuation and in Hitchcock a perfect matching of shock and suspense. Her reaction shocks at first because it is so unexpected, but thereafter we are also waiting until it next happens, or to see if it actually will happen. We are waiting for the source of her fear, the colour red, to come back. At the same time we are also spectators performing the same function as Marnie's suspicious employers. We are encouraged to monitor her as a 'pathological' case and her subjective states of mind are always filtered through our distanced witnessing. Hitchcock's film thus frames its subjective and expressive moments within a broader continuum.

If these examples of Hitchcock's expressive moment come from his later films, this is no coincidence; it is only here, in the period between *Rear Window* and *Frenzy*, that the German legacy come to fruition. The more distant from Weimar, the closer Weimar becomes. Thus we have, in relation to German cinema, two 'Hitchcocks'. The first is the Hitchcock of short-term gain who drew from early Lang the poetics of dissembling, flight and suspicion to be found in the Mabuse films and Lang's espionage classic *Spione* (1928). The second is the Hitchcock who reinvented the expressive moment of the 1920s for his more abstract modernist period three decades later. Here there is a true reckoning with *M*'s serial killing in *Frenzy*, with the fatality of *Der Müde Tod* (*Destiny*, 1921) in *Psycho* and in *The Birds*, but equally in most of Hitchcock's films of the period a reckoning with that unique fusion of love and catastrophe to be found in *Sunrise*. Before we turn to these connections let us reformulate the aesthetics of the expressive moment that he inherits in a more precise way.

Expressive aesthetics

The most perceptive critics of Hitchcock's reworking of expressionism are André Bazin and John Belton. Both are brief but succinct. Bazin, a reticent admirer, preferred Welles and Wyler, Renoir and Rossellini for their use of deep-focus and long takes. He had clashed with Hitchcock's young admirers on *Cahiers du Cinéma* for what he took to be their uncritical adulation. Yet, after a brief interview with Hitchcock on the Riviera during a break in the shooting of *To Catch a Thief*, Bazin began to change his mind. From this interview and conversations with Hitchcock's collaborators he formulated a critical insight that is both enigmatic and succinct. Hitchcock, he claimed, had 'a permanent notion of *mise-en-scène*, that of a tension in the interior of a sequence', a tension that leads to 'an essential instability of image'; 'Each shot', he added, 'is like a menace or at least an anxious waiting' (1982: 153). It is a tension both visual and dramatic. The spatial framing lights and places characters and objects in a precise way that generates tension in the viewer, and this is not a matter simply of atmosphere but of impending disequilibrium, an unbalancing act rather than a balancing one. Hitchcock's stylistic variations often consist in new and ingenious ways of formulating incipient menace and the anxious waiting that is a feature not only of his characters onscreen but also of the suspense-fix of his audience viewing that screen, a moment of mutual identity that does not demand empathy or shared emotion but still has the sense of a common fate. But with one or two exceptions, like *The Lodger* or *Sabotage*, the true creation of menace was a long-term outcome of the Weimar legacy that really did not kick in until the start of American Hitchcock. It was not until he had left Europe that Hitchcock really honed his European influences to perfection.

As a critic Bazin notoriously set out his stall against the poetics of montage, which he saw as cheating the autonomous judgement of the spectators by imposing an artificial order created by fast-shot editing. However, Belton has noted Hitchcock's ability to blend expressive *mise-en-scène* with poetic montage, or more precisely, Murnau with Eisenstein. If Murnau used the shot as a unit of expression within which reality is transformed, Hitchcock linked it to a form of dynamic editing in which the cut – or *découpage*, the visual composition of successive cuts – can distance the viewer from the mood or emotion the shot has established. 'Hitchcock's point-of-view editing', Belton contends, 'combines the subjectivity of Murnau with the analytical objectivity of Eisenstein and Kuleshov' (1980: 10). This means that not only does he transform an expressionist aesthetic into an expressive moment circumscribed by montage – he also does the opposite. He transforms an editing experiment with Constructivist aesthetics, Belton continues, into 'an expressionist tool shot within a non-expressionist frame' (ibid.). As a narrative device suspense cannot be seen merely as an offshoot of expressionist aesthetics or the manipulation of an audience. It is also a process of formal construction that lays bare the device. Suspense in films like *Rear Window* becomes a reflexive form since it points to its own origins in narrative construction. It is not invisible, but increasingly transparent, so watching expressive moments of Hitchcock suspense is not a way of forgetting that we are watching a film; it is a way of reminding us more clearly that indeed that is what we are doing. In the title of his essay Belton refers to this reflexive formalism, a little unkindly, as 'dexterity in a void'. Hitchcock himself used the terms 'cheat' or 'cheating' as technical slang for suddenly cutting from a character's point of view, without ever dwelling on the etymology of the word. But such 'cheating' does indeed characterise his technique. We never get too cosy with anyone's adventure. There are always key moments when the director will cut to a more objective shot, and compose a dynamics of exchange between characters, and characters and objects, that is best seen as intra-realist, not subjective or expressionistic. This, as noted, was the basis of Hitchcock's wider aesthetics, intra-realism as the mode of constructing the dynamics of exchange. This was *his* 'new objectivity', and one that is distinctly his own.

While Bazin and Belton seem to explore different aesthetic dimensions of Hitch's achievement, they are in fact closely related. We can see this clearly in the *découpage* of the most underrated of the Kammerspiel films, *Dial 'M' for Murder*. Here Hitchcock adjusts the 'menace' and 'anxious waiting' evoked by the 'instability of the shot' (Bazin's insight) with his trademark blending of expressive moments and constructivist editing (Belton's template). In the key early sequence of the film, we are waiting for Grace Kelly's would-be killer to come at her from behind the curtain covering the French windows without knowing the outcome, which of course is that expressive moment where her hand reaches back in wide-angle shot for the scissors to stab her assailant in the back. Yet Hitchcock prepares the way for this and other expressive moments in the apartment by the tautness of his editing, where he constantly shifts the angle of shot and hence the angle of vision by the sudden cut. Even on a second viewing we often cannot second-guess the shift. Nor can we second-guess the duration of any one shot. Hitchcock will sometimes hold longer than we expect, sometimes less. There is no crossing of the 180-degree line; on the other hand there is scarce use of shot/countershot conventions where the spectator is easily sutured into the dynamics of plot. Intimately we are in the room but spatially we are moved around so much that our gaze cannot settle or our position feel assured. We are not allowed to be fully naturalised observers, for we are there only at the director's invitation. Hitchcock's technique here complements the suspense of the situation, as style blends with content. Will Kelly be murdered, or later when she survives, will her husband's ruse to incriminate her convince the police? The menace of the waiting is matched by the unpredictability of the cut and the placement of the following shot. We know where we are. This, after all, is a ground-floor apartment in Maida Vale, a modest living room with adjoining rooms and an external hallway. Yet the sheer fixity of place, where Hitchcock often uses static camera shots, makes the instability of editing uncanny. Perceptually we know where we are, but cinematically we are shifted, decentred to an extreme degree. In this way, Hitchcock adapts a stage play by notionally retaining its set but in fact liquidating its proscenium arch theatricality. We are, metaphorically speaking, watching not only from the wings but also from centre stage, from backstage, from the footlights, the curtains, the rafters and the balcony and at times we are everywhere at once. At the same time everything is near and tight because the apartment is a studio stage apartment whose removable fourth wall is constantly changing. It is an artificial space and Hitchcock preserves the artifice along with the naturalist illusion. Out of it he creates extraordinary editing rhythms that allow the film to be watched pleasurably again and again.

Hitchcock and Lang: the short-term effect

While Hitchcock was often prepared to name Murnau as an inspiration, he failed to do the same unambiguously with Lang, feigning scant knowledge of Lang's *M* years later with Truffaut, when every film buff knew that he had cast Peter Lorre in his 1930 films on the basis of Lorre's great role in Lang's picture. Speaking of the violent end to his *The Man Who Knew Too Much* Hitchcock named as history model the anarchist Sidney Street Siege in London of 1911. True, yet any close observer could also see the inspiration for his *mise-en-scène* in the virtuoso shoot-out between police and conspirators that ends *Dr Mabuse, the Gambler*. In career terms we can take the similarities further. In the 1930s both directors left Europe to try their luck in Hollywood for different reasons and with differing outcomes. Key themes overlapped too with Hitchcock usually following in Lang's footsteps: themes of suspicion, flight, dissembling, madness, betrayal. Both linked the teeming labyrinth of the modern city to images of deceit and darkness, to social unease and political subterfuge. In Lang sharp images of the political were forged powerfully on the rebound from a Weimar society permanently in crisis. In Hitchcock, hemmed in by the fake grandeur of a still Imperial Britain and by archaic censorship, such images became suitably vague and were suitably curtailed so that in *The 39 Steps* Hitler's Germany could only be described as a 'certain foreign power'.

The difference lay in milieu. Born in 1890 and nine years older than Hitchcock, Lang lived through a post-war Germany in near-permanent crisis. Yet he was also part of a thriving art-cinema with a commercial bent that did not exist in inter-war Britain. In 1919, he had been a key contributor to the box-office hit *The Cabinet of Dr Caligari* before he left for another project. Then, in his early films between 1920 and 1927, the Austrian with an architectural eye made his mark as one of the great directors of the decade, along with Eisenstein, Murnau, G. W. Pabst and Carl Theodor Dreyer. One great film followed another: *Die Spinnen* (*The Spiders*, 1920), *Destiny, Dr Mabuse, the Gambler, Die Nibelungen*, and then the big-budget *Metropolis* that opened at Berlin's UFA-Palast am Zoo in January 1927. If the young Hitchcock was ever to overshadow him, he had somehow to overtake him, a truly formidable task. Racing metaphors suggest themselves but just as quickly dissipate. Try to imagine Lang getting off to a brilliant start and Hitchcock ghosting past him well before the finishing straight. The image of the portly Hitchcock running in any kind of race, let alone against the tall, energetic Lang, makes the metaphor ridiculous. And critics differ about the respective merits of the two. Both had a European Period and an American Period. Are these continuous? Does one director rise while the other falls? Let us look at the parallels more closely.

On first sight it would seem that Hitchcock came to Hollywood by choice, Lang by necessity. One gladly took advantage of bigger budgets and better studio conditions despite the hands-on intervention of David O. Selznick: the other was a refugee, via Paris, from a regime that banned his last Weimar film, *Das Testament des Dr Mabuse* (*The Testament of Dr Mabuse*), due for release in 1933 just months after the Nazi seizure of power. Both directors, however, had qualms about leaving the country where they had started their careers. Hitchcock was stricken with guilt at making the move across the Atlantic in 1939 as war threatened Europe. His long-time producer at Gaumont-British Michael Balcon, who had earlier encouraged the Weimar connection, now accused him of desertion (Spoto 1983: 235–6). Yet during the period of American neutrality Hitchcock began making key anti-Nazi films to turn the tide and in 1944 returned to London to make two short propaganda films about the Free French at the behest of the Ministry of Information. Lang's case was more compromising. His 1920s films, especially *Die Nibelungen* and *Metropolis*, were much admired by top Nazi leaders. His wife and screenwriting partner Thea von Harbou became a party sympathiser, as did two of his greatest actors, Rudolf Klein-Rogge (Rotwang in *Metropolis*, Mabuse in the *Mabuse* diptych) and Gustaf Gründgens (Schränker in *M*). In 1933 Goebbels offered Lang a key role in the German film industry but Lang declined. According to his version of events, recognising the perils of Nazism, he had left the country the very same night. Passport records show, however, that he returned to Germany several times and did not finally leave until three months after the fateful meeting with Goebbels (see McGilligan 1997: 178–81). Lang's attitude to the new regime, it appears, was more than ambivalent.

By the start of the Second World War, however, both directors were alert to the dangers of a fascism they found repellent. In 1939 they aided the struggle to convert a neutral USA to the anti-Nazi cause, their propaganda drive well under way before the bombing of Pearl Harbour. It duly continued as the Allied war effort gained momentum and lingered on after final victory. In those hectic years Lang gave us *Manhunt* (1941), *The Ministry of Fear* (1943), *Hangmen Also Die* (1944) and *Cloak and Dagger* (1946). Hitchcock's pictures made the bigger public splash with a wider range of themes in *Foreign Correspondent, Saboteur, Lifeboat* (1944) and *Notorious*. In general though, their careers diverged. Hitchcock worked on a broad canvas well financed by Selznick and moulding new stars like Joan Fontaine, Cary

Grant, Ingrid Bergman, Gregory Peck and Joseph Cotten. Lang worked on more constrained budgets with Walter Wanger, often casting the same actors again and again. Early on Hitchcock started to gain directorial control of his projects through his deft handling of Selznick, who could be persuaded to loan him out to other studios for a smart profit, and even though he rewrote and cut up the last of their collaborations, *The Paradine Case*. Lang was also hamstrung by studio demands and in the case of *The Ministry of Fear*, a hands-on producer Seton Miller who was also the writer and thus able to refuse alterations to his screenplay. While Hitchcock ventured out of doors in a big way, using good location photography for spy narratives like *Saboteur*, Lang's contemporary films remained studio bound, a feature that defined his American period from *Fury* (1936) right through to *Beyond a Reasonable Doubt* (1956). In 1943 Hitchcock filmed *Shadow of a Doubt* on location in Santa Rosa, a small town north of San Francisco. With Lang, one senses such a project would have remained on sound stages and in the back-lot. His great use of Monterey harbour locations for *Clash by Night* (1952), superbly filmed by Nicholas Musuraca, proved sadly to be an exception to the rule.

It was Weimar Lang that still inspired American Hitchcock. His first spy-flight thriller in the US, *Saboteur*, opens with a factory *mise-en-scène* in Los Angeles that echoes and transforms the opening of *Metropolis*. With young art director Robert Boyle on his first Hitchcock venture, Hitchcock designed a studio defence factory that is both hierarchical and democratic at the same time. Shot from the workers' canteen, the gate rolls back like a cinematic wipe across a dark screen to reveal the factory behind, framed as a horizontal and recessional shot, then augmented by a cut to a documentary insert of an 'adjacent' aircraft hangar full of planes just off the assembly line. The low, wide look, geometric and modernist, counters the vertical monumentalism of *Metropolis*, and just as Lang had begun with the start of the workers shift in the Underground City, the massed, uniform ranks marching robotically forward to their task, so Hitchcock starts with a break in the factory shift, the aircraft workers casually dressed, ambling towards the vast canteen for some well-earned nosh. Armed guards patrol, so this is wartime mobilisation, a place of strict surveillance. As a young workmate of Robert Cummings is distracted by an eye-catching blonde, the worker behind (Norman Lloyd) bumps into him dropping a hundred-dollar bill in an envelope with an incriminating address. This is the plot-trigger. Cummings will soon be framed for sabotage by Lloyd but knowledge of the name and address on the envelope will save him. For the final virtuoso touch to the *Metropolis* make-over Hitchcock echoes the wipe of his gate roll-back with something even more dramatic, a plume of thick dark smoke that rolls horizontally right to left across the screen, turning it black. He then cuts to the source of the fire and to Cummings handing his young buddy an extinguisher to quell the flames. The extinguisher has been tampered with. It contains not water but gasoline that explodes and wreaths the luckless fire fighter in flames. Instead, however, of the mass slaughter that follows Lang's factory explosion with workers hurtling to their death and Freder as delirious survivor, he is the single victim of the sabotage and Cummings the fall guy who must fight to prove his innocence.

As Hitchcock prospered in the 1940s, the problem for Lang was that his genre films often ended up as stylised back-lot features, hybrid versions of Hollywood New Objectivity. This Hawksian formula – fast, functional, economic – would have worked if Lang had Hawks' humour in tow, but he clearly did not. It is Hitchcock, not Lang, who renews the European *Kammerspiel* tradition in the age of sound and Hollywood colour. Single room or apartment films were not in Lang's scheme of things, yet *Rope*, *Dial 'M' for Murder* and *Rear Window* are all so stylistically inventive in their use of single interiors, they show up the *mise-en-scène* limits of Lang's American thrillers. (In his atmospheric Gothic excursions like *House by the River* (1950) or *Moonfleet* (1955) the studio design of the picture is far superior and creates a sense of mystery way beyond its laboured plots and limited acting.) Compared with the monotony of Lang's office and home interiors, Hitchcock's *Kammerspiel* aesthetic would give his single interior an identity of its own, turn it in effect into a leading character in the film. Yet it is also a space in which the spectator is immersed. You watch *Rope* and for sure, it is *their* apartment, *their* room, but after a while it is also *your* apartment, *your* room. And you are part of it. You are there. And after a while it does not bother you that you do not move out of it. While French critics have always championed Lang's American films, and Raymond Bellour (2002) has recently suggested American Lang could be preferable to American Hitchcock, their changing reputations at the time suggested the opposite. In Hollywood Hitchcock waxed as Lang waned, to the extent that in 1948 when Lang made the haunting *Secret Beyond the Door*, sumptuously photographed by Stanley Cortez, the plot seemed a straight composite of *Rebecca* – which he openly admired – as well as *Suspicion* and *Spellbound*. Lang's casting of Joan Bennett in the style of Fontaine in the starring role was also a giveaway. If Hitch had once followed Lang the roles were now well and truly reversed.

One step backward: one step forward

Let us now go back to *The 39 Steps*, Hitchcock's first major reckoning with Lang, and then forward in time to his penultimate film, *Frenzy*, his final reckoning with the Austrian director. In the 1930s the inspiration of Lang had kept British Hitchcock going. The strength of *The 39 Steps* lay in the lessons Hitchcock had learnt from Lang's spy movies, the bewildering changes of tone and the rapidity of movement. It also lay in something more original: a brilliant inversion of the figure of Dr Mabuse, who is Lang's Weimar puppet master of disguise, a demon of many personas pulling the strings and putting people under his spell, bringing chaos to the world. Mabuse in a word is the demonic Other who preys on human weakness in a decadent culture yet has no core to his being. Dissembling is the speciality of Lang's villains and in *Spies* he had taken the role more clearly into the world of espionage, through the persona of his Trotsky look-alike, Haghi, another master of disguise. In *The 39 Steps* Hitchcock and screenwriter Charles Bennett transfer the disguise components of the Langian villain to their fugitive hero Richard Hannay, falsely accused of murder and forced to hide his identity to survive arrest. In the course of his flight, Hannay 'becomes' or acts out the roles of milkman, motor mechanic, religious evangelical, crowd-pleasing politician and eloping lover. Irony has it that only when he tells the truth about being wrongly accused does he get into serious trouble. The double pursuit he endures, chased by spies and police alike is reminiscent of the double pursuit of Peter Lorre in *M* by the police and the city underworld. But the Langian stress is entirely different: for Lorre is a compulsive child-killer, guilty of multiple murders. By contrast, Hitchcock's hunted man is innocent and his villains sinister at times, but hardly demonic. In a shock sequence, Hannay is 'shot' through the heart without warning by the charming Professor Jordan (Godfrey Tearle). Jordan is all too normal: just a moment earlier he had been hosting pre-Sunday lunch drinks in his elegant country home. Hitchcock chooses to taint him by just a single detail – the missing joint of his little finger. The images of the deformed finger and the unexpected shooting are key expressive moments. But here they are fully integrated, early on, into the momentum of the plot. In a touch of comic irony, the Bible Hannay has previously taken from a devout crofter and placed under his jacket saves him from the professor's bullet. The book-under-the-jacket device is another lift from Lang, this time from *Spies*. Yet Jordan is no Mabuse. He is the master of a *single* disguise that makes him the pillar of a Highland community, while Hannay is the chameleon of Mabusian proportions, disguising not his guilt but his innocence.

The power of Hitchcock's narrative comes through its fusion of metamorphosis and flight. Hannay improvises with his back against the wall by pretending to be whom he is not and also pretending not to be a prime suspect. Lang's Mabuse was Mephistopheles earthbound, or a version of the Nietzschean *Übermensch* targeting the rich and the weak of his age – in Thomas Elsaesser's succinct phrase 'a Weimar disguise artist ... a principle of negation and corrosion' (2000: 155–6). Hitchcock's disguise model is the opposite: Everyman with a touch of class in the wrong place at the wrong time, and wrongly accused. This inversion of Mabuse, supreme autocrat and disguise-artist, is anti-Nietzschean. By dissembling, Hannay proves himself to be democratic and flexible, to be ever taking on the role of the other and shedding aristocratic pretension. While Mabuse the mover is orchestrating the fate of his victims, Hannay is the victim on the move, being moved around by his persecutors but forever defying victimhood. The kinetic style and rhythms Hitchcock required was not easy to attain. In adapting Buchan's text he had to make his Canadian hero's Scottish flight episodic and jagged for it to be cinematic, cutting elliptically, jumping from one situation of risk to the next. The film's expressive moments are made possible only through Hitchcock's debt to Soviet montage. After all, he did not have the literary advantage of John Buchan, the fluent and continuous line of written first-person narrative that is such a perfect form for the adventure romance. But neither did he want it. Instead his model is the jagged editing of *Dr Mabuse*, zigzagging and shifting, weaving back and forth, editing that gives us one of the great pictures of pre-classical narrative, so impressive that Eisenstein used it as a model for his dialectic montage (Eisner 1976: 67).

True, Hannay is still the narrative core. There is barely a sequence in which he is not present, but this is continuous questing without discursive linking. We are where we are and for Hannay this is a pragmatic world, not an expressionistic one. He is not the puppet-master like Mabuse, forever pulling strings, but a fugitive improvising, learning by trial and error, embroiled in a set of perceptual confusions that seem more comic than deadly. When order breaks down, whom do you trust? And how do you second-guess your adversary's move? On both these counts, the fallibility of trial and error and the centred narrative thread, Hitchcock moves away from Langian expressionism. Where Lang contributes is in New Objectivity mode, through his use of documentary detail: the model is *M* where he drew not only on serial killer cases of the time, but also on police investigation methods, on stories of the unique Beggar's organisation in Berlin, as well as anecdotes of the Berlin underworld (see Kaes 2000: 30–48). *The 39 Steps* is the one early picture in which Hitchcock tries to match *M* through richness of variation, and creates a social panorama unusual for that time in British film: the seedy music hall in London's East End with the chaotic response to Mr Memory, the brawling then the panic as Annabella Smith (Lucie Mannheim) fires shots to distract her pursuers. We then switch to the cool modernist interior of Hannay's flat in Portland Place where the spy plot is flirtatiously half-revealed by the pursued woman before she is assassinated. After Annabella's nocturnal murder by unknown intruders Hannay escapes from his apartment block by dressing up as a milkman and hightailing it to King's Cross. In the Flying Scotsman heading north we then follow the droll 'corset' conversation of the two salesmen whose company Hannay has to endure. In the Highlands with

Hannay in full flight we move quickly from the crofter's cottage with its love-less couple where the dour husband betrays him, to the Professor's elegant country home, then to brusque arrest in the police station upon showing the bullet lodged in the pages of his Bible, then to escape by mingling in the street with a religious parade followed by impromptu speech at a local rally when he is mistaken for a famous politician. Finally we have the comic scene of his second escape, and the handcuff scene with Pamela on the remote Highland bridge where the spies' car is stalled by sheep.

Here Hitchcock moves away from Lang by absorbing the dynamics of a new Hollywood genre: screwball comedy. Apart from its update to the 1930s the central change in *The 39 Steps* from Buchan is the invention of Pamela (Madeleine Carroll), a role that grew in production as the spark on set between Donat and Carroll ignited (see Glancy 2003: 36–7). Hitchcock would surely have noted the drawing power of Frank Capra's *It Happened One Night* (1934) with its hapless couple Clark Gable and Claudette Colbert stuck in the same motel room. With Gable look-alike Donat in the starring role this seemed to be British cinema's response, while Carroll in tenacious defiance of the 'male threat' more than matches Colbert's example. For Pamela manages to betray Hannay twice, once to the police, once unwittingly to the enemy who proceed to handcuff her to him to prevent escape: such propinquity prompts her reluctantly to aid him, an early victim we might say, of Stockholm syndrome. Shortly after Lang came to show us full-blooded romance for the first time since *Destiny*, first in *Fury*, casting Sylvia Sidney with Spencer Tracy, and then *You Only Live Once* (1937) where she is opposite Henry Fonda. Yet the tone is shrill and sombre. The burning issue of a mis-carriage of justice is so great in both films, heroes condemned to death for crimes they did not commit, there is no room for humour. Yet neither is the false sentimentalism marring *Metropolis* any longer in evidence. The differ-ences in approach are fascinating. Hitchcock's film is a spy thriller that treats complicity and transference of guilt in a wryly comic idiom. Lang's films are social justice or 'wrong-man' melodramas that burn with conviction but also depend for their dramatic outcome on the love of a good woman. Nota-bly, Hitchcock was to use Fonda in his own 'wrong man' docudrama twenty years later. In Hitchcock love is ambiguous and unreliable, if not treacher-ous, before it redeems itself – if indeed it does. In Lang it is unwavering but one-dimensional.

When Hitchcock finally moved back to London in 1972 with his serial-killer film, *Frenzy*, it was a homecoming not only to his native city but also to European themes. If it was his final reckoning with his birthplace, it was also its final reckoning with Weimar. Just as *The 39 Steps* had been a *Dr Mabuse* reversal, so *Frenzy* was an *M* reversal, an oblique reckoning with Lang's masterpiece. It was well and truly an English picture, a completion of uncompleted business and atonement above all for the many limitations of his 1930s studio cinema. It did so not by homage to early expressionism but through a ruthless reworking of New Objectivity cinema. *Frenzy* is a naturalistic horror film that dispenses with distorted POV shots or subjective impressions. It shows an actual world in no way hallucinatory, one that on the surface of things would be mundane and ordinary were it not for the existence of a serial killer and another wrong-man solution from the dilatory arm of the English Law. This is rape and serial killing without any melodrama at all. There are no handsome heroes or ugly villains, no random hysterics and no glamorous victims. Its villain is a cheerful salt-of-the earth cockney, its 'wrong man' a morose ex-RAF squadron leader: its fearful killings induce not so much panic as prurience and idle curiosity, adding spice to local gossip. This, then, is the opposite scenario to *M*, where the killings and the reaction to them are a dark sign of a collective pathology soon to come, where mass hysteria prevails and collective vengeance is the order of the day. Hitchcock's killer is also the inverse of Lang's killer. As Hans Beckert, Peter Lorre is the outsider, the loner, driven to distraction by his pathological compulsion. His killings are all offscreen and he is a hunched shadow in the folds of the city. As Bob Rusk, Barry Foster is the opposite. He is at the heart of things, the man-about-Covent Garden, petty baron of the fruit-and-veg market, loud, conspicuous, nattily dressed and with a word for everyone. As if to assuage any shadow of doubt about being 'normal' he parades his cheery visiting mum at the window of his flat early on for his pal Richard Blaney. Hitchcock is showing this is not *Psycho*. Mother is no longer the menacing wheelchair silhouette in the window of a Gothic pile. She is flesh-and-blood, salt-of-the-earth just like her lovable boy. And yet this is just as disturbing as anything in *Psycho*. The first murder sequence he shows is the most graphic and detailed in Hitchcock's entire cinema. Meanwhile the Law, as usual, tumbles arse about face: the killings multiply; the cops are clueless and duly arrest the wrong man.

A film made just after *Psycho*, Michael Powell's *Peeping Tom*, mediated the long transformation from *M* to *Frenzy*. Central London locations, a psychotic killer of women, narrow streets, cramped flats and offices, menacing passages and backyards: what Hitchcock did for Covent Garden Powell had already done for Soho and Hitchcock knew it. He cast Anna Massey, murder victim in *Peeping Tom*, as a murder victim in his own film thirteen years later. Yet Powell's film has more in common with *M* in one vital respect. His killer is also a complete outsider, Carl Boehm his equivalent of Peter Lorre, here vaguely bohemian but also Germanic and clearly out of place in 1950s London. The killer's photographic studio is a claustrophobic crime scene with its bayonet knife a killer attachment to an obsessive camera. The pathology is part of an eerie and enclosed world and Soho, centre of the capital's film world but also of its seedy pornography, is a perfect setting. Thus Powell's reflexive use of the obsessive camera updates expressionist aesthetics but in his film Hitchcock eliminates them almost entirely. For Rusk's world is everybody else's, the Covent Garden market a place of transaction and people ever passing through, of to and fro and coming and going, on the face of it, a transparent spectacle.

Though a big box-office success, critical reaction to Hitchcock's film was mixed. He was accused of treating London as if in a time warp, as if it was the same city as when he had left it thirty years earlier. The film was seen by some, after the stir created by the defining modernist films of 1960s London (*The Servant* (1963), *Repulsion* (1965), *Blow Up* (1967), *Performance* (1970)), as somewhat old-fashioned and out of touch. In a sense it was. Apart from brief shots of New Scotland Yard and the Hilton Hotel there is no modernist architecture to be seen in this vision of the metropolis. Yet what Hitchcock had achieved here was similar to what David Lynch would achieve with *Blue Velvet* (1986) in the following decade. Lynch had made a film that was simultaneously past and present, blending two different American time zones, the 1950s and the 1980s. Hitchcock did the same with a film that simultaneously evoked the London to which he returned in 1972 and the London he had left in 1939, the 1970s and the 1930s within a single film; this despite brief post-war returns for *Stage Fright* (1950) and *The Man Who Knew Too Much*. While Lynch was lauded as postmodern for his eternal present and his folding of time, Hitchcock had been criticised for his. And true, Hitchcock's London here is a double-edged sword. Like his expert use of Covent Garden as a market bustling with life yet earmarked to close down shortly after, the film seems a valedictory lament to a disappearing way of life soon to be super-seded by a class of new professionals, a new service economy and a growing multi-ethnic world. Yet at the time that Hitchcock shot the film there was an authentic way of life in London, and Covent Garden proves the point, more in touch with the past than the future. Not everyone was suave, bohemian, gangsterish or modishly professional. The documentary feel of the film was a continuation of what he had known from a different era: but with continu-ous location shooting he could also give it a richer texture that his 1930s films had lacked. It took on board the lessons learnt abroad and used them in the homecoming, which itself was spectacular. The opening helicopter shot with its bird's-eye view of the Thames takes us right down through Tower Bridge and almost lands us on the Embankment where Rusk's current victim will be washed to the shore with a tell-tale tie around her neck. *Frenzy* is thus the necessary completion of something that had been incomplete, the completion of British Hitchcock.

Of course Hitchcock does use off-screen murder (like *M*) but blends it with his flair for the macabre, featuring a strangled, naked corpse (anonymous) at both the start and the finish of his film, bodies of women whose murders we do not see. But his necktie strangler is the exact opposite of Jack the Ripper, with whom local gossip compares him, or to use an update, the post-war serial killer John Christie who had featured a year earlier in Richard Fleischer's biopic, *10 Rillington Place* (1971). Rusk is not shown as a killer of prostitutes, as they had been, but of women as well known in the locale as he is: it makes him a killer of those in his own social network. The double murder witnessed, first of Blaney's ex-wife Brenda (Barbara Leigh-Hunt) and then Blaney's casual lover, barmaid Babs Milligan (Anna Massey) is a shock to the system because there is no get-out clause. The two women cannot be written off as they might in Hollywood thrillers, as drunk or degenerate or naïve or demented, or even too sexy. They are normal working women, old-fashioned perhaps, but the rhythms of the film establish the pattern of their daily lives. Here Hitchcock's fascination with the English class system is as strong as ever in the crossover effect it creates. Rusk, the wholesaler, is the flash working-class cockney become possessive and petit-bourgeois. Blaney, ex-RAF officer, is down on his luck and now proletarian, sleeping in a Salvation Army hostel and flitting from one bar job to another. Blaney's bar associate is now the working-class Babs, while the middle-class Brenda reluctantly numbers Rusk (disguised under a pseudonym) as one of the difficult clients in her marriage bureau.

The social detail in the film is as strong as in *M*. While Lang specialised in the collective – the neighbourhood women, the organised gang, the beggars' network and the Berlin police department – Hitchcock individualises social differences. He also plays on audience identification. Rusk is secretly psychopathic but openly bluff and hearty: Blaney is openly aggressive, distrustful and full of resentment at social misfortune. Hitchcock makes us realise how much we feel at ease with his serial killer and yet dislike and distrust his 'wrong man'. Film referencing here would place Blaney as an update of Trevor Howard's framed ex-Air Force officer in *They Made Me a Fugitive* (1947); Rusk is a sly inversion of Michael Caine's cockney Don Juan, *Alfie* (1967), the mouthy seducer of that film transformed into psychotic womankiller with ginger-haired Foster as a dead ringer for Caine, whom Hitchcock had wished to cast in the role of Rusk. Inversion is also mirrored in the shooting technique. There are few reassuring close-ups of Blaney to draw us into his unjust predicament: Hitchcock reserves his close-ups instead for Brenda's horrific killing and most of these are profile shots of Rusk's demented face. Where we are close in we are distressed witnesses of terror. Where Blaney's injustice scenarios demand sympathy we are kept at arm's length and too distant to give it. Blaney assumes the aura of his class pedigree should protect him with little effort on his part and though technically the transfer of guilt is part of the doubling effect of the plot, where Rusk is always Blaney's shadowing double, it is made here alarmingly devoid of substance. Blaney feels no real guilt about the deaths of the two women he has known intimately, or remorse that he had not prevented them. His anger is purely egocentric, anger at false accusation of himself, not the rape and murder of innocent women.

In the framing of the onscreen murders Hitchcock uses a continuation of the repetition techniques he had shown in *Psycho, The Birds* and *Marnie*. All are variations on his expressive aesthetic, in which montage is crucial but not always essential. In *Psycho* we noted earlier, in the murders of Marion and of Arbogast, a style-contrast at the heart of repetition. In *The Birds* we noted the contrast in the two big attack-sequences, the assault on the children outside the schoolhouse and later, the final assault on Melanie in the attic. In both cases the use of cinematic space differs radically. For *Psycho* the shower sequence is enclosed, the staircase sequence open. In *The Birds* the schoolhouse attack is open, the attic attack enclosed. In *Frenzy* we have a like pairing of opposites. The killing of Brenda in her office is enclosed, and shown in graphic detail. The prelude to the killing of Babs in Rusk's apartment is open in its spatial framing but the killing never shown. In the first case, Rusk appears in Brenda's office by surprise and without appointment. He is already there, Brenda already trapped before either she or the spectator realise what is about to happen. Here Hitchcock starts with separation framing to indicate distance and tension: in shot/reverse-shot Rusk at the files by the far wall and Brenda at her desk implying the presence of her troublesome ex-client searching out masochistic women. As he moves to the desk, the two-shot takes over and as Rusk's banter turns to sexual advance and that in turn to force and violence, Hitchcock starts to cut rapidly between altering angles of shot. According to Bill Krohn, Hitchcock shot the murder in a single day from fourteen angles, discarding only two in the edit: twenty of the forty-three shots are tight close-ups of Rusk, with only four of Brenda from Rusk's point-of-view (see Krohn 2000: 272–3).

Later there is a brief reprise of quick-fire montage in the killing of Babs, with near-subliminal flashback images as Rusk tries to work out the whereabouts of his missing tiepin. But the *mise-en-scène* of the murder is very different, the antithesis of montage. It starts as Babs leaves the pub after a row with her boss over Blaney. Hitchcock's camera zooms in on her suddenly as she stops outside and the ambient sound fades down to nothing. The static moment is almost a silent freeze-frame, yet the camera is still rolling and reverse-zooms to reveal Rusk, who had been drinking inside, now standing behind her as the street noise comes up again. It is a superb subjective shot (and one of the few in the picture), her awareness of his presence shown as if she had eyes in the back of her head. The camera then switches to objective mode, tracking them head on as they cross the road to go into the market arcade, and the rest of the shot is done from the same frontal angle to complete a single mobile take through the market and out the other side towards Rusk's flat. It is an eye-level backward shot with even lighting, a friendly prolonged walking together for all to see, no dark shadows or strange colours, – nothing to create obvious menace. The menace, rather, lies in the casual ease with which the whole thing takes place, in Rusk's easy friendship and offer of a place to stay, in Babs' open and trusting nature. The ease of the contact is intimated by the unbroken fluency of the camera. Hitchcock then cuts to the second long take, shot from inside the hallway of the flat. The camera backtracks ahead of the couple as they walk up the stairs and then follows them on up as they pass towards the door of the flat, stopping as the door opens and closes behind them with Rusk's words to Babs that had also been his words to Brenda: 'You're my kind of woman.'

But there is no cut. After a pause, the camera backtracks in silence down the stair and pulls out of the front door in one fluent take: a cut from studio interior to Covent Garden location is then (echoes of *Rope*) disguised by a passing porter with trolley that fills the lens. The street is bustling once more with the market and its sounds are faded up again. We are left to imagine the murder we know is now taking place because we have already witnessed its predecessor without respite. We may have escaped the second time around but then not really escaped at all for dire probabilities still haunt and linger. At this point we can think back to *M* and the disappearance of Elsie Beckmann, first the close-in following shot after she leaves school and bounces the ball along the pavement, soon after the anxious mother's high-angle POV shot as she walks out of her apartment and looks right down the empty tenement staircase. We can think too of Lang's experiments with sound: Peter Lorre's whistling and his uncanny use of offscreen sound. So while the look of *Frenzy* is very different from *M* and Bob Rusk is the complete antithesis of Hans Beckert, key connections can be made. And here is another: both killers like munching fruit.

We can find other Lang connections too, notably in *Destiny*, one of the first great Weimar films by Lang for which Hitchcock expressed open admiration. But equally important and less well remarked upon was the imprint of American Murnau on American Hitchcock. *Sunrise*, one of the great German-American debuts that failed, however, to give Murnau a head-start under the new Hollywood studio system has been less considered a source for American Hitchcock. As noted, it was almost certainly an inspiration for *The Manxman*. But along with *Destiny* it was also a key source for Hitchcock's later work. These were the two films that inflect that powerful quartet of late Hitchcock masterpieces – *Vertigo, Psycho, The Birds, Marnie* – and to this we must now turn.

Love and catastrophe: the long-term gain

In *Sunrise* Murnau created an entire social world, a film text as a living organism that links imaginary country to city on a back-lot belonging to Fox Film Corporation. Nature and culture are locked in symbiosis: a tram links the two of them and we follow its journey from village to city. Arrowhead Lake by which it passes is actually there, a short distance from Foxhills where Murnau built his modern outdoor metropolis. The re-creation of this world on an expansive back-lot has been unmatched anywhere for its delicate play on the encounter of tradition and modernity. Only Federico Fellini in the 1970s with *Roma* (1972) and *Amarcord* (1974) – the latter set in his hometown of Rimini and re-created on a back-lot at Rome's Cinecittà – comes close to matching it. Hitchcock in his career never attempted anything with the same astonishing scope. Yet Murnau's topography is immediately suggestive for Hitchcock's later work. We can look at the journey from the country village to the large metropolis that the Man (George O'Brien) and the Woman (Janet Gaynor) undertake. It is a journey into a different world and each world is constructed with exact detail. The lakeside village is Germanic, expressionistic. The city, which seems on first sight to be a continuation of the design Murnau had used at Neubabelsberg for *The Last Laugh*, is something else: not a place of rain and darkness and shadow, but a city of shimmering glass, luminescent and teeming with life, vibrantly New World and embodying the active promise of the American Dream. Many critics take the Gothic funfair of *Dr Caligari* as the model for the one that ends *Strangers on a Train*. Yet surely it is Murnau's vast exploding fireworks display of a funfair where the couple do have fun that is the firmer precedent, naturalistic in detail but framed and shot with such compelling energy as to transcend naturalism altogether.

Murnau was spare and economical with his naturalist illusions. On the remarkable tram ride right into the city, his set designer Jochus Gliese recreated a fast-changing landscape – forested, bucolic, suburban, industrial, asphalted – and compressed it into a few minutes of film time, designing only those things that would be seen by the camera lens on its moving journey. To the inquisitive naked eye, looking around, the artifice would have been instantly exploded (Eisner 1973: 180). In the nocturnal city Murnau created the illusion of depth of field by using floors slanting upwards and ceilings slanting downwards for interiors, and for recessional long-shots of city streets, miniature cars in the background surrounded by diminutive extras, often children in adult clothing or dwarfs. Moreover there is, strictly speaking, no inside and outside. Every exterior shot has buildings that seem transparent; every interior shot has an open vista. Deep focus illusion is a trick Hitchcock repeats with the caravan train of the circus performers amongst whom fugitive Robert Cummings hides in *Saboteur*. The caravan stretches as far as the eye can see through the use of miniature trailers and cars that are quite literally just a few yards up the road.

Sunrise starts in the country then goes to the city, before returning to origin. In Hitchcock's quintessentially Californian films, *Vertigo* and *The Birds*, he inverts the process with variations. Both chart the movement in reverse, from city to country. *Vertigo* has a double movement: it roams the topography of San Francisco before the romance of Scottie and Madeleine takes them out to the Big Basin Redwood Park and then onto the Mission at San Juan Bautista· in compressed form Scottie repeats the movement with Judy (the same woman) in the picture's second half. *The Birds* begins in San Francisco then moves out to Bodega Bay. To this we can add *Marnie* with its studio East Coast settings which start in Philadelphia, go out to rural Virginia with its hunting locations, then back to a studio Baltimore in the form of a double return, a return to a different city that is also for Marnie a return to childhood. In the opening sequence Hitchcock shoots Marnie's train arrival on location in San Jose, California as a stand-in for Philadelphia's 32nd Street station (McGilligan 2003: 648). In the Baltimore homecoming he uses an artificial studio set for tiny row houses framed against the painted backdrop of an ocean liner in harbour. Thus he starts with the simulation of a real city but ends with a purely imaginary one. In *The Birds* too the final sequence cues ambiguously the chance of return. Will nature's winged creatures – still waiting to pounce – allow nature's privileged humans to return from the coast to the refuge of the city? *Vertigo* and *The Birds* both beg the question: does the city corrupt nature, or is nature too vast, too implacable for civilisation? It is a question for which at first sight Murnau's film had simplistic answers, but then he stunningly turns it around into a breathtaking leap of faith. What begins in clichéd Germanic fashion with polarisation between the simple uncorrupted life of a rural village (proto-German) and the corrupting city figure (proto-American) of the Vamp who tries to seduce the Man into killing his spouse, ends up ninety minutes later in reconciliation and affirmation. The Man and the Woman renew love through their adventures in the city, which they must 'conquer' symbolically without corrupting their nature. In doing so, however, they must endure on their return a further trial of destiny, the cruelty of nature that seems a cosmic force beyond moral consideration in Murnau's magnificent storm sequence on the lake. They are still creatures of country life but all the stronger for their city odyssey, and thus steeled for a future life in America.

Murnau's effects are uncanny. The brief tram ride into the city, filmed in real time, seems to stand in for a transatlantic journey from rural Germany to urban America. It is a supreme example of Murnau's aesthetic alternation between the real and the unreal, an alternation shown to great effect in

Nosferatu, where he matches expressionist interiors to incisive locations, the vampire-figure in the Carpathian Mountains (rural) set against his later image in the streets of medieval Bremen (urban). In *Sunrise* we expect at first an old-fashioned story of rural virtue versus city corruption: the man who must choose between his pure peasant wife and the city vamp with flapper fringe who seduces him into attempted murder. Yet Murnau's mythic resolution of the social contradiction is indeed a bold one. In his vast, quasi-naturalist meta-set, the Man and Woman prove their love for one another by coming to love the city which at first sight appears a web of corruption and decay, but turns itself into a source of affirmation and renewal, a shining beacon of hope.

Murnau's Vamp, however, is no cliché. Margaret Livingstone's sensual performance is almost on a par with that of Louise Brooks as Lulu in *Pandora's Box* (1928), so we could say that the two great *femme fatale* roles in Weimar film were American! Yet their lure is pitched differently. Lulu is surely the Weimar model for American film noir of the city, while Murnau's ambiguous Vamp could be viewed, indirectly, as prototype for Hitchcock's later women of the modernist period, of Madeleine Elster, Marion Crane, Melanie Daniels and Marnie Edgar who circulate freely between city and country. Murnau's city, moreover, is crystal, opalescent. Hitchcock's San Francisco is nearer to Murnau than it is to film noir. Kim Novak and Tippi Hedren are not straight vamps but at best desolate, deconstructed women dressed in haute couture who prey amidst the disquiet of uncertainty, hunted as much as hunting, gradually losing the sense of who they are. This fragmentation of the vampiric image means that Hitchcock's resort to artifice is greater than Murnau. *Sunrise* remains an integrated and organic composite, a silent hymn to visual unity. In that respect its closest successor, technically speaking, is Michael Powell's *Black Narcissus* (1947) a pure studio movie of expressionist lineage so expertly designed it blends convent interiors with Himalayan exteriors to perfection in three-strip Technicolor. Hitchcock's inversions of *Sunrise* go beyond the organic, however, to a modernist fracturing of style. They draw attention to difference; the location shot versus the process shot or the matte composite, or in the case of *The Birds* a sense of place bombarded by an array of special effects. *The Birds* and *Marnie* alternate at times jaggedly between the real and the unreal, the organic and the artificial. They confront and challenge, optically and sonically unsettling. Where *Vertigo* blends together more fluently and poetically in the spirit of Murnau, Hitchcock still makes breathtaking leaps of locale. Murnau's studio city constructed on wasteland, only possible because Los Angeles was in its relative infancy in 1927, is replaced by the topography of a developed city that gives Hitchcock everything he needs. The car replaces the tram: the movement is constant as Madeleine never stays in one place. She is, as it were, always passing through. In both films, movement recreates the sense of journey as a dream world, oneiric in its own space-time continuum, sensual and complete.

Thirty years later, Hitchcock crucially inverts the terms of Murnau's romance. His post-romantic agony is as much a response to *Sunrise* as to his earlier films. Biographically speaking, there is irony a-plenty here, and paradox. Murnau the gay director created the greatest fusion of heterosexual love and marriage in film history. Hitchcock the monogamous husband created the greatest film about ocular obsession, a film that denies, like *Rear Window*, the heterosexual engagement, the promise of union. The ever-faithful and homely Midge, consigned to a life indoors, is sacrificed for the image of Madeleine as a beautiful ghost everywhere in the metropolis, a ghost who then becomes flesh. (If the ghost of Rebecca haunts a country house, the ghost of Madeleine haunts an entire city.) Murnau's film takes up the Man's reunion with the Woman after his fateful encounter with the Vamp. Midge, however, disappears from the second half of *Vertigo* and Scottie's 'reunion' takes place with the double of the ghost, the real Madeleine otherwise known as Judy Barton. One earthbound woman is thus substituted for another, but only because the good looks of the substitute give her the potential of being made over, in Scottie's act of compulsive repetition, as a double of the ghost.

The other connection to *Sunrise* lies in the redemptive power of the kiss. The true embrace with the Woman in the second half of the picture redeems the Man's false embrace with the Vamp in the first half. In *Vertigo* the repetition is with the same woman and here it marks the recovery of the first embrace not its denial. The rotating embrace with Judy in the hotel room lit from outside by green neon and framed by the hallucinatory image of the stable at San Juan Bautista repeats the embrace with Madeleine by the ocean with its natural textures of green and blue. But it cannot redeem it. Save for *North by Northwest*, which reinstates romance on a valedictory note, it is the last romantic kiss of any note in Hitchcock's cinema. In contrast the snatched embrace of Tippi Hedren and Rod Taylor in *The Birds* seems like an afterthought in the downward spiral of the Hitchcock romance where love is finally extinguished. *Psycho*, *The Birds* and *Marnie* are all inheritors of the doomed romance in *Vertigo*. At the start of *Psycho* the lovers embrace intimately in a forlorn Phoenix hotel room, but only in the backwash of an ebbing desire. Hitchcock told Truffaut that in the scene he had wanted 'to give a visual impression of despair and solitude' (Truffaut 1986: 415). Thereafter love is barren. In *Marnie* the cold neurasthenic heroine blocks the honey moon kiss of Mark Rutland with closed lips and clenched teeth. In *The Birds* screenwriter Evan Hunter had carved out a melodramatic love sequence for Melanie and Mitch complete with full-blown embrace. To his annoyance, his director omitted it from the final cut of the picture. Hunter had referred to his scene quaintly as 'our screwball lovers kissing seriously and passionately'

(1997: 49). Yet Hitchcock knew this was a distraction the film could not afford. Under the shadow of catastrophe and the menace of the birds, no romance can ever flourish. It can struggle to come into existence but remains stillborn. The tantalising questions remains? Is it catastrophe that destroys it or, on the contrary, prolongs its chances when daily life would soon have ground it down?

On the other side of the gender divide things get even stranger. Like Scottie, Mark Rutland and Mitch Brenner are males in no-man's-land, ever stranded between contrasting women, gravitating towards one of them but with no final conviction. Yet casting Sean Connery and Rod Taylor as opposed to a laconic James Stewart also gives the later pictures a fascinating edge. For these are muscular masculine stars – Connery straight out of his James Bond pictures – who by convention would stand to get their women without trying. Hitchcock bravely goes against the formbook and denies his audience with this shattering of icons. Yet artistically he triumphs. Both films are post-romantic yet there are traces of *Sunrise*'s magnificent storm sequence in each. It is a key visual source for the framing of sudden catastrophe that dominates the *mise-en-scène* in *The Birds*, especially the graphic creature attacks on Melanie that wound her and shred her clothes. It also finds a strong echo in *Marnie*'s sudden storm, where the redness of lightening convulses the heroine, alone and helpless in Mark's Philadelphia office. Like Murnau's Woman saved from drowning, Marnie and Melanie must 'come back' from the dead. In *Sunrise* the Woman is saved for the Man she loves. In *The Birds* and *Marnie* the woman is saved by the man she cannot fully bring herself to love and by implication, never will.

In these events too lies the seed of fatality that takes Hitchcock in the making of *The Birds* back to his Weimar source, to *Faust* and *Nosferatu* but above all to Lang's *Destiny*. The English title of *Der Müde Tod* says it all. Yet closer even than *The Birds* – the only Hitchcock film that echoes the silent Langian spectacles of *Die Nibelungen* and *Metropolis* – is Hitchcock's other fable of tragic destiny, *Psycho*. In a way, *Destiny* is to *Psycho* what *Sunrise* had been to *Vertigo*. Part allegory, part fairytale, Lang's film co-written with Von Harbou is both archaic and modern. Its dark, morbid opening recalls the tales of the Brothers Grimm. Yet the visitation of Death (Bernard Goetzke) – Lang's prime allegory of 'the Destiny Machine' (Gunning 2000: 16–17) – to a small German town would also resonate with a country traumatised in 1922 by the aftermath of a lost war, and for many, a lost nationhood. Lang's story comprises three related tales set in three different continents, linked by a framing narrative. A young woman (Lil Dagover) solicits the aid of Death to save her lover from his clutches. Showing her three candles, he offers her three chances of rescue, which the three tales set respectively in Baghdad, Renaissance Venice and Ancient China then fabulate into a triad of poignant failures. Goetzke – whom Hitchcock cast subsequently in *The Mountain Eagle* (1926) – not only plays Death but the figure in each of the three tales who frustrates the rescue-attempt, so that Death, like Mabuse, has many faces. After the failure of the last attempt Death reaps his reward and the woman herself is sent to share her lover's fate. Lang's silent feature strikes a consistent note of fatality he then translates to the trio of contemporary sound films he made around the spectre of Nazism: *M* his most decisive and compelling, *Fury*, where tragedy afflicts both the perpetrators and their victim and *You Only Live Once* where the Law abjectly fails to serve the cause of justice.

The most disguised figure of Destiny in the modernist phase is Melanie Daniels, the most opposite figure to 'Weary Death' it is possible to imagine. For the poised, playful and vivacious Melanie is accused by the panicking mother in the Tides diner of bringing the birds to Bodega Bay and is seen briefly by all those hiding there as a harbinger of death. The identification can also, of course, be made through the caged lovebirds she brings for Mitch's young sister. Yet Hitchcock rejects the expressionist trope that he sets up so tantalisingly. His subsequent strategy is to show Melanie as the bloodied *victim* of avian attack. In the onslaught of the birds against the Brenner house and finally the attic where she is trapped, her suffering is a sign of her human frailty, her lack of disassociation with her fellow-beings, the absurdity in extreme circumstance of the higher social status she may possess. There is a crossing-over in the narrative from an allegorical scale (of death) to a concrete empirical one (of surviving death). Hitchcock is not attempting to humanise the figure of Death but to invert it, as he is also inverting a favourite expressionist trope, the demonisation of the outsider. It is a common construct cruelly conferred by others in the process of exchange, blaming the outsider, but Melanie's ordeal turns it around. By enduring catastrophe she becomes a surrogate member of the bruised and battered family.

Hitchcock's previous film, *Psycho*, had been a different matter altogether. Like *M*, *Psycho* is a film that turned *Destiny*'s early model of tragic fate into a contemporary setting: it did so ingeniously on the Universal Studios backlot. Yet this is no fairytale. This *is* the American West in 1960 and Hitchcock also uses key settings: the bird's-eye view of downtown Phoenix that starts the picture, the sleazy hotel room, the bland office interior, Marion's fin-tailed car on a remote highway in Southern California, the Bates location with contrasting structures of Gothic house (vertical) and timbered motel (horizontal). And *Psycho* is more powerful than any of Lang's American pictures. What intrigues and is overlooked is the parallel structure to Lang in the *Psycho* narrative. While Lil Dagover in *Destiny* wishes to rescue her *lover* from the clutches of Death, Marion (Janet Leigh) wishes to rescue her *love affair* from a similar fate, after the indecisions of the hotel assignation. In this she fails because her quest ends abruptly, halfway through the film, with her own death while, departing from Lang Hitchcock permits her ex-lover to survive and with perfect dramatic irony, track down her killer with the sister Lila (Vera Miles) who clearly resembles her.

Marion's road to salvaging the lost affair is perilous and ends in disaster. Here as in *Destiny*, there is a triangular figuration of Death: the Visiting Businessman, the Highway Patrolman and the Motel Clerk. All are in normal social roles but also cast as social types in the expressionist mode of German drama. But of course they are more, they are naturalised and given detailed definition. Or are they? At a time when Hitchcock had his own television series, the drunken businessmen in the office who gives a fortune to Marion to bank for him, is a cliché of Television Drama. The Highway Patrolman, eyeless behind Polaroids and nameless in the plot, is the opposite, a menacing abstraction with an irksome presence, a smart American update on a long European tradition. And what is Norman Bates? Marion makes the mistake of treating him as a shy introverted variant of the Boy Next Door. Some mistake. Yet Bates evades definition entirely. The psychiatrist's attempt to nail him down at the end of the picture can only be treated as one of Hitchcock's elaborate spoofs. All three men are visible, transparent, social. Yet all are elusive to the eye in one way or another and that is because they are the three Faces of Death.

Psycho, however, is no allegory. The figures it presents to Marion on her journey are all normal in terms of their manner and their body language. The businessman's wad of dollar bills is a clumsy male ploy in a drunken play for a younger woman. The patrolman's dark glasses are clearly meant to intimidate any errant motorist, and Norman's stutter at critical moments is the first giveaway of dark things to come. This deft surplus in the image shows us that all three are pointing Marion along the Road to Death. The Businessman places temptation in her hand, the Cop panics her into further flight, and the Motel Clerk 'delivers' her to his Mother. Or, put differently, the businessman 'delivers' her to the highway out of town, the Cop 'delivers' her to the Bates motel, Norman delivers her unto 'Mother' and Mother 'delivers' her unto Death. We recall Rohmer's astute remark about Murnau as the director who turns contingent moments into forms of necessity. Hitchcock is a true successor. There is a naturalist reading of Marion's fated journey that attributes disaster to her failures of choice. Indecisive, neurotic and guilty because she has taken the money, Marion panics herself into further wrong decisions and one thing leads to another. Night has fallen, she cannot see the highway ahead for the storm and so, a lone woman, she seeks sanctuary rather than spend a second night in her car. Yet the pattern of the film is masterly. On a first viewing we do not see the murder coming, the shock effect, yet looking back or re-viewing, all events assume the cast and hue of inevitability, as if nothing could have happened otherwise from the moment she fails to take the money to the bank. But then, if she wanted to save her relationship, would she really look a gift horse in the mouth? Where does choice begun and end? Where, for that matter, does morality?

These are questions that Hitchcock makes us ask ourselves, not only about his film but also about existence in general. The Freudian formulas that many Hitchcock critics have used in discussing the film add little to Hitchcock's own, his knowing sense of derangement in extremis. Let us remember that he got there first. Marion is the neurotic female who makes the wrong decision, which leads her to Norman, the psychotic male who does not even know what decision he is making, or that he is actually making one. She is retreating from an actual world she can longer bear. Meanwhile he has created an imaginary one to replace an actual one with which he no longer connects. If the Unconscious drives both of them, coming from different paths that cross to transact murder, this is the Freudian formula that frames it, Norman's psychotic child-disturbance and mother-compulsion that is a 'disaster waiting to happen'. *Psycho* makes of this a genuine horror but also a macabre joke. Yet the stakes could not be higher. If the Unconscious here offers us nothing more than a reassuringly individualised form of Destiny, and Destiny is a wider and deeper force altogether, where then do we stand? We stand perched on the edge of a precipice and that is where Hitchcock is happy to leave us. He has, after all, pre-emptively inverted the formula of his Freudian critics. If they want to read through his cinema the fate of Western modernity as that of a psychoanalytic Unconscious, his cinematic vision suggests the opposite. In his view of things, the 'unconscious' is but a modern coding of Destiny, which still remains an enigma to be resolved or, conversely, an enigma that can never be resolved at all.

chapter 4

THE FLIGHT AND THE GAZE: HITCHCOCK
AND THE BRITISH CONNECTION

Many things mark the transition from British to American Hitchcock but
the most important is the persistence of British writing. John Buchan's novel carried Hitchcock forward beyond *The 39 Steps* to American narratives
of flight that still bear its imprint. In *Foreign Correspondent*, *Saboteur* and
North by Northwest the resemblance is tight: with *Shadow of a Doubt*, *Spellbound*, *Strangers on a Train* or the remade *The Man Who Knew Too Much* it is
a touch looser. The surge of Buchan's fiction and the makeover of its flight
(or chase) theme into contemporary life by great screenwriters – Thornton Wilder, John Michael Hayes and Ernest Lehman among them – nudged
American Hitchcock into box-office currency. Hitchcock himself saw motif
with a slight difference. In 1950 he called the core of the feature film 'the
chase', which he claimed 'was indigenous to the movie technique as a whole'
since it is someone 'running towards a goal, often with the antiphonal motion
of someone fleeing a pursuer' (Gottlieb 1995: 125). The flight therefore often
has a *double chase pattern*, the hunter being hunted generating a pattern of
suspense in which both aspects of the chase converge. As the police close in
on Richard Hannay he, in turn, closes in on the spies who are after him. The
pattern is also a matter of pace and rhythm and, as we have seen, of trans-
acted relations. For Hitchcock also engages in Humean reflection: 'In the
ideal chase situation', he speculates, 'the tempo and complexity of the chase
will be an accurate reflection of the intensity of the relationships between
the characters' (Gottlieb 1995: 129).

The 39 Steps was a tribute to a favourite writer and to a genre, the adventure romance, made powerful through its Scottish settings, settings
Hitchcock still thought of as wild and primitive. His other peripheries were,
of course, the Isle of Man and Cornwall. He shot on location in Cornwall,
which doubled for the Isle of Man, in *The Manxman*, adapted from the novel
by Hall Caine, and again in rural England for *Young and Innocent*, which re-
prises three years later in gentle, almost lackadaisical mode the flight-narrative taken over from his Hannay film. Meanwhile in 1937 Michael Powell
– once Hitchcock's assistant – made the first of three Scottish island features,
a location film set in the Outer Hebrides and called *The Edge of the World*
(1937) after the term 'Ultima Thule' used by Roman explorers. The expressionistic framing of Powell's film had a lasting impact on Hitchcock's use

of the dramatic sublime. The dramatic rock-face sequence with its vertigo shots that climax the cliff-top race of the two rivals, Andrew and Robbie, was echoed with different variations of American landscape in *Saboteur*, *Vertigo* and *North by Northwest*. Yet the hand-rescue motif that begins *Vertigo* and ends *North by Northwest* also has its source in the Cornish quarry sequence (strictly studio bound) in *Young and Innocent* where the fleeing Derrick de Marney rescues Nova Pilbeam from her collapsing car. The same film also contains the children's game of blind man's buff that will feature more dramatically on the Bodega Bay cliffs in *The Birds*.

Outside the flight narrative other British writers proved vital. From these he would create something Buchan could never give, the edge of erotic subtext and a poetics of the gaze. Before we look at his ontology of flight, let us consider some of these fictions. *The Manxman* is the most poetic and least discursive of his British features, with sparse use of inter-titles and early signs of that stress on the visual, which Hitchcock inherited from Weimar cinema. In this silent film, disparaged by Hitchcock in his Truffaut interview but well received at the box-office, he moulds the embryonic power of the gaze and its strange triangulation of desire: male/female, male/male, female/male. Through Jack Cox's sensuous photography the gaze alternates in a shifting of allegiance between Hitchcock's three lovers, two life-long friends and the girl that both cherish. In this triangular choreography and spacing of the gaze, unaided by inter-titles, all three look longingly at the other two, and a lot more than once in the course of the film. Yet Hitchcock subtly varies levels of innocence and complicity in the framing of the gaze so it operates at two levels, conscious and subconscious. The gaze of fisherman Pete is naïve and bright, the eyes of lawyer Philip downcast and devious, and the look of barmaid Kate is shifting and flirtatious. If Philip knowingly swaps allegiance from his 'best friend' to his best friend's girl, his best friend in contrast does not even know the nature of his own (split) desire. Homoerotic subtext here paves the way for the more complex re-emergence of the desiring gaze in his filming of *Rebecca* for Selznick.

The remoteness of the Scottish and Cornish landscapes that attracted Hitchcock had been matched by the Cornish landscapes in the novels of the young Daphne du Maurier. After the gross misfire of *Jamaica Inn* (1939), his truly feeble adaptation designed as a vehicle for Charles Laughton, Hitchcock's American makeover of du Maurier's other Cornwall fictions – the best-selling *Rebecca* from 1938 and her 1952 story *The Birds* – produced two of his greatest films. The Winston Graham novel *Marnie* of 1961, set in adjacent Devon, was transposed to America's East Coast but again was mainly a studio picture. There were other sources too for the Atlantic transfer. Hitchcock transferred a 1929 Patrick Hamilton murder drama with an Oxford setting to an apartment in post-war Manhattan. *Rope*'s cryptic gay intimacy was soon reinforced by his intriguing turn to an American source, Patricia Highsmith's stunning *Strangers on a Train*, with its boldly queer agenda and its subtle variations on the transfer of guilt. This, for example, is Guy falsely protesting his innocence over the murder of Bruno's father to Ann, and facing nemesis near the end of the novel: 'But whether she believed him or not, he thought, he was finished. It seemed the basest lie he had ever told, the basest thing he had ever done – the transferring of guilt to another man' (Highsmith 1999: 218–19). In the film things differ of course. Guy is ambiguously innocent and Hitchcock concentrates on the obverse transfer – the transfer of guilt from Bruno to Guy. And here the transfer of guilt is not the basest thing ever done but rather part of the natural order of things in the Hitchcock universe. Yet the phrase 'transferring guilt' crops up in the text of Highsmith's novel some years *before* it emerges in the critical text of Rohmer and Chabrol as key concept for the work as a whole.

The film of the book exuded a new sexual daring that Hitchcock was prepared to try out in Hollywood, testing censorship to its limit when, one suspects, his British experience with producers and censors had made him more timid. Though American Hitchcock was ruthless in commodifying literary properties – Highsmith knew nothing of the pre-sold film rights on her debut novel – his use of American fiction was in fact restrained. A key novel Hitchcock could well have adapted but did not was Elisabeth Sanjay Holding's *The Blank Wall* (1947), filmed by Max Ophuls as *The Reckless Moment* in 1949. One of Hitchcock's favourites, this was a wartime Long Island story of murder, guilt and cover-up from the female point-of-view, with a plotline that ran very much in tandem with his own work and that of du Maurier. But in eight breathtaking years, 1940–48, Hitchcock had already made his post-literary mark. There seemed no special reason for him to film Holding's novel: in retrospect we can see that *Rebecca* had marked a watershed in his career. He had forged a new kind of contemporary film – intimate spectacle – that met with popular acclaim. He had also teased out of du Maurier nuances that would have passed by many of her readers and his viewers. A contemporary audience would see the film differently and surely read the signs of a bisexual milieu at Manderley where, in the novel, Mrs Danvers claims the adulterous Rebecca 'despised all men. She was above all that' (du Maurier 2003: 382). It was a charged atmosphere brought to life on screen by Hitchcock's abstract Gothic design. Stylistically the film lent to his cinematic profile a different structure of feeling, the vision of a perverse sexual stress on the power of the look and the gaze. Just as Buchan's novel had given him a structure for onscreen flight, so *Rebecca* allowed him to expand upon *The Manxman's* triangular desire. Here he sets up a sinister *four-way* nexus – young second wife, older husband, deceased first wife and forbidding housekeeper – enabling him to weave an intricate pattern of sex-power transactions. The film's poetics of look and gaze could never be mistaken as the work of another director. Later he went further. *Vertigo*, *North by Northwest*, *Psycho*, *The Birds* and *Marnie* are all *fusion-films* in which the flight and the gaze finally come together.

Less successful than *Rebecca* was Hitchcock's version of Frances Iles' *Before to the Fact*, adapted to the screen as *Suspicion*. He and his screenwriting team were unsure how to convince Selznick and the American censors of their ending for a very English novel, where a duplicitous husband (Cary Grant) is suspected by his fearful spouse (Joan Fontaine) of cold-blooded murder. Under studio constraint, scriptwriters Samson Raphaelson, Joan Harrison and Alma Reville could not end the film satisfactorily. Could they get away with making the suave and handsome Johnny Aysgarth (Grant) a cold-blooded murderer? They decided not. As a result the film's ending in its post-preview cut lacked all conviction. Just as disappointing was its simplistic portrait of rural Sussex, its picture postcard villages and fake country house warped by a glossy studio look and a Californian coastal highway back-projected with scant plausibility. Yet whichever ending Hitchcock used, the film presented him with a genuine dilemma because of the very suspense he had cleverly generated. If Grant turns out to be innocent of murder, he loses his unerring menace to anti-climax – which in fact he did. If, however, he turns out to be guilty Hitchcock loses the power of the agonising look on the face of Joan Fontaine as Lina, a look whose anxieties convey a delirium of suspicion that goes beyond the evidence of the senses. Selznick and the Studio Code may have placed harsh constraints upon Hitchcock's options but the quandary remains as a dilemma of the new psychic ambiguities in bourgeois life that Hitchcock had begun to explore in *Rebecca*. Fontaine's false perception strengthens her performance, but undermines that of Grant who wanted a villainous ending to strengthen his own. The problem thus lies not only with the censors but also with the structure of ambivalence the film creates and which no ending can truly resolve.

Yet in Hitchcock there is no such thing as unfinished business. Two years later, *Shadow of a Doubt* more than redeemed the suspicion motif of its predecessor. Its transition of suspect intimacy from studio to location, and from troubled spouses to uncle and niece was a masterstroke. Hitchcock had to wait more than ten years, though, before he could fine-tune his stillborn vision of the murderous husband, although the asking fee of Cary Grant had by this time excluded him from acting in the role he coveted. Though based squarely on Frederick Knott's play, the cold, calculating performance of Ray Milland in *Dial 'M' for Murder*, plotting the end of Grace Kelly and then framing her for killing her would-be killer after she survives, is a gem of suspense. It accomplishes everything that *Suspicion* could not. In the short term Hitchcock, however, had to move on to things and places American, though even here he would always carry British motifs with him. This was especially true of the Hitchcock murders. He had remarked in 1950 how the murder rate in the US far exceeded that of the UK, yet for that very reason perhaps, those back home always seemed more distinctive and notorious (Gottlieb 1995: 133–8). In *Rear Window*, for example, the dismembering and decapitation of the wife's body was based on the methods of the notorious English killer, Patrick Mahon (Truffaut 1986: 333). Yet English social manners, backed by Hitchcock's insistence on formality in dress, also shine through for many years afterwards. Two decades on from *Suspicion* we can note the ambience of Mark Rutland's country house and the social manners of its riding set in *Marnie*. The locations are real, the house unmistakeably American in style: yet the customs and costumes of the wealthy seem very English, more Old World than New.

The look and the gaze: Hitchcock and du Maurier

In his film of *Rebecca* Hitchcock could well be accused of excess caution: he sticks very closely to the book. Yet his first screenplay version, which Selznick rejected, showed many key deviations that clearly irked his powerful producer (see Spoto 1983: 212–16). In the end irony and censorship struck a common blow. The Motion Picture Production Code that enforced Hollywood censorship refused to accept the idea, faithful to the book, of Maxim de Winter's hushed-up, unpunished murder of Rebecca. Hitchcock was forced to use a tamer ending – her death through accident – that did no justice either to book or film. Prevented from inventing when he wished, he was forced to invent when he had no impulse to do so. Despite this the film is a clear breakthrough, the instance in Hitchcock's work where for the first time since *The Manxman* the power of the emotions consistently matched the power of the image, and in this film had a deeper complexity.

In the passage from book to film a restricted Hitchcock invented his own trade-off to limit the damage of censorship and producer interference. The complicity of husband and second wife in concealing Rebecca's murder, a sure-fire Hitchcock theme, was sacrificed for a different stress, a bolder emphasis. This was a relationship of look and gaze between two women haunted by the absent presence of a third. Housekeeper Mrs Danvers (Judith Anderson) casts a perennial gaze, a gaze that judges, upon the interloper whom she hates and desires at the same time. After having nurtured and loved Rebecca, she preys upon her substitute, the young spouse whose look betrays anguish, uncertainty, doubt, insecurity. Hitchcock's casting of Joan Fontaine in this respect – over Vivien Leigh fresh from Selznick's *Gone with the Wind* (1939) and wanted in the part by husband Laurence Olivier – is vital. Fontaine has the perfect malleable look. It is photogenic and yet diffused, a neurotic response to the new tests of a new role in a new household where she is still seen as a young girl but has to satisfy a middle-aged husband and fill the shoes of a dead woman much older than herself. In this rite of passage her adversary is Mrs Danvers whose judging (and desiring) gaze is always based on her sudden appearance in a room: a woman with no footfall, her dark, still form often watching with face and eyes half in shadow. It is a performance of mute eruption that Judith Anderson hones to perfection, ugly yet statuesque. The gaze insinuates: it is not direct, usually in profile and seldom frontal in shot. Yet with precision it crystallises the nervous look of the Girl With No Name. Moreover relations are triangulated. In any encounter, the dead Rebecca always seems present, an invisible witness; always *there* as the text or subtext of any conversation between them, and always watching both of them. The Girl With No Name is thus stranded between the *judging* gaze of the ubiquitous Danvers and the *absent* gaze of the dead Rebecca.

Because he was refused that which is explicit in du Maurier, a marital love strengthened by complicit knowledge of murder, Hitchcock looked elsewhere at what is implicit – the makeover of one woman by another in the image of another. Fontaine is the first true predecessor of Kim Novak in *Vertigo*. While Novak is the focus of the male gaze – that of James Stewart – Fontaine is the focus of the *female* gaze. A whole generation of critics, who have misread Laura Mulvey, use Hitchcock to obsess with great pedantry about a generic male gaze on the female 'subject'. But they have entirely missed the point about the direction of his cinema. After *The Manxman*, with its triangulated gaze, the Hitchcock genealogy runs from *female to male*, not the other way around. Three key variations of the female gaze rapidly follow *Rebecca* in Hitchcock's wartime pictures, in *Suspicion, Shadow of a Doubt* and *Spellbound*. With Cary Grant, of course, Hitchcock half-reverses it in *Notorious* but there establishes a parity of gaze and look between the two lovers. Only with James Stewart in *Rear Window* and *Vertigo* does it become fully male. In the meantime, however, he had generated a third variation – the gaze of *male on male* that comes out of *The Manxman* and finds fruition in *Rope* and *Strangers on a Train* is then echoed obliquely in *I Confess* and repeated in a minor key by the Soviet spies tracking Cary Grant in *North by Northwest* where Martin Landau in hot pursuit certainly gives Grant the eye. As far as *Rebecca* goes, the gaze-structure is clear. Maxim de Winter hardly seems to notice his second wife except when she's a social irritant, and thus the female gaze – the housekeeper's gaze – always comes first. In fact the housekeeper cannot take her eyes off 'Madam' and yet we, the audience, cannot really see her eyes. We are uncomfortably present at the genesis of a perverse eroticism, the eroticism of an eyeless gaze. But the perverse is only effective because it repeats the banal gaze at the start of the film when Fontaine's suffocating employer has a judging gaze as she watches Fontaine's clumsy courtship with Olivier.

Fig. 6 Looking the other way: Joan Fontaine and Laurence Oliver in *Rebecca*

Her censorious eyes are ever open and prying, though in fact she does not see the half of what is going on. It is Danvers' gaze in shadow which is relentless and much more sinister. Having been born 'blind', however, in the figure of Danvers, the Hitchcock gaze is quickly modified in later films. He converts it to the frontal and fanatic stare of eyes, nowhere more so than in Bergman's first sighting of Peck in *Spellbound*.

Heterosexual, Constance Pederson succeeds where Danvers fails. The latter's sinister try at 'makeover', unlike that of Scottie Ferguson, goes nowhere. The play for seduction takes place in the deserted west wing when Fontaine discovers her predecessor's bedroom preserved immaculately as if she were still alive. Disturbed by Danvers and caught in the act of prying, this is the make-or-break moment. Before Fontaine's eyes the housekeeper lovingly extracts and fondles Rebecca's underwear as she reminisces about her departed mistress. The insinuation is that Fontaine might wish to wear it too, that is be 'made over' intimately into the desirable image of the woman she has succeeded as mistress of the house, the woman Danvers has loved. When that innuendo fails, cruelty takes over. The housekeeper's next ploy is to fool Fontaine into wearing a shepherdess outfit for the de Winters' fancy dress ball in order to resemble one of Maxim's ancestors, whose portrait hangs on the wall by the stairs. The idea for the second wife is to please Maxim but since, unknown to her imitator, Rebecca has also worn the same outfit at the previous ball before her death, it backfires horribly. With wife number two – the substitute – a humiliated Danvers has won a Pyrrhic victory, punishing her resistant object of prey through the ploy of double imitation. Fontaine becomes 'Rebecca' by imitating the ancestor Rebecca has previously imitated, and Rebecca is brought back from the dead by default. The visual aspect of the double imitation had a strong appeal for Hitchcock and of course he re-peats it in the portrait imitation of *Vertigo* when Madeleine goes to the art galley, tracked by Scottie, to look at the portrait of her 'ancestor' Carlotta Valdez whose hair she has meticulously copied. Here though the shepherdess portrait stands in for the film's most stunning absence. Manderley possesses no visual memento of Rebecca, no clinching image by which her successor can nail her down and define her.

Originating in *Rebecca* the Hitchcock gaze embodies not only desire, but also judgment and surveillance. The look precedes it but is also its reactive complement. It embodies not only uncertainty, but also guilt and suspicion. In this way Hitchcock provides us with a cinema of the Humean passions, very much adjusted as his own, and mediated through his subject, his new Anglo-American heroine. For in her two Hitchcock roles Fontaine displayed a kind of fragility that was precisely what her director wanted. In *Rebecca* the look – nervous, shifting, labile – reveals the anxiety of being judged. But in *Suspicion* it is transformed to live up to the title of the film. Here the look is integral to the gaze itself, so the two can barely be separated. Before their marriage Grant's gaze is directed at Fontaine; the opening train sequence is its strongest expression. After, there is gradual transfer until the reverse becomes true, but that is because the gaze is assimilated into Fontaine's look as deepening suspicion. For the vulnerable woman, suspicion is the active gaze-component of the look of fear. Hitchcock had already done this in *The Lodger* with the look-gaze of the daughter, anxious and ambivalent about the handsome intruder. But here there is greater subtlety. The variation that Hitchcock rings on Fontaine's look/gaze as his plot thickens is the redeem-ing feature of the film, so we are looking less to the machinations of the confidence man and more to their effect; to a female response which is also a surplus of affect, to a look/gaze that will surmise and speculate with grow-ing delirium.

Shadow of a Doubt continues the formula but gives its context much greater conviction. Teresa Wright's gaze starts out loving and admiring but as Cotten's crimes are revealed to her, and his deviousness grows, the gaze is transformed into a look of fear and loathing. Suspicion corrodes: and once Cotten arrives in Santa Rosa we see things filtered mainly through her eyes, not his. The same is true of *Spellbound*. Bergman's sudden rapture announces

Peck's arrival at Green Manors. As he gradually cracks up, that rapture is strengthened rather than weakened by Bergman's look of compassion that goes beyond solicitude. Unlike Grant in *Suspicion*, Peck's imposture elicits sympathy because it is an illness not a subterfuge. Fontaine's look/gaze of suspicion is turned around into Bergman's look-gaze of rapture, a compassionate rapture that is unique in Hitchcock's cinema. Hitchcock thus transforms the possibility that germinates in *Rebecca* as pure fiction into his own medium – pure cinema.

It was appropriate that du Maurier also provided 'The Birds' feeding Hitchcock's final reckoning with the Blitz, which his family had painfully endured in his absence. The story itself, though it takes place in post-war Cornwall, may well have been prompted by the war experience and we should note that du Maurier's birds finally descend on London. If her fiction had opened a new chapter in Hitchcock's cinema with *Rebecca*, it all but closes it here: fear and flight under a watchful gaze that terrifies and whose outcome is terrifyingly uncertain. Yet from *The Birds* onward Hitchcock's literary sources were nearly all British – in Winston Graham's *Marnie*, in the choice of novelist Brian Moore to write an original screenplay for *Torn Curtain*, in adapting Arthur La Bern's novel as *Frenzy* and finally in his choice of Victor Canning's *The Rainbird Pattern*, a novel set in the English countryside, as the basis for Ernest Lehman's very Californian screenplay of *Family Plot*. It was a homecoming of sorts, an indication that, deep down, part of him had never gone away. In the twilight of his career, he may well have been very distant from British cinema but in general the British connection loomed as large as ever.

Hitchcock and Conrad: shock, suspense, cover-up

There is a third name besides Buchan and du Maurier in the filmed fiction of British Hitchcock, sometimes overlooked. One of his boldest moves, where he challenges censorship and convention came, in adapting Joseph Conrad's turn-of-the-century novel *The Secret Agent* to the screen as *Sabotage*. Conrad's book is one the great Europeans fictions of late nineteenth-century terrorism, a masterpiece of tragic irony; Hitchcock duly updates it for his own time with comic and macabre interpolations. In the novel a motley group of European anarchists use a simple and demented boy for an act of terror that is more symbolic than effective, a plan to 'sabotage' the Meridian line at Greenwich that organises our modern conception of time. The boy is the impressionable brother-in-law of Verloc, the chief conspirator. The bomb explodes at the wrong time and the boy is killed. When she finds out about this callous dispatch of her brother on a death-mission, Mrs Verloc takes homicidal revenge. Hitchcock keeps the contours of the plot but changes the detail and the dénouement. Verloc's first terror target in 1930s London is Battersea Power Station; his camouflage is no longer the seedy bookshop of the novel but a seedy cinema that becomes a victim of the subsequent power-cut when the lines go down. In despatching Stevie to commit another act of terror at Piccadilly Circus, Verloc (Oscar Homolka) conceals the time bomb, and the motive, from him by putting it next to a can of film in a parcel. Hitchcock thus introduces a motif that is organic and reflexive at the same time. Verloc's cinema runs off the very power source he is trying to eliminate while his cheap neighbourhood cinema is surely Hitchcock's private joke, an inverted mirror held to the 'congested' conditions under which he claimed to work as a director, in a medium still seen by many English literati as something of a low-life occupation.

Unlike Conrad, Hitchcock is not interested in a revolutionary politics gone wrong, nor its attendant ironies. What fascinates him is the death of innocence created by Stevie's tragic 'accident'. His *mise-en-scène* for the bus bomb, which kills the other passengers too, was a calculated outrage on his part. Let us quote from his reflections on the film a decade later. First the outrage: '...the episode in *Sabotage* was a direct negation of the invisible cloak of protection worn by sympathetic characters in motion pictures' (Gottlieb 1995: 121). Second the film's unusual combination of shock and suspense: '...because the audience knew the film can contained a bomb and the boy did not, to permit the bomb to explode was a violation of the rule forbidding a direct combination of suspense and terror, of forewarning and surprise' (ibid.). Hitchcock wryly added that lack of surprise left audience and critics the space to be outraged by his tactics, where pure shock would have left them emotionally numb. This is the high point of British Hitchcock: two violations on Hitchcock's part that yield cinematic fruit. The first is the fusion (not separation) of shock and suspense, a fusion that he repeats to perfection in the shower and staircase sequences of *Psycho*. The second, the murder of innocence, is more problematic, the one thing that he *cannot* repeat in Hollywood. Even in *The Birds*, where the attacks on the local children are graphically depicted, it is two local adults, a farmer and schoolteacher, who die, off-screen, from the attacks.

For the ban on the murder of innocents, American Hitchcock compensates in sly ways. In *Rear Window* the backyard dog who digs up the severed head of the murdered wife in the garden and duly gets poisoned by Thorwald for his curiosity, is the pampered child its doting owners never had. In the remade *The Man Who Knew Too Much* the child kidnapping has a curious middle section where doting and distressed parents James Stewart and Doris Day appear for a brief time to have forgotten their son's existence and are more relaxed in a new childless ambience. This, of course, is fleeting subtext, and Hitchcock's happy ending duly compensates. Yet with Hitchcock you never know. In *Shadow of a Doubt* the 24-year-old Teresa Wright is an uncanny version of a girl-child so physically developed but yet so short she could pass for being pubescent. After all, how old is she? Officially 18 but at times, we might feel, passing for 14 or 15. Hitchcock plays on this ambiguity and gives us the glint in Cotten's eye of possible seduction of a vulnerable minor who also happens to be his niece.

Stylistically, *Sabotage* establishes the *doubled montage sequence* that attends violence not only in *Psycho* but also in *Vertigo, Marnie* and, as noted, *The Birds.* The knife montage of Verloc's killing doubles the bus montage of the explosion: dynamic editing not only generates suspense but intensifies it the second time around. In both sequences Hitchcock presents a tight repetitive focus, cutting between core images. In the bus sequence his cutting alternates between the seated Stevie, the traffic lights he sees outside, the clocks the bus passes in the street counting down his fate, and his parcel beside him on the seat. In the killing sequence that follows montage is again minimal, a mosaic of body fragments. There are matched cuts from Verloc to his dinner plate, to his numb and distraught wife, to the roast from which she absently carves a portion to put on the plate set for the dead Stevie. At one point the camera tracks in on her desperate expression. Seconds later it tracks in again but this time from Verloc's point-of-view as he moves towards her. Hitchcock then cuts to a reverse-angle profile shot of the two moving in close, followed by a close-up on their hands as she snatches the knife ahead of him. Montage then bisects their bodies in half. First the camera watches their uncertain faces chest-high as the knife goes in. Then it cuts down to their stomachs as she steps back to reveal the blade implanted in his flesh. Finally it cuts to a floor shot of her legs departing around the outstretched feet of her dead husband.

This is not only for audience effect, a display of virtuoso technique from the cockney Kuleshov. It can also be viewed as pure *transfer-of-guilt montage*; the second killing stems from a response to the first one as Verloc's lack of remorse transfers guilt to his hapless spouse (Sylvia Sidney) who duly suffers remorse on behalf of her dead brother. The tensions of montage over the dining table, where the spectator is placed tight with the action and never released from that position, quickly transform her guilt into unspoken rage so that exchange becomes reciprocal. She kills the hate figure whose guilt she has absorbed, because he himself has none. Yet the Rohmer-Chabrol formula seems at this point a little too simple. The tensions are precisely about the impossibility of moving forward as a couple and also, because of the enormity of Verloc's crime, the impossibility of finding a way to go on living. Hitchcock produces crystalline images of indeterminacy that are unbearable not only for the Verlocs but also for us. By killing her husband 'by accident' at knifepoint, just as he had killed her brother 'by accident' with explosives, Mrs Verloc transfers guilt back, under the Rohmer-Chabrol formula, in disguised form. But the act also brings to a head a situation that is unbearable and changes it utterly.

For sure, the fusion of shock and suspense in the doubled montage acts to facilitate violent exchange: to make it not only more dramatic but also more poignant, not only more shocking but also more tragic. But in the knife-killing sequence, Hitchcock also uses montage in a way *antithetical* to expressionist *mise-en-scène*. He remarked that the wrong way to proceed would be for Sylvia Sidney 'to convey her inner feelings to the audience by facial expression' (Truffaut 1984: 152). It lies instead in kinetic transaction, the tensions of conflict as collage of spatial relationships that his montage gives. Here montage is not used in Eisenstein's sense to forge a new and transparent meaning, but the opposite: to render a situation unbearably *enigmatic* until violence resolves it. The new situation for the survivor is also enigmatic: she is now alone. Yet aloneness is the only way forward even if it will end in her own death.

Here Hitchcock effects a cynical but profound change in Conrad's ending, where Mrs Verloc had tried to escape by boat train to France but then kills herself in despair. Hitchcock provides the safety-cushion of the handsome detective (John Loder) who covers for her because he desires her. This is yet another trade-off similar to that which ends *Blackmail*. For sure Verloc deserves to die and she feels that she deserves to live, but there is complicity here and the embryo of the desiring gaze. Putting Verloc under surveillance from his greengrocer's stall Loder is drawn to his younger wife so conveniently he lets the obvious pass him by. For Hitchcock the irony is clear. The detective has allowed the outrage to happen by faulty surveillance, or rather by the transfer of the gaze out of the domain of the law (watching Verloc) into the arena of desire (gazing at her). She is redeemed by love, but only from someone who might have prevented her brother's tragic death, who is already compromised by incompetence and resolves complicity in that death through further complicity that means the saving of a life. Is the end, then, a macabre emanation of the detective's wishful thinking where he gets the girl only by permitting the crime of her husband?

The fourth man: Hitchcock and Graham Greene

In 1939, Hitchcock took the flight motif out of England to California. In the hands of others, the leitmotif stayed behind in post-war British film. Here, after the key figures of Buchan, Conrad and du Maurier, we have a rivalry. In Hitchcock's career it hovers beneath the surface of things, a contest with a 'fourth man' that went beyond the boundaries of film and continues to fascinate. It did not involve Michael Powell, who remained a close friend, or David Lean, who made the defining film of English wartime experience, *Brief Encounter* (1945); at the same time it did help create a British cinema in Hitchcock's absence. Graham Greene was an English writer who appealed, like Hitchcock, to the idea of the popular, not the highbrow, often writing books he called 'entertainments'. Yet his fiction was deadly serious. He was a rival for Buchan's legacy and stated openly his wish to update *The Thirty-Nine Steps* in his own fiction, dragging it out of an imperial, Edwardian straightjacket into a new age of modernity. Where Hitchcock adapted it for the screen, Greene reformed it ambitiously into a series of contemporary novels written throughout the 1930s. In *Stamboul Train, A Gun for Sale, The Confidential Agent* and *Brighton Rock* he uses flight to explore the changing cities of 1930s England and, more obliquely, the turbulent politics of a changing Europe. Later, when Hitchcock spent the war in Hollywood, Greene spent the time of the Blitz as a fire warden on London streets, witnessing anxiety and courage amidst destruction. Having 'made over' Buchan for his gangster thrillers, he reformulated him again for that wartime experience in *The Ministry of Fear*; and for post-war Europe he forged a story of subterfuge and flight that was to become the buoyant, precise screenplay for an astonishing film directed by Carol Reed, *The Third Man* (1948).

To set this achievement in context, let us look more closely at two great English artists born within five years of one another. Hitchcock, the older, was from the East End, lower middle-class, a greengrocer's boy in a Catholic family and schooled by Jesuits. Greene grew up in rural Hertfordshire, the son of a headmaster whose wealthy public school, Berkhamstead, he attended before going up to Oxford; soon after Oxford he converted to the Catholic faith. In Greene's writing the conjoining agony of faith, sin and remorse is an open wound that never heals. For Hitchcock, it is equally powerful but fully absorbed, for it was in the blood. If Greene was always searching for an elusive something throughout his life, a material and spiritual quest that took him restlessly around the world, Hitchcock was more sedentary, moving out of working-class Leytonstone and then from the West End to rural Surrey (Shamley Green), then onto California (Bel Air and Santa Cruz) from where he ventured mainly for holidays or film shoots. Greene became as close in his own life to the ontology of flight as Hitchcock was distant from it. Hitchcock filmed spy thrillers at one stage removed. Greene wrote spy thrillers, but also became a spy. He joined British military intelligence in London during the war, was sent to Portugal and then to Sierra Leone where he wrote *The Ministry of Fear* in 1943. As he travelled widely after the war, according to recent biographers, he became a freelance operative for MI6 in Europe, Latin America and South East Asia (see Shelden 1994: 19–44; Sherry 1994: 481–7). As far as politics went, Hitchcock's work rose to the challenge of the Nazi threat and then moved back to familiar obsessions: Greene's fiction never left politics. It confronted new Cold War enemies but more often the corruption and dictatorships that the West supported in the new world order, and it produced great novels like *The Quiet American* and *The Comedians*.

Yet the early Greene of the 1930s had already set out the motifs that Hitchcock later used to give his cinema its special stamp. The train setting was one that he enjoyed filming because it always allowed characters to be hemmed in, yet in constant motion at the same time. Unhindered by the primitive medium that was British cinema, Greene, however, had published his early thriller *Stamboul Train* six years before Hitchcock made *The Lady Vanishes*. Moreover, Greene gives us the chapter and verse of a changing Europe, naming and reflecting on countries through which his Orient Express is steaming onward. Such kinetic melodrama propels us through the twinned fates of a Serbian revolutionary and a Viennese killer, early models perhaps for different aspects of Harry Lime, while Greene observes in turn the fatuous English abroad and, tongue-in-cheek, boldly finishes with a lesbian affair in the making. En route he takes us out of the train into the city of Vienna then later into the Serbian countryside, tapping into the brutalities of a turbulent Europe for key moments in the plot. In his studio-bound *The Lady Vanishes* Hitchcock plays safe and remains on board, amusingly so at times, yet no countries are actually named in this spy saga, for this is a fantasy Balkania.

Things between them were not helped by Greene's film reviewing in the 1930s, which had praised Lang, Griffith and Renoir but disparaged Hitchcock at nearly every turn. After seeing the leaden and contrived *Secret Agent* in 1936 Greene comments acerbically:

> His films consist of a series of small 'amusing' melodramatic situations: the murderer's button dropped on the baccarat board; the strangled organist's hands prolonging the notes in the empty church; the fugitive hiding in the bell tower when the bell began to swing. Very perfunctorily he builds up to these tricky situations (paying no attention on the way to inconsistencies, loose psychological absurdities) and then drops them: they mean nothing: they lead to nothing. (1972: 75)

He expressed disappointment with *The 39 Steps* and slated *Jamaica Inn* three years later, yet he also praised *Sabotage* for its tight focus on the Verlocs and its tragic ending (1972: 122–3, 222–3). While he had damned Hitchcock for feebleness in earlier scripts (blaming the director as though he were screenwriter Charles Bennett) he praises the dialogue here co-written by Ian Hay and Helen Simpson. Hay, crucially, had also written the colloquial dialogue for *The 39 Steps*. But with Greene this would have cut no ice. Towards the end of his life he would confirm his disappointment with *The 39 Steps*, which he saw as a chance lost. Yet Greene was mistaken. It was a chance gained. In the 1930s, as he was starting to find his true touch, Hitchcock was guided out of the narrative maze by the *preformed* fiction. He followed on from Conrad just as he had followed on from Buchan and would follow on from *Rebecca*. He had absorbed three different literary sources, all British, to create a template for his mature cinematic vision. Hitchcock seemed not to hold Greene's critical reservations against him. In 1951 he asked the writer to collaborate on the screenplay of *I Confess*, and a decade later tried to buy up the film rights to *Our Man in Havana*. In both cases, Greene politely declined his requests.

Greene's criticisms had come from an obvious rivalry but also a greater sense of assurance in a medium – fiction that was largely autonomous and individual – while British filmmaking as Hitchcock well knew, was collective and constrained. It was the cruel response of a kindred soul increasingly in full control of his art when Hitchcock was still groping toward his. With clear and detailed eye Greene's flight motifs had given fresh, unusual insights into English life in the 1930s. They had forged a new kind of anti-hero, not suave, upper-class villains, but rough-and-ready fallen angels – Raven in *A Gun for Sale*, Pinkie Brown in *Brighton Rock*. This updated Buchan to the decade of the hunger marchers, who seemed to Greene 'more real than the politicians' (1999: 69). It was an act that Hitchcock could never hope to follow so he took a different route. In Hollywood his villains become more complex, more enigmatic as bourgeois renegades, fully-fledged products of modernity. While Greene invited sympathy for his street-wise murderers through their tangled conscience and buried faith, Hitchcock distanced us from his middle-class transgressors who were largely amoral and secular, letting us admire their technique and their sang-froid but disallowing empathy, that same empathy Greene could always evoke through intimations of guilt and remorse. Greene's fiction gravitates towards the gangster underworld: even when Hitchcock takes murder out of the drawing room, he still locates it in the bourgeois home, or in American parlance, on the right side of the tracks.

Greene's eye for detail, narrative drive, naturalist's accuracy and streamlined prose made his work perfect for the ninety-minute feature film. *Brighton Rock* became a box-office hit in the post-war version – 1947 – made by the Boulting Brothers. *A Gun for Sale* was turned into American film noir as *This Gun for Hire* (1942) with Alan Ladd and Veronica Lake, and *The Confidential Agent* with Lauren Bacall followed in 1945. His bittersweet romance of the Blitz, *The End of the Affair* (1954) became a late post-war film directed by Edward Dmytryk and was remade in 1999 by Neil Jordan, the Irish director and fiction writer whose many flight-narratives bear the imprint of Greene's influence. Greene's 1943 thriller *The Ministry of Fear* went to his cinema idol Fritz Lang in Hollywood the following year even if the end product was not to his liking. Closer at home, his wartime story about Nazi sabotage in rural England 'The Lieutenant Died Last' was transformed by Alberto Cavalcanti into Ealing's full-scale film of traumatised village life, *Went the Day Well?* (1942), a work co-written by Angus MacPhail that makes a fascinating contrast to *Saboteur*.

As a wartime friend of Greene's and planning a follow-up project with him that came to nothing, the Brazilian Cavalcanti then went on to make *the gangster-flight film* of post-war England, *They Made Me a Fugitive* (1947), featuring Trevor Howard in one of his great roles, a demobbed RAF officer at a loose end on civvie street who is sucked into black-market crime. In this Greene had no part, but his spirit was there and his mark was all over it. But then it is a story that comes back into play when Hitchcock returned to London to make *Frenzy* at the start of the 1970s. The connections here are fascinating. The Hitchcock film is adapted from the 1966 novel *Goodbye Piccadilly, Farewell Leicester Square* by Arthur La Bern (who had earlier penned the novel adapted in 1947 as a convict flight film *It Always Rains on Sunday* directed by Robert Hamer and co-written by Hitchcock's collaborator, Angus MacPhail). Set in London and featuring an escaped convict on the run, Hamer's film was in the same flight idiom as Cavalcanti's film of the same year and it is hard to think that La Bern has not run back narrative aspects of *They Made Me a Fugitive* into his later novel. After all we have an almost identical hero, an ex-RAF officer down on his luck in London, who is framed by a misogynistic criminal and sentenced for crimes he did not commit only to escape and seek revenge. In returning for *Frenzy*, Hitchcock's work had not only come full circle in terms of his career. It also came full circle in terms of his enduring connection with the post-war cinema that emerged in his absence and proved to be one of the great moments of British film history.

For Greene, meanwhile, his screenwriting career had begun to take off: first, the collaboration with the talented Carol Reed on adapting his story 'The Basement Room' for the screen as *The Fallen Idol*, followed in the same year, 1948, by the great collaboration in Vienna with Reed on *The Third Man*. It was a remarkable portfolio. The 1940s moment of Hitchcock – Britain's greatest triumph in Hollywood after Chaplin – is matched back home by the film-fiction moment of Greene. Here three comparisons remain momentous, and in each the boundaries of film and fiction are crossed and re-crossed during that crucial phase between 1935 and 1948 – pre-war, wartime, post-war, thirteen years that seemed a lifetime. Let us take them one by one: (i) *The 39 Steps* and *Brighton Rock*; (ii) *Spellbound* and *The Ministry of Fear*; (iii) *Shadow of a Doubt* and *The Third Man*.

Comparison starts with a paradox. In the 1920s Hitchcock, with his cinephile membership of the London Film Society, had early on absorbed, as noted, the innovating achievements of silent film – Griffith, Eisenstein,

Kuleshov, Lang, Murnau, Buñuel and Dalí. Never strong on plot construction at that time and with little flair for dialogue, he relied on limited screenwriters like Charles Bennett to absorb the construction rules of classical narrative in the sound era and so flesh out the visual epiphanies of modernist invention which had become his early trademark. Greene, by comparison, was a natural storyteller with a good ear for dialogue, a keen observational eye and great love of cinema. From this foundation he began to push at the edges of the modernist text, which from Joyce and Dos Passos onward responded to the perceptual advances of the moving image. *Brighton Rock* and *The Ministry of Fear* were truly cinematic texts. Both used daring forms of flashback, montage, ellipsis and crosscutting, absorbing film techniques into the modernist fiction much as William Faulkner had done in the 1931 gangster novel he deemed his 'pot-boiler', *Sanctuary*. The quick bold switches that Greene used in flight-narrative, his mastery of the double-chase pattern both he and Hitchcock had taken from Buchan more than matched the new pace and rhythm that Hitchcock had shown in *The 39 Steps*. There was in Greene a greater sexual boldness, political wisdom and emotional complexity. But then Greene did not feel the same constraints of censorship. Hitchcock's moral ambiguities might challenge, as he did in *Sabotage*, cinema's golden rule of melodrama, namely that good and bad should finally be separated and that only bad be punished while good is rendered triumphant. But with Greene there was a different kind of provocation. In *Brighton Rock* Pinkie Brown, precocious gangster turned killer, at first repels us then locks into our emotions as he becomes the hunted one and his haunted conscience shows through his taut amorality. Here Greene comes close to insinuating sympathy for the devil and he is nearer to Dostoevsky's *Crime and Punishment* than any other English writer of the period. That it is to say he perfects the dilemma of reading response in the moral inquiry of evil – sympathy for the doer, revulsion at the crime

The 39 Steps is a chase that takes us back and forth across national borders, that opens up spaces and places. *Brighton Rock* is tightly set in a small seaside city, 1930s Brighton, during the period of the racecourse gangs who had made their way down from London to establish their betting rackets. Greene's story has its special take on the double chase pattern. Having hunted down and murdered a corrupt journalist he accuses of double-cross, the 17-year-old Pinkie Brown panics and retraces his steps to cover up incriminating evidence. Here he charms and courts the gullible Rose to prevent her, as possible witness, turning King's Evidence. Tactical courtship ends in brief marriage. While Hitchcock's Hannay works hard to convince a quizzical Pamela of his innocence, and hence his goodness, Pinkie works hard to conceal from the naïve Rose his murderous nature and flair for evil. In the double chase pattern, Greene provides his own variation. Pinkie's arrogance ebbs away not only as the police start to suspect him but as other gangs turn against him and his own gang takes fright. As his enemies close in, Greene's bold strategy is to enhance his hero's inchoate conscience in equal measure to his precise cruelty. His tactical scheming grows with his Catholic guilt. Yet his terror is played out: attacked and wounded by gangster-enemies he is reduced to killing one of his own gang and chasing down witnesses to his crimes. The innocent Hannay turns around his female adversary in order to chase down the spies that hunt him; Pinkie terrorises women because his petty kingdom is already in ruins.

Brighton, the new place of weekend escape for Londoners with its beach, pier, funfair and leisure arcades, is an apt site for Pinkie's fate. It is where he pursues and is pursued in topographical spiral, so the openness of flight that Hitchcock prizes is taken in the opposite direction. The teenage hoodlum is gradually forced out of the glare and bustle of the seafront and the grandeur of its Grand Hotel into the dark refuge of a lodging house near the station. It is a movement that John Boulting's film tries to capture but the complexity is something no film can fully encompass, that is to link the interior and exterior aspects of Pinkie's predicament in a way comparable to Greene's sinuous prose. Nonetheless in shooting the film on location and giving it a documentary flavour Boulting makes a post-war film complete with cars and 'spiv' fashions that contradict the preface of a scrolling text claiming it as a 1930s story. Boulting in fact updates the novel for a new decade and a new era that also makes it part of a new genre the book had actually helped to instigate. Yet this is not a narrative Hitchcock would have adapted, even if Greene had not written it! Its subject is too raw, its back streets too seedy, its hero too demonic and yet too banal at the same time.

Greene's narrative goes steadily forward and resurfaces in the 1960s. Pinkie is one prototype in British cinema for the menacing changes of a new consumer age, for James Fox's villainous Chas in *Performance* or Malcolm McDowell's Alex, leader of the Droogs in Kubrick's futuristic *A Clockwork Orange* (1971), the *mise-en-scène* in both highly stylised, the overtones clearly Satanic. Both films, however, break with the naturalistic template and that is what still links Greene to Hitchcock in the earlier period, as do the questions of conscience and the trauma of war. Greene's response to wartime experience came from the front-line of the Blitz, Hitchcock's from the seclusion and safety of Hollywood. Yet the espionage factor of war, its treachery, double-bluff and ruthlessness that Greene had tapped into so well, also surface in the short films Hitchcock made for the Free French in London in 1944, a homecoming of sorts and the very opposite of Greene, who had written his story of the Blitz from the distance of Sierra Leone in West Africa. On the one hand, distance and retrospect for the writer with first-hand knowledge, on the other homecoming for the absent filmmaker, the trauma of family bereavement mixed with a dark witnessing of havoc wreaked by German bombing on his native city (Spoto 1983: 270–1).

We do not know if Hitchcock had read *The Ministry of Fear* before making *Spellbound* or if Angus MacPhail had, since MacPhail worked with Hitchcock in 1944 on the treatment from the Gothic novel *The House of Dr Edwardes* before the director went back to Hollywood to hand the screenwriting to Ben Hecht. But the overlap is extraordinary: the male protagonist with memory-loss that is the result of wartime violence, the country asylum controlled by madmen who appear to be sane, the ineffable traumas of the hero's past, both near and distant, and finally, in the midst of paranoia, the healing power of love. If Lang's flawed film took the asylum out of Greene's masterpiece Hitchcock's film restores the asylum motif with a vengeance. In both Greene and Hitchcock, the asylum madmen are closer to Lang's Dr Mabuse than anything Lang produced in his film of Greene's novel, and equally close to Mabuse's predecessor in the film that Lang never got to direct, Robert Wiene's *Caligari*. The insane 'doctors' of Weimar film posturing as sane: a formula that Greene and Hitchcock both remove from its Gothic entrails and in doing so look elsewhere for inspiration in the modernist labyrinth, where they trade upfront expressionism for intimations of the surreal.

In his book Greene shows his debt to Weimar cinema but also his leave-taking. He switches around the framing device of *Caligari*, where poor Alan turns out a delusional patient demonising his calm doctor as a murderous hypnotist in a bygone age. Instead Arthur Rowe (turned by Lang's screen-writer into the anaemic 'Stephen Neale') is a 'mercy killer' who has terminated his sick wife with buried malice (not malice aforethought) and served a prison sentence that may have been perversely just in his sentencing. Certainly he has reasons for wishing to lose his memory before he actually does lose it, the victim of the bomb planted by a Nazi agent – a bookseller no less – who gives Rowe a case full of 'eighteenth-century folios'. Yet this outrage is already well into series of surreal disconnections. The first concerns a cake Rowe wins from the 'free mothers' at the fete in a Bloomsbury square surrounded by bombed buildings but still reminding Rowe of childhood Cambridgeshire. It is a scene both serene and sinister, the repetition of a country idyll in a damaged city. The cake contains microfilm – a true Hitchcock MacGuffin – that the Enemy wants. Rowe is the Chosen One – delusions of grandeur – standing in their way, but is then hunted down – delusions of persecution – with ruthlessness that turns out to be very real.

Rowe's leaps of logic as he tramples past the rubble and dust of the Blitz are as unnerving as Hamlet's worst nightmares, 'between sleeping and wak-ing', like 'dreams we remember on waking so vividly that we continue them and so fall asleep again and wake and sleep and the dream goes on' (Greene 2001: 63). This captures precisely the spell of Greene's writing, and is not too distant from the effect Hitchcock seeks in *Spellbound* with the amnesiac Gregory Peck – but which he only matches a decade later in *Vertigo*. The parallels between the amnesiac Peck and the amnesiac Rowe are fascinating. The trauma of memory-loss is tied into erroneous guilt: both think with recovered memories they are guilty of a murder they have not committed. Both have two identities. Rowe, the bomb victim, is renamed 'Digby' by Dr Forester, the Nazi director of the asylum where he is being kept against his will, after 'killing' Cost, who is still alive. Peck's character impersonates Dr Edwardes, the analyst he later believes he has killed once his memory returns to him his real name: John Ballantyne, American fighter pilot injured after bailing out over Rome. Further back erroneous guilt also has its trauma back up. Rowe has poisoned his wife in a 'mercy killing'. In childhood, Ballantyne has 'accidentally' killed his brother by impaling him on the house railings, an event Hitchcock shows us in brief and chilling flashback. The key variations from the novel of Francis Beeding uncannily point to one source: all seem to have filtered themes of paranoia and redemption through a sensibility that has come from elsewhere, and possibly from Greene's novel.

For Rowe the figure of Anna Hilfe, who does indeed help him, is a wish-dream, the good Austrian girl trapped in the nest of vipers that includes her own brother. Yet Anna is a secondary figure as Greene dwells on his hero's agonistic journey. While Hitchcock's *Spellbound* foregrounds romance, Greene's thriller is a dismembering of the male psyche from within, creating a scattergun effect of disconnected events and perceptions that all miraculously tie together in the end. Surreal incongruence comes through Rowe's waking dream of a journey, by juxtaposing English eccentricities with Nazi treachery and then soldering them together. The fete, the spiritualist séance, the antiques bookshop and the staid department store, once repositories of reassuring Englishness, are now sites of treachery in troubled times. Ten years later, in the remade *The Man Who Knew Too Much*, Hitchcock was to use a like preciseness of imagination in the *mise-en-scène* of deceit. For Drayton (Bernard Miles), to be preaching at Ambrose Chapel in South London and leading its revivalist hymns in service is perfectly English for its time, and apparently harmless; but it is also perfect cover for a Cold War spy and kidnapper who had many personae and many lives.

In *Spellbound* by contrast Hitchcock created a site of abstraction in his country asylum, Green Manors, as he had done with *Rebecca*'s Manderley. There is no war or society near at hand, nor is there Greene's attention to social detail. Moreover he begins with analyst Constance Pederson a woman in an all-male establishment; then shifts back and forth between the two lovers, Ballantyne and Pederson, the one who is damaged and the one who cures. That is to say, Peck's psyche is dismembered and put together again but always under the aegis of Bergman's gaze.

Hitchcock's surreal disconnections are strictly in studio and subtext. His asylum images at times are fighting against the film's official version of the new science, psychoanalysis, in which Selznick, his producer, was a strident believer. Selznick had after all enlisted advice from the profession for the film's making. Yet the best of intentions still go awry. Often towards the end the psychobabble of Ben Hecht's dialogue overwhelms Hitchcock's powers of invention. The director's attempt to compensate through Dalí's dream images also gets lost in the convolutions of the subconscious as the plot unravels like a bad detective story of the mind's misadventures.

What shocks, looking back, is the sly insolence which undermines the official story and which suggests, obliquely, that 'Green Manors' may be Hitchcock's cryptic version of Selznick International Pictures. At the very start, the muscular male orderly and the glamorous patient (Rhonda Fleming), who are flirting in the corridor on their way to Bergman's office, look like Hollywood starlets. But it is clear audience misrecognition. The predatory Fleming is soon labelled as 'disturbed'. She has, after all, bitten off a suitor's moustache. Yet in the next sequence the greasy-haired analyst, who makes a clumsy pass at Bergman and implies she is frigid, seems to be indulging in what passes for normal office behaviour. Such sexual double standards work in two ways. Not only are there doctors who are as bad as patients, the crossing of the line makes the severe, ascetic Bergman aware of untrammelled (and censored) desire. The sequence makes for a sly allegory of Hollywood double standards, severe censorship of sexual material by front office offset by the casting-couch mentality that ran through many of the Hollywood studios. Moreover Hitchcock, who was later said to model the physical appearance of murderer Raymond Burr in *Rear Window* on boss Selznick, with silver hair and spectacles prominent (Belton 1980: 7–8), may well have been up to his devious tricks here too. Dr Murchison the asylum director (Leo G. Carroll) is the real murderer, ever jealous of the rising reputation of other analysts: here Peck his replacement is yet another rival, a young impostor taking over the asylum and 'taking over' Bergman as well. The Selznick/ Hitchcock rivalry is obliquely translated into the Murchison/Ballantyne rivalry. Here Peck could well be a knowingly idealised version of Hitchcock's body adrift in Hollywood: young, lean and handsome rather than short, stout and immobile.

It is certainly the 'body' which Bergman falls for. Her feelings agitated by her 'promiscuous' patient and her lecherous colleague, this is the perfect launch pad for the entry of Peck, the baffled impostor who appears as a dream lover, the youngest analyst of distinction in the land and hence the most desirable. This transfer or exchange of desire sets the scene for the most subversive element in the film's subtext. This is not so much anti-Oedipus as Oedipus-in-reverse. Loving the young romantic Peck also involves for Bergman – as her colleagues jokingly point out – the risk of mothering him. As Peck is discovered not to be a doctor but a traumatised ex-pilot on the verge of breakdown, Hitchcock intensifies the romance through ambiguity. Even stranger things happen. Peck, who is disturbed by fork lines on the white tablecloth at dinner, breaks down at the excess of whiteness in the operating theatre, where he has suddenly turned into a medical surgeon complete with facemask and scalpel ready to operate on a disturbed patient. (The readied scalpel suggests on the 'studio' reading, an upstart Hitch ready to 'cut' his first picture in the House of Selznick.) As Peck swoons and faints in moments of crisis, aided by Miklos Rozsa's theremin vibrations in the musical score, Hitchcock brings in pieta framings that establish a strange erotic triangle. Bergman is not only Peck's lover: she also becomes his analyst, and in her caring smothering role, the figure of a surrogate mother. If Peck is an Oedipal figure, he is the one who is actively loved, the object of desire. The young 'Mother-Analyst' initiates him, after all, into the joy of love. His false displacement of Carroll as new asylum director could be seen, therefore, as Oedipal desire, the wish to displace the Bad Father who in fact turns out as the murderer of the real Dr Edwardes. This symbolic killing is answered by its reversal much later when Bergman spirits him away from the asylum to see the good shrink, the Good Father (Michael Chekhov) who analyses him and draws out his trauma, thus 'curing' his amnesia and guilt. In a reprise of *Suspicion*, Chekhov calms him late at night by giving him a glass of milk, which actually contains bromide, knocking him unconscious. The good father thus symbolically 'kills' the prodigal son while professing to save him, revealing the covert jealousy perhaps, that he and Murchison as shrink doubles of one another feel at Bergman's love of the younger Peck and not either of them.

Curiously Hitchcock repeats an extreme close-in POV shot in the dénouement, giving us two shots almost identical in their framing. When Chekhov offers Peck the milk laced with bromide, we see the upraised glass and the swallowing from his point-of-view, the preface to blackout and oblivion. When Carroll is found out by Bergman as being Edwardes' murderer, we have a close-in POV shot of his gun pointing towards her as she leaves the room – then swivelling round 180 degrees to point at his own eyes (or the camera) and detonate. Again blackout and oblivion, but also death; for his brains are blown out. There are thus alternate endings. In the first the Son is symbolically murdered, but rises from the dead to be redeemed by the talking cure. In the second the Bad Father dies at his own hand. The affinity of Bad Father and Good Son is also established by repetition: Peck roaming around in half-light with an open razor may be off to kill the sleeping Bergman or slit his own throat. In the final shot Carroll points the gun at Bergman before turning it on himself. Hitchcock's sub-text inversion of the Oedipal myth is so bizarre – the surrogate mother seduces the son, the surrogate father symbolically kills him – as to undermine all rational claims that Selznick thought the film might be making. Of course there are too many loose ends and ponderous sequences to generate the tension Hitchcock wanted. The tension is less between desire and action, which is what he aimed at, than between cluttered dialogue and faltering images, which is what he wanted to avoid. It is not until *Psycho* that his vision is tightly controlled and fully effective with the same material. But then, fifteen years on, there is no longer any Selznick to prevent him. *Psycho* is fully Hitchcock's film.

We could take a neat shortcut here and say our final comparison hinges around Joseph Cotten. He is the central figure in *Shadow of a Doubt* – Charlie Oakley – and in *The Third Man* – Holly Martins: indeed these remain the starring roles for which he is most noted in his career. Yet the connection goes deeper, especially as Cotten was such a late choice for Reed's film. Let us try something else. In Hitchcock's film the key flight sequence takes place at the beginning. Charlie Oakley evades two men in the street watching his upper-storey room – shades of Hannay in *The 39 Steps* – by escaping through industrial wasteland. In *The Third Man* the flight-spectacle takes place at the end as the forces of order catch up with Harry Lime (Orson Welles). Then there is the complement of image-difference, height and depth: Oakley escapes in broad daylight over Philadelphia rooftops while Lime fails to surface from the dark Vienna sewers. Or we have the final comparison for our fugitives – both are loved, obsessively, and both are coldly evil.

Technically, too, there are similarities. Both are films with literary writers and prestige directors: and there are clear instances of great mutual respect. Hitchcock was as grateful for Thornton Wilder's contribution to his film as Reed was for that of Greene, whose story it was. Both are location films that use their exteriors to evoke a detailed sense of time and place. Studio interiors are strictly matched. In directing Reed used a practice that would stand Hitchcock in good stead for most of his American career: for studio interiors detailed photographs of actual interiors and matching exteriors as the basis for production design. The meticulous nature of his preparation for the studio work at Shepperton after the Vienna shoot showed how far English studio design had advanced in the few years since Hitchcock's departure. Around 75 sets were built, mostly small realistic sets that matched the Vienna originals and the film's most famous shot, the doorway shot of Lime revealed for the first time, was the shot by the production team's second unit at Shepperton (see Drazin 1999: 82–5). Taken with his earlier films, *The Fallen Idol* and *Odd Man Out* (1947), Reed showed himself to be just as meticulous in design and *mise-en-scène* as American Hitchcock. His use of exteriors was, if anything, bolder. Though many of his following shots were complicated and demanding, in Santa Rosa Hitchcock had the neat coherence of a smalltown shoot. *The Third Man* was more adventurous, an exhaustive exploration of city locations including much footage that was greatly admired but could not finally be used.

We can also notice differences in approach. *Shadow of a Doubt* takes place in wartime. There are soldiers in uniform around town but there seem no restrictions on civilian life, everyone is relaxed and friendly, and there is no mention of the war. This is a film of suspicion and betrayal without politics, the antithesis of *Saboteur*. *The Third Man* takes place in a post-war Vienna still under international control with attendant tensions between the Allied powers. Civilians remain tense and wary. The political maelstrom seems to echo through every sequence and every frame. Lime may be a crook dealing in diluted penicillin but the Russians for whom he does favours in return also protect him. The 'Third Man' was the term used much later to describe the *cause célèbre* of Kim Philby, the British intelligence chief who defected after Guy Burgess and Donald MacLean to the Soviet Union, and many have seen it as an apt transfer of labelling. Yet some critics have suggested there was no transfer at all. Harry Lime *may well have been* Greene's acerbic portrait of Philby, whom he knew well in MI6 during the war, and Greene, who worked in his department, was possibly one of the very few to know Philby's secret from an early stage (see Wollen 2002: 138–42). In Reed's film crime is inseparable from politics. Suspicion and betrayal make no sense without it.

Hitchcock's film is different. Though this is wartime, this is still an orderly civil society, a small town under no danger of attack. It is with some conscious intent – perhaps to compensate – that Hitchcock later set *The Birds* in a small coastal town just along the road from Santa Rosa as, at one level among many, an allegory of the wartime Blitz he had escaped. But Santa Rosa remains an ordered world where the outside threat is Uncle Charlie. Here Hitchcock's film pits innocence (the loving niece) very starkly against experience (the malign uncle). Niece Charlie is, to start with, both naïve and gullible. In Reed's film, such innocence has been lost, buried under the ruins of total war. Holly Martins may be naïve but he is never innocent, and Lime's lover Anna Schmidt (Alida Valli) is indubitably neither. Yet niece Charlie and Holly Martins do have something in common: both want to believe the best of the forbidding object of their affection, and then have to make the painful adjustment of believing the worst.

The objects of their affection have something in common too. They have lost all respect for humanity: so distant in their contempt they compare humans to insects or animals. Looking down from the top of the Big Wheel at the Prater, Lime sees the moving specks below not as people but as 'dots'. Deriding the leisured life of wealthy widows, Oakley tells his niece they are nothing but 'fat wheezing animals'. 'Do you know the world is a foul sty?' he asks her rhetorically. 'Do you know if you ripped off the fronts of houses you would find swine?' There are strands here of social Darwinism, and of vulgarised Nietzsche that Hitchcock brings out in *Rope*, his study of evil contemporary to *The Third Man*. There, his preppy villains are precociously demented. But in Lime and in Oakley there is something else: world-weariness, a hatred of the present, a deep fatigue beneath the buoyancy and the enigmatic smile. This deceptive world of bodily signs where the very signs have been corrupted is something that as actors Cotten and Welles enter into with relish and conviction.

In an American vein, Oakley and Lime are the heinous younger brothers of Hickey the evangelical salesman in Eugene O'Neill's tragic drama *The Iceman Cometh*. Like the barflies in O'Neill's waterfront joint waiting for iceman Hickey, Charlie is willing her charismatic namesake, her 'iceman' to lift her out of her narrow world: in late adolescence that torpor of smalltown life already hemming her in. Likewise, Martins is searching out his old friend for a role in life to lift himself out of the alcoholic rut into which he has sunk. It is right that Martins and Lime should be made over as Americans by Greene for the film, not simply because of the two Mercury Theatre players who act out their roles so well, but also because there is in this a version of the American Dream gone sour. Though set in the heart of Europe *The Third Man* would never have had the same resonance if Greene and Reed had cast fellow-countrymen in the lead parts. And the lure of the American Dream, promising so much, leads onto the depth of destruction when it fails to deliver. Yet it retains its feel, its shape and its force even when the substance is gone. Like Hickey, Oakley and Lime dispense their nihilism with immense charm, and with no conscience.

If Cotten is a crucial link, even in antithetical roles, there is one instance in which he suffers an identical fate in both pictures. For both have splendid walk-by sequences complete with camera hold that display true cinematic daring. The first starts with Teresa Wright. Outside the family home, she and Cotten have just found out from the local detective that Cotten is no longer a suspect and all is relief and smiles. But Cotten has already recklessly confessed his crimes to her. As the cop walks away out of shot the camera holds on the back of her head, then gradually she turns to look back at the house with a terrible recognition in her eyes. A reverse angle shows Cotten standing in the shadow of the porch, watching her. Both know that she still knows the truth. She walks towards him and then hesitates where the path forks. Then she takes the right fork round to the back entrance of house without looking at him. The more famous walk-on-by is the one with Anna after Lime's funeral. The Hollywood convention, or even the British one at the time, would be reconciliation, of burying the past and building a new life. In the endless long shot where Anna walks along the tree-lined route out of the cemetery following Lime's real funeral, Martins, having overtaken her

Fig. 7 The end of innocence: Teresa Wright and Joseph Cotten in *Shadow of a Doubt*

in a jeep, is now standing, waiting, to the side by a cart in the foreground. Autumn leaves are drifting to the ground (even though the trees are bare). We expect an encounter and the long take encourages that expectation. After all the shot is way too long, we get to thinking, as Valli's distant figure slowly approaches, for *nothing* to happen. But nothing, of course, does happen. Without a sideways glance Valli keeps on walking and perched against the cart, Cotten is helpless in watching her go. Yet Cotten gets the brush-off for opposite reasons. In Hitchcock's film he is a diabolical killer: in Reed's film he is a romantic loser. Charlie trades the uncle she loves and hates for the easygoing cop who arouses little passion. Anna Schmidt is different: still more attached, perversely, to the dynamic spirit of Lime, her betrayer, than to the drunken sentimentalist at the side of her who is heading into entropy.

In one sense *The Third Man* is a kind of feature film Hitchcock never made. His one serious foray into the continental Europe of the Cold War, *Torn Curtain* (followed by the risible *Topaz*), is superbly designed by Hein Heckroth but is a film without focus, at best a travesty of Reed's masterpiece. For the latter is primarily European in its sensibility, a connecting link between *M* and *Le Jour se lève* (1939) that preceded it and the great films of a reinvigorated European modernism that followed it – Antonioni's *La notte*,

Godard's *Vivre sa vie* (1962), Bergman's *The Silence*. The Reed/Greene film is one where evil commands fascination but also where good is no guarantee of true intimacy. Harry's rival admirers cannot come together after his killing because his hold in death, his 'second' death, remains as strong as it was in life. By contrast Hitchcock's great spy thrillers, *Notorious* and *North by Northwest*, are ones that stress the redeeming power of love. That is why *Shadow of a Doubt* remains the best comparison since it too is a story of deep fascination deeply betrayed. Yet there is another unlikely comparison, often overlooked, where Hitchcock and Reed/Greene converge. This is Hitchcock's buried gem, the flight narrative of *Bon Voyage* only 26 minutes long and one of two studio shorts – the other is *Aventure Malgache*, set in Madagascar – made with Angus MacPhail for the Free French in 1944. It anticipates *The Third Man* by four years, remains Hitchcock's most European picture, and was shot very quickly with émigré French actors at Welwyn Studio. But it never got a release at the time in France or anywhere else and Hitchcock, already back in California after his flying visit home, was powerless to intervene.

Since it is about the dark world of the French Resistance in Northern France confronting the Gestapo in 1943, it goes against two trends in the emerging war movie genre – the stoic patriotism of the unassuming British, and the heroic awkwardness of the wartime romance. In this respect it is nothing like *In Which We Serve* (1942), *Brief Encounter*, *A Matter of Life and Death* (1946), *The Captive Heart* (1946) or *Against the Wind* (1948), which deals more directly with spying and double agents. As an escape-flight film, its main theme is the symbiosis of naïvety and betrayal, the unhealthy *absence* of suspicion. An Anglo-Scots officer in the RAF escapes from German prison aided by a Polish compatriot, who turns out, unknown to him, to be a member of the Gestapo using him to transmit messages and reveal identities of Resistance contacts. Shot in flashback from a debriefing of the escaped POW by Free French Army officers in London, it becomes a story of dawning realisation, though in its dense layering Hitchcock ensures that the 'authentic version' of events offered to him by his French interrogators is never authenticated. Nonetheless up to that point the officer has thought himself the beneficiary of an act of sacrificial comradeship from a Pole who allows him to become a special escapee. He finds out the 'Pole' is actually German and using him as bait, as the unwitting go-between for a contact in London. He hopes to be reunited with the Resistance woman who has aided his escape. He finds out his 'comrade' has shot her after his departure. He hopes his 'Polish' comrade will survive to aid the Resistance: he finds out the Resistance have assassinated him.

The film is darkly lit, sombre and poetic, a form of studio realism reminiscent of Marcel Carné, but on a topic which Carné, after the war, did not really touch. (It also has strong echoes of Hitchcock's Weimar heritage in the atmospheric photography of Austrian Günther Krampf, who had worked in the 1920s for Murnau, Robert Wiene and G. W. Pabst.) Given the absence of a Resistance 'genre' in post-war French film the nearest thing to Hitchcock's film, its full realisation, comes twenty-five years later, *after* the New Wave. This is Jean-Pierre Melville's astonishing *L'armée des ombres* (1969). Like Hitchcock, Melville at his best deals brilliantly in the currency of comradeship that shades into suspicion and betrayal. While *Bon Voyage* is unusual for its French setting it does track the enemy within that the American wartime films had also done. More than that, it fits completely into the philosophy of flawed exchange. The escaped officer, by intent but not outcome, is 'delivered' to a spy in London to whom he unwittingly delivers instructions, while the delivering 'comrade' stays behind, by intent and outcome, to kill those who have really helped him. The farmer's daughter, who helps with his escape and kindles his affection, is a woman the doting officer inadvertently 'delivers' to her death. His naïvety, we might suggest, is echoed in the naïvety of Holly Martins just as the cunning and duplicity of his 'comrade' is echoed in the cunning and duplicity of Harry Lime. If Greene and Reed fleshed out the motif in British cinema's greatest-ever feature, we could say that Hitchcock in this modest short that still lies neglected had clearly got there first.

If the British connection, as we have now seen, served Hitchcock well in one form or other throughout his Hollywood career, one thing American ambience – and finance – provided that British cinema could not was the power of the star system. Hitchcock, however, had no intention of slotting in to any existing studio system. Like any truly ambitious director he wished to cast, to mould and to configure his own 'star' system, in which his lead actors work in very specific ways, tailored to his precise intentions. In American Hitchcock this pattern of distinctive acting was developed in the 1940s to reach new heights in the casting and making of *Notorious.*

chapter 5

HITCHCOCK'S ACTORS: *NOTORIOUS*, VALLI
AND THE TRIPTYCH EFFECT

In American Hitchcock one thing is clear. The gaze is institutional, the look individual. And for that he needs great actors, or actors he can make great, starting with Joan Fontaine and Judith Anderson. In *Rebecca* Anderson as Danvers is the pivotal figure in Manderley's household – all domestics – who gather in the Great Hall to welcome the newlyweds. From Fontaine's point-of-view, all she sees as she enters is a sea of staring eyes. She is being watched curiously, courteously, deferentially, but still dissected, the target of a shared gaze in a British institution now at the heart of heritage culture – the country house between the wars. It is a setting Hitchcock exaggerates in scale to create maximum effect. Fontaine has to respond without acting like a drama queen or a frightened rabbit. Her reactive look is all it should be: anxious, uncertain, restrained, a newcomer unsure of her new role and self, a bride isolated from husband Maxim by that shared gaze, yet to come to terms with marrying into opulence. The later gaze of Danvers is individuated to be sure, but it stems from a given role and that primal gaze of 'welcome'. It is the perverse refinement of a generic 'housekeeper's' gaze, a bona fide derivative, not just an egocentric obsession. It is a refinement that Anderson delivers brilliantly. *Quod Est Demonstrandum.* The institution is the springboard to desire.

Even the fanatic gaze of James Stewart in *Rear Window* and *Vertigo* springs from social convention: in the first case the prying eyes of an immobilised action-photographer, in the second the tracking eyes of a cop-turned-private-investigator and stricken by vertigo. In both instances the gaze becomes individuated, breaking out of its collective shell and then transgressing. In *Shadow of a Doubt* Teresa Wright shares in the admiring gaze of her family, and the locals, who see Joseph Cotten as a bit of a character come to shake them out of smalltown torpor. As her admiration turns to a love unspoken that goes beyond affection, a counter-gaze emerges from the two cops posing as survey-researchers who suspect her uncle of murder. On the one hand the admiring gaze that is the springboard for teenage love: on the other the suspicious gaze that becomes the trigger for love's disillusion. Yet in each case the power of Wright's acting lies in transforming the collective gaze into unique variations that take over at the centre of the film. The key exchange of the film is to transfer her from one gaze to another, to deliver her out of trust and into suspicion. Yet that suspicion is then refined as *her* suspicion. Wright's acting brief is to make it all her own. Much later, in *Marnie*, Hitchcock inverts the function of suspicion. Right at the start Sean Connery is privy to knowledge of Tippi Hedren's compulsive thieving but on meeting her turns around his suspicion into a stark curiosity mingled with desire. His gaze is the maverick continuation of official surveillance by other means, until complicit knowledge and coded blackmail push him to cross the line. As for Hedren, her reactive look, in all its plasticity, has no institution to rely on at all. She is very much on her own.

Grant and Bergman: *Notorious*

All of which brings us to *Notorious*. It starts with the transfer of guilt from a Nazi father convicted of treason in Miami to his anti-Nazi daughter Alicia Hubermann where, under pressure of the public gaze her guilt has turned volatile. And there is no letting up. The controlling gaze of the film's first half derived from that public gaze of approbation. It is the mediating gaze of FBI agent Devlin (Cary Grant) on the distraught daughter, played of course by Ingrid Bergman. It is one of surveillance made oblique, governed by organisation strategy. Hitchcock's *mise-en-scène* translates the relationship precisely into spatial affect. Yet initially, for this to work, the subjective gaze has to belong to Bergman – how she sees herself being watched – but the objective gaze belongs to the camera, which turns a clinical eye onto her gaze. This constant alternation of the gaze between the face of the actor and the medium of the camera, as well as alternation between protagonists, illustrates an aesthetic of 'intrarealist' effect, as we noticed earlier in *The Birds*.

We can spot this clearly in a sequence near the start of *Notorious*. At a drunken party in Miami before the boating trip where she hopes to forget her father's conviction, the film frames her standing over-lit in middle distance, watching a man in silhouette seated left foreground, his dark back to the camera. We see her eyeing him while talking to guests, moving shakily in front of him. The camera pans left to right then right to left as she walks across him and back again, pouring drinks. Immobile, he remains silent. There is a fade out at the party's end on his silhouette and then a fade back in for the same position in the early hours of the morning. The couple are still together, and almost alone. This time the camera tracks right and forward to catch him in profile, revealing the face and gaze of Grant for the first time. Their conversation begins. Some have seen this sequence as an instance of Devlin's oppressive male gaze, others as a surrogate positioning into Devlin's point-of-view of the spectator watching the film. Both approaches are wrong. Typically Hitchcock proceeds with a *double positioning*. We are watching Alicia and seeing what Devlin sees, but we are also watching *her*

Fig. 8 Surveillance and desire: Cary Grant and Ingrid Bergman in *Notorious*

gaze, sharpened by drink, flickering over him while his, conversely, remains withheld from view. Thus the primal gaze is *hers*, but seen objectively and not from her point-of-view and we are left to imagine his response. With the time-lapse we do finally see a response from him but this is now directed at a potential lover, deeply drunk and whose look remains focused by his gaze, explicitly desiring.

From Grant, who is one of cinema's great maestros of the reaction shot, there is something missing here. Initially we get no reaction at all. And because Hitchcock frames the conversation in profile, an intimate two-shot, we do not, strictly speaking, get a reaction shot the second time around either. The mystery lingers as dramatic suspense. But then in a set of reverse-angle close-ups, reaction becomes inseparable from action, the look inseparable from the gaze. Both Grant and Bergman express their own desire while reacting to the desire of the other. This is the pure look-gaze in operation, an intimate parity of transaction, both gazing and reacting at the same time, *in the same expression*. It is a clinching moment in cinematic body language, which in this film is 90 per cent *eye-language*: we sense already the affair-to-come is a done deal, strong enough to survive Alicia's discovery of Devlin's true (official) identity during the car ride.

In the morning-after sequence Hitchcock again stresses the primacy of Bergman's gaze with the famous hangover POV shot. As she slumps at an angle in bed still half-asleep, we see face and tousled hair in full close-up then cut to a rotating shot of Grant walking upside down and then right side up around the bed towards her, thus intimating the swivel of bleary eyes. After Grant delivers her to the Bureau, however, Hitchcock prefers to film the couple in intimate but objective two-shot, frontally or in profile, where the look away from the lover often takes precedence over the look towards the lover. They are together in the same shot, but uncomfortably so, because by now the relationship is double-barrelled and political, linking passion to conspiracy. It is secret: it dissembles in public. To fool the FBI, it must appear as conspiracy not passion, business not pleasure. To fool the Germans in Rio it must appear, whenever they get too suspicious, as a closet passion but never a conspiracy. Caught out spying by Alex (Claude Rains) on the Sebastian wine cellar at the party, Grant embraces her like there is no tomorrow. The liaison must be pleasure and not business. As in *Shadow of a Doubt* there is a gaze-transfer halfway through, a poetics of exchange. Bergman starts off being watched by the FBI. But made over by Grant into an reluctant American agent, she is then placed under the scrutiny of their German enemies, first Alex Sebastian, the man she is forced to marry, then his fearsome mother and finally an ensemble of spies and scientists still working for the ignoble cause. Before the dinner party in the Sebastian household, Hitchcock frames the social introductions as a gaze-series of instant judgements passed on the Huberman daughter and seen from her point-of-view. Grant has delivered her from an FBI gaze of which his own is a maverick variant, into a collective Nazi gaze of whom the enchanted Rains is an old-fashioned precursor. In the riding-sequence outside Rio, Grant, acting on instructions, delivers her into the arms of her old admirer, thence to marriage and to his bed. His organisation that 'defends' the Law but is always above it, forces him to act like a pimp when he wishes to be a lover.

Because their world is walled in by espionage the close shots and long shots of Grant and Bergman, on the park bench or the outdoor café in Rio, their sites of secret assignation, are often three-quarter shots. Technically the direct gaze at the other seems subject to a prohibition order. Their look must be stranded between camera and lover, bisecting the two. Conversation cannot appear too intimate or animated or even serious. It has to be casual. For Hitchcock's actors, the cue is palpable. They have to act with great discipline the part of a couple forced to be casual. You look frontally but down, just past the camera, and then glance sideways at your partner from time to time. When taken back into a distant two-shot the awkwardness of situation is further exposed. But with great actors that awkwardness is always rendered fluently, without seeming effort. Grant and Bergman hone their own manner of expressing it to perfection. In *Spellbound* Hitchcock had taught Bergman that in close-up shots the power of the shifting glance away, either left or right, to reveal anxiety or reflection, can have enormous power (Spoto 1997: 169). In *Notorious* she shows she has mastered the technique. If anything, Grant is even more minimal. The face barely moves because the eyes do all the moving. To signify reaction or reflection – thinking on his feet in tough situations such as getting unnoticed into the wine-cellar or reclaiming Bergman whom he suspects is being poisoned – Grant will flicker his pupils left and right, first one way then the other, while keeping his body perfectly still. His face remains supple but its movement is always slight, almost imperceptible. The eyes, in contrast, work overtime in precise gestures.

Like James Stewart, Grant has piercing eyes, but dark, not blue. They work better in the black-and-white of *Notorious*, we might speculate, than in the colour of *To Catch a Thief*. Stewart's blue-grey eyes on the other hand are perfect for close-ups in *Rear Window* or *Vertigo*. In *Notorious* we are always aware of the darkness of Grant's hair and eyes, the darkness of his suit; or where his suit is light in colour, the dark tie or hatband: all is offset by the luminous greys and whites of Ted Tetzlaff's photography, and by the soft textures of low-contrast film stock. The sharp look of the eyes is never statuesque but always connected to movement. Even when stationary, we feel Grant is poised to uncoil. As he kisses Bergman right across the hotel room while answering the telephone or later guides her poisoned, suffering body out of the marital bedroom and down the main stairs to eventual safety, he glides on air like the acrobat he once was, halfway between the walk and the run. That final scene, with Bergman semi-conscious, out on her feet, is one to cherish as plot considerations fade away. The fluency of movement that Grant enacts and Bergman follows and Hitchcock choreographs turns cliché into the sublime; as poetry in motion that is never pure effect but also drama and a felt suspense. In the vast hallway of the studio set, courtesy of David O. Selznick, masquerading as some house in Rio into which the film claustrophobically retreats, it is the culmination of stage two in the journey of intimate spectacle Hitchcock had begun six years earlier in *Rebecca*.

In *Notorious* we also have the complementary features of voice, equally important. Here there is breathtaking contrast. With Bergman we can mark the soft cadences emotionally accentuated by the effort of vowel movements that have to be made in a second language, as English would be to her native Swedish. Everything is emotional when it has to be and perfectly pitched. Nothing is husky or guttural as it had been with Dietrich and Garbo. Nothing is too knowing either: everything is open to the slings and arrows of outrageous fortune. Grant offers the perfect contrast, a voice that is Anglo-American but never mid-Atlantic. It is a double accentuation that makes it instantly recognisable, not to say unique. It is not soft like compatriot James Mason but guttural and sharp; yet always resonant. Grant never cuts off his words. On the other hand he stresses without ever lingering on the syllable. This was because he was never a well-spoken English gentleman before he became an American actor. He was Archie Leach, a working-class lad from the West Country, who came up the hard way in life and the entertainment industry. Moreover, he was an actor who was never sure at what point, despite an official name change, he really became Cary Grant. The voice always seems pitched at that liminal point of persona, a sound that reassures in the middle of nowhere.

In this picture, Grant and Bergman achieve the impossible. In their (public) exteriors they make acting out forced roles seem quite natural. In their (private) interiors they make acting out complex romantic gestures seem equally natural. In the famous long embrace sequence, the couple moving across the hotel room from balcony to door in one shot, Hitchcock wanted to fool the censor and create the longest screen kiss on record. As the camera moves in close on the gliding, rotating couple, they seem held together by invisible glue. In unison they must move and talk and kiss, and Grant must use the telephone at the same time, in one continuous movement. Hence they naturalise the unnatural, or give to film a new convention of 'nature'. The style is anti-naturalist, a new artifice created in order to persuade us the intimacy is natural. The kiss, after all, has a natural foundation, the culmination of a warm romantic day by the coast, but is then interrupted by the phone call and followed by unwanted exit, a romantic climax left on ice.

On the return, when Grant has learnt of his mission, to 'deliver' Bergman to Claude Rains, the evening is dark and cool, already too cold to eat on the balcony. The soft warm contours enveloping the daytime kiss are replaced by harshness akin to film noir: yet the noir feel is anything but steamy. The balcony is cold and forbidding as Grant lurks silent in its half-light. Hitchcock's framing repeats the two-shot of late afternoon. Yet now Grant's body is still and icy: there is a sudden deadness behind the eyes. Hitchcock cuts and mixes his angles of shot, intimating jaggedness in the growing tension as Bergman finds out the worst. This is the Kuleshov effect taken to a new level of

sophistication: repetition of the first balcony scene, but total transformation of mood through minute alteration of the figure. Here the unwitting
Bergman prolongs the loving warmth of the first scene even when Grant
has changed from fire to ice. For this is the key: Bergman as the same, Grant
as transformed. Yet Grant's transformation is nuanced and lies in the detail:
slight modifications of glance and gesture, deft adjustments to the movement of the eyes. Where Grant had been 'all eyes' for his lover earlier in the
day, now he can no longer look her in the eye. Yet the photogenic register
of change is minimal and in this, paradoxically, lies its strength. Grant, in
medium shot or close-up, specialises in the deflection of the gaze, a gaze close
and intimate that will not lock on to the face of the other. It holds, typically,
for a brief instant then flickers away. Bergman's look by contrast is modulated, changing by degrees. Hers is the fluid transition of the re-active look,
absorbing bit-by-bit the bad news Grant has given her, forced to be free in
the worst sense: either to choose against the mission and lose him, or choose
for it and also lose him. Thus she registers in real time the agony of the
dilemma that montage has cut elliptically in two in the double figuration of
Grant, before and after.

The power of *Notorious* has affected many films but only two have come
near to showing themselves equal to the influence it has upon them. Hitchcock's film is South American in setting: these unusually, are both Asian.
In *The Year of Living Dangerously* (1987), Peter Weir replicates the motif
of dangerous liaisons in the Indonesia of the 1960s in a political setting
where context is duly altered. While Grant and the FBI are sweeping up in
the aftermath of world war victory, Weir's Aussie hero, amoral journalist
Guy Hamilton (Mel Gibson) is looking for political secrets about impending
communist revolution when events are fluid and uncertain. His relationship
with British secret agent Jilly Bryant (Sigourney Weaver), very much after the same information, is an erotic adventure based on addiction to risk.
Certainly, they try to exploit each other's knowledge, yet there is parity between them that goes beyond manipulation: no equivalent here of Bergman's
degrading makeover. Weir's film is a euphoric release from the constraints
of Hitchcock's studio movie, which is in effect a brilliant study of extreme
confinement. It also has the advantage of location shooting and the *cinéma
vérité* look of newsreel politics. And it also has its own take on the chase and
the surveillance gaze. The gaze is that of diminutive Billy Kwan, Hamilton's
jealous photographer-double and voice-over of the film narration, watching
the affair that is nobody's secret. The chase is the curfew-chase that echoes
from *Notorious* the drunken coastal-road chase (pure back-projection) of
Bergman and Grant after the film's opening party. Bergman drives drunk-
enly at speed and Grant's FBI card is produced to save her from the clutches
of the motorcycle cop, and from humiliation. But Weir opts for a chase that

epitomises the year of living dangerously. His couple burst through a curfew roadblock late at night and accelerate away to escape the following gunfire. It is a roller-coaster ride – erotic, foolhardy, exhilarating – but then passion here is a level playing field that in Hitchcock's film does not exist because politics has dictated otherwise.

If Weir teases out the politics of surveillance in Hitchcock's film, Wong Kar-Wai's *In the Mood for Love* does the opposite. It makes surveillance operate through the living space of confinement, a communal apartment in 1960s Hong Kong, replacing the collective gaze of Hitchcock's Rio mansion. Every movement of neighbours Maggie Cheung and Tony Leung takes place under the composite gaze of other residents and the prying gaze of the landlady. Weir had tried to open up the Hitchcock passion out of its confinement but Wong locks it in even tighter. This is a passion that dare not whisper its name, especially since it is doomed to be a copy, a mere imitation of the affair their betraying (and unseen) spouses are discreetly having elsewhere. The enacted slow-motion glide of Hitchcock's lovers (shot in real time) is taken to extremes: Wong turns it into a general trope, keyed by the soundtrack, where the slow-motion is literal not acted. At the slightest hint of passion the walk of both lovers is slowed by frames-per-second, yet there is no embrace, barely a touch. Since they cannot express it for themselves, the camera and the music must do so for them, it of course being the mood for love. Wong takes the acting down to an intense minimum in order to bring it up again as pure emotion through soundtrack and *mise-en-scène*. It is a bold move, not always successful, but Hitchcock's anti-naturalism has shown him the route that he has taken even further in contemporary cinema than anyone else.

The acting of Grant and Bergman is such that it suggests no one else could do it. But Hitchcock, a director with a mania for control, could not always get the actors he wanted. After *Under Capricorn* Bergman left him, professionally speaking, for Roberto Rossellini and a different kind of cinema: more important for Hollywood she also left her husband and her children to become Roberto Rossellini's lover, a public scandal that caused her vilification throughout the American press. One of her lone defenders in the industry was Grant himself who argued for her right to privacy. But Hitchcock, who had unusually filmed a costume drama, *Under Capricorn*, mainly as a vehicle for her immense talent, was devastated. Meanwhile Grant, also to Hitchcock's disappointment, decided he was not available after *Notorious* for the part of Rupert Cadell in *Rope*. Instead James Stewart played the role with an element of sexual naïvety that is rescinded, dramatically speaking, only in the last sequence. The loose, unsubstantiated gossip about Grant's sexuality then floating around in Hollywood may well have influenced his decision not to take the part. Certainly Montgomery Clift, who was known in the industry to be gay, also turned down the part of one of the young murderers.

The decision of both actors pointed to the fragility of reputation over such delicate matters, more so then when it would have been ruinous but still so now when it remains a salient issue in Hollywood.

The star enigma: Valli and *The Paradine Case*

In his own mind Hitchcock could find no substitute for Bergman until the casting of Grace Kelly. Kelly was a high-class American from a wealthy Philadelphia family and her stardom was different, and Hitchcock turns her into a serenely *performative* icon for a 1950s generation. Yet earlier he had used two Europeans in his pictures with English settings, the mature Marlene Dietrich in *Stage Fright*, the young Alida Valli in *The Paradine Case*. It is the case of Valli that merits a closer viewing. He had cast her, reluctantly, in his last film for Selznick while already thinking forward to his next collaboration with Bergman in *Under Capricorn* for Sidney Bernstein's Transatlantic Productions. These were films in which Hitchcock was able to explore new techniques, especially what he called 'the roving camera', free from Selznick's editorial control. With Valli in place, Hitchcock was already starting his affair with the roving camera. Yet the casting of the film was largely beyond his control. He told Truffaut that he would have preferred Garbo to Valli (in the novel by Robert Hitchens the accused woman is Danish not Italian), Olivier or Ronald Colman instead of Gregory Peck, and Robert Newton for Louis Jourdan (Truffaut 1986: 254). Yet despite his dislike of the cluttered dialogue that Selznick imposed on him and then often rewrote during the shoot, Hitchcock's camera sets up a quizzical adoration of Valli as intriguing as anything he accomplished with Bergman. Using the new multidirectional crab dolly developed by his cinematographer, Lee Garmes, for its fluid camerawork, he repeated long tracking shots around her still figure as Maddalena, the enigmatic Neapolitan from a poor family, now charged with poisoning her rich English husband, the blind Colonel Paradine. These takes are long, circular glides that move in close on the inscrutable face that is severe in its beauty and imperious in defeat, not only in the arrest sequence that begins the film but also in the prison and the court sequences that follow.

Two long takes that top and tail Valli's arrest in her West End townhouse define the scene. The first tracks into the drawing-room behind her servant and then circles around her from medium to close shot as she plays on the piano, before pulling back to reveal the huge portrait of her dead husband on the wall above at which she glances briefly, and inscrutably. The second semi-circles her, again left to right but from medium shot into extreme close-up, as the arresting officer reads the charges against her. The face is not a mask yet restrains its reaction: a sign that even at close quarters she is giving nothing away. She is dressed in black, her hair brushed straight back, curled high into a bun. A spot illuminates her face but on one side the sharp line of the cheekbone is contoured by shadow. It is the camera set-up that Hitchcock will use again for the trial. In Holloway prison her hair changes: it is brushed out and down in one brief shot where Hitchcock makes it straggly, her face unadorned. Yet for her courtroom appearances it is brushed back again, the status quo ante of hairdressing, more Hollywood than Holloway. Yet Hitchcock had based his prison studio set on the actual lay-out of Holloway and nothing stresses the solitude of his heroine more than the echoing sound of the barred cell door clanging shut behind her. In that sound we have the summation of a fate that is irreversible. After Valli we can think forward to another actor Hitchcock used only once, Kim Novak, whose blonde hair is brushed back as Madeleine and comes down as Judy only to return to its original style at Scottie's behest. Dark hair – blonde hair, same difference: Maddalena become Madeleine.

In the Old Bailey court scene Hitchcock replays the circular shot around Valli in the dock as Louis Jordan, Paradine's valet André Latour, walks behind and around her towards the witness box. This time it is not just a moving shot, technically speaking, but a process shot with Valli in studio foreground on a revolving platform, a prelude to the famous platform kiss cum process shot in the Vertigo hotel room with its green neon-reflected walls suddenly changing into the old stables at San Juan Bautista. But Hitchcock does complement the statuesque shots of his fallen heroine with dolly and crane shots too, along to her prison cell after her arrest or later making her entry with her warder up the stairs into the courtroom (uncannily echoed by Scorsese in the Steadicam dressing-room to boxing-ring take of De Niro in *Raging Bull* (1980)) In fact we see the only long distances she walks from the point of arrest to the end of the trial. Hitchcock is thus fascinated by her confinement and her separation: her only intimate scenes are with her defence lawyer Anthony Keane (Peck) in the visiting room where her warder observes them through a divided glass partition. In other words there is no privacy at all: her world is public and panoptical. The open and circular structure of the prison is replicated in the high-angle shots of the studio courtroom (a faithful reproduction of the Old Bailey) and the multiple camera set-ups that Hitchcock used for shooting there. This is a film of one-way love, Peck for Valli, Valli for Jordan, that becomes a public spectacle of humiliation for all three. Yet the transactions are through interrogation, always at a distance. And Valli is always a woman framed in grand isolation, spatially separate, always solitary but never alone, always under surveillance. The film also shows, again as prelude to *Vertigo*, the singularity of a male obsession that ends in abjection and is revealed in court to be witnessed by all.

The situation creates a unique imbalance in Hitchcock's work. The aura of Valli he had created, perhaps without realising it, makes of all its other

Fig. 9 'a severe, solitary beauty...': Alida Valli and Gregory Peck in *The Paradine Case*

characters, lesser mortals. She dominates the film in part through her absence, as her co-star Orson Welles was soon to do in *The Third Man.* We wait
for her to re-appear. Like Harry Lime, Maddalena is discussed endlessly in
her absence, a clear threat to the ailing Keane marriage, a secret role-model
for the daughter of the Paradine family solicitor who would like to snare
Keane despite her close friendship with Gay, Keane's wife. (She is first seen
dressed as a double of the accused woman, all in black, hair brushed up, and
donning a fur coat as Valli does at the time of her arrest.) The narrative
sets up a tension it cannot resolve: we are almost wishing to see Valli in the
huge open spaces of Selznick's studio rooms but she is doomed to circulate
between court and prison. Though he was wrong about Valli Hitchcock was
right about Peck: hamstrung by Selznick's leaden script he is too wooden to
convince as an English barrister or take on the emotional challenge of the
part. Yet there is a precedent for this gender imbalance in the films of Josef
von Sternberg with their debasing of the male lover at the hands of the
aloof heroine – with Dietrich rampant in *The Blue Angel* (1930), *Dishonored*
(1931) and *Shanghai Express* (1932). Valli's performance is in that tradition;
yet here it is naturalised and grounded by Hitchcock's use of detail. The
camp and baroque elements in von Sternberg's films are replaced by a severe,
solitary beauty in the image of the accused woman set against the barren in-

teriors of confinement and a panoptical arena of judgement. There is nothing wilful or knowing in Valli's performance. Arrest, trial and unexpected confession are dimensions of an authentic and painful fate. Like Keane, we are made to wish she is innocent and her lover is guilty. But it is not to be. It is one of Hitchcock's darkest films not only because he cheats his audience in this way but also because of his tight framing of unrequited passion and the impasse in transaction. Peck's feeble look of adoration contrasts not only with Valli's final gaze of contempt from the dock but also with the gaze of hatred that Jourdan gives the back of Valli's head as he leaves the court. Valli is inconsolable, still loving the man who hates her, who 'despises all women', and after Latour's suicide hating quite unconditionally the lawyer who loves her. Valli is thus an exception to Hitchcock's trans-active rule: a heroine in solitude, a heroine as murderer. There are echoes of her predicament in *Under Capricorn* where Bergman (also guilty of murder) stays loyal to the complicit Joseph Cotten at the expense of the enamoured Michael Wilding. But this drama is trans-active: Australia may have started as penal colony yet Bergman has already avoided Valli's fate when the action begins. It is the forbidding aloneness of Valli's role that makes her star persona unique in the Hitchcock oeuvre.

Stewart and Kelly: *Rear Window*

In 1953 Grace Kelly then made her auspicious debut in *Dial 'M' for Murder*. Soon after, Hitchcock harnessed the considerable talents of a young New England screenwriter, John Michael Hayes, who had been a fanatical fan of *Shadow of a Doubt*. In two of the films Hayes famously wrote for him, *Rear Window* and *To Catch a Thief*, Hitchcock cast Kelly in lead roles. Her triptych of Hitchcock films made her a genuine replacement for Bergman not only in the eyes of her director but also in the eyes of Hitchcock's public. Thus Hitch was equally devastated when she left him for Prince Rainier of Morocco, American wealth marrying into European royalty. He tried to tempt her back for *Marnie* but failed and she was killed in 1982 in a car crash on roads close to those used by Hitchcock for the daring car chase in which she centrally figures for his Riviera film. Life had partially imitated art, and personal tragedy taken over from Hitchcock's light comic touch. Let us look closer at her acting with James Stewart – the greatest contrast that Hitchcock has given in the style of two actors confined to the same living space.

In *Rear Window* the polarities of stillness and movement are at the core of *mise-en-scène*, a summation perhaps of the contrast in acting styles. Jeffries is wheelchair-bound: Stewart, at the film's centre, a figure who cannot stand let alone walk, contravening the appetite for motion that drives much of Hitchcock's cinema. It was a shift sideways in career for Stewart who had just finished a series of rugged and visually spectacular westerns with Anthony Mann where he perfected his new image as a leathery, tenacious outdoor hero. Here he retains the tenacity but this is the enclosed cityscape, a cyclorama in a studio picture. Some have seen Stewart as a stand-in for the cinema spectator, his gaze flickering across the array of rear windows opposite like someone entranced by multiple screens. But his role is more complex. If he is a surrogate spectator he is also a Peeping Tom, an active voyeur whose role-play teases out the daily curiosity that exists in us all. And there are his third and fourth roles as well. Technically he is like a programme editor confronted by a bank of screens and flicking the switch from one to the other as fancy takes him. Finally he is a version of Hitchcock himself seated in the director's chair, sedentary choreographer of multiple movements, the matrix-figure. His acting has to intimate all of these things at the same time. To be mute, robotic, affect-less would be an acting disaster. Through Stewart the film takes Hitchcock's preferred acting style to its ultimate point, the actor as someone doing nothing and therefore doing something. And he does move. His bodily powers articulate confined motion. He rolls his wheelchair back and forth at key moments: he uses his camera's telephoto lens at key moments. Confronted by Grace Kelly or housekeeper Thelma Ritter his detective voice breaks out of its watching silence to work overtime; when alone again his watching eyes cease only with the onset of sleep. When murderer Lars Thorwald (Raymond Burr) breaks the cinematic frame by coming across the courtyard to his apartment, he dazzles the intruder with flash bulbs. He is in a sense still and hyperactive at the same time thinking faster as his movements slow. He is also trying to annihilate the returned gaze of his cross-courtyard target, blinding the eyes that have finally 'watched back'.

As Lisa, Grace Kelly must provide a deft contrast in style, moving at different speeds around the room, performing for Stewart as much as she does for us, but always self-aware; aware of her attention-seeking devices and lightly mocking her duplicity. As someone who reads *Harper's Bazaar* and could well be on its cover her stride is easily narcissistic, as if she were practising for the catwalk. Eventually she breaks the frame, crossing over into the courtyard and entering Thorwald's apartment by climbing the fire escape onto the apartment balcony. If this works as a rupture with the film's three-walled convention and sees her outside of the apartment for the first time, it is also a continuation of the performing self, an accentuation of that fluent presence she presents inside and makes effortless. Their first encounter establishes Lisa in Jeff's eyes as a lithe dangerous figure from whom he must deflect his gaze. When she ambushes him in the room Hitchcock shoots from Stewart's point-of-view, a close-in low-angle shot of her approaching face and body, then a quick cut to a profile shot as she plants the kiss in slow-motion on his unprepared lips. It is a predatory gesture. We have already seen him react to moving images from the windows opposite but here he has no time to react at all.

After her constricted movements in *Dial 'M' for Murder* Hitchcock wanted Kelly to open up in style, to create the illusion of perpetual yet graceful motion. No longer frightened and confused, a double-victim of violence and betrayal as she had been in the earlier film, her character exudes a sensuous, self-confident air. There is openness to experience and yet a muted disappointment in the limitations of her lover. Kelly's special gift is to shift easily and quickly between one posture and the other. She is forever role-playing and yet her performance is never mannered; witness her self-introduction in timing her name, Lisa Carol Fremont, to a trio of side-light switches that illuminate the room and then the charade of a surprise dinner delivery that follows. Charm, posture and movement always seem perfectly natural. Yet her purpose is clearly to catch Stewart off guard and to keep him guessing. Kiss, light switches, door opening to the dinner tray: three fluent movements unpredictable in nature and sequence, yet a physical tour de force.

While Kelly must seem natural when performing, never too theatrical, Stewart must exaggerate restraint. His reactive look must never seem over-the-top since the film's edifice would crumble. It has to be instant and fleeting and played out in contrast to the necessary over-acting of the courtyard neighbours. Forced to play out their long-distance dramas before us, surrogates that we are of Stewart's relentless gaze, they have to act manically, as James Naremore points out, like characters out of silent movies; when Miss Lonely Hearts in her ground-level living-room stands to raise her wine glass flamboyantly and toast a fictitious dinner guest, Stewart half raises his in lame reply, the slightest of gestures (see Naremore 1988: 241–3). The action is played up, the reaction played down. Yet suspense suggests this will not be the same forever and at the end chickens come home to roost when the motionless Stewart enters the arena of fear.

In a telephoto shot the apprehended Kelly puts her hand behind her back in Thorwald's apartment to indicate to Stewart that her finger now wears the wedding ring of the murder victim – a superb instance of involuntary doubling. In the same shot the camera shows the double gaze of Thorwald, who first cranes his neck to rumble the furtive gesture and then looks out and across at Stewart's rear window for the first time. Stewart's gaze is returned, if with not with a vengeance then definitely with the prospect of vengeance. Thorwald will also return Kelly's visit but with more criminal intent. The final sequence that takes Stewart 'out' of his apartment against his will is one that seems to lead naturally into the opening sequence of *Vertigo* three years later, placing him at the side of a building, waiting for him to drop. The fear of falling Stewart's eyes convey in both sequences is fanatic and overpowering. Colonel James Stewart after all had been an Air Force officer flying countless missions over Germany in 1944 and seeing many of his comrades not coming back. Plagued by nightmares for several years after his return home in 1945, he refused all roles offered to him in war pictures. Yet he came to see the deep fear of falling his acting conveys in these two films as a powerful residue of war-experience, a form of paralysis by fear (see Fishgall 1997: 172–3, 266). Hitchcock must have realised the strength of the emotion as he filmed the ending in *Rear Window*, and that in turn must surely have clinched the casting of Stewart for *Vertigo*.

Diptych and triptych effects

Before we continue we should not forget the role of the supporting actor in the Hitchcock equation. Thelma Ritter shines as the garrulous housekeeper in *Rear Window* and from Leopoldine Konstantin in *Notorious* we have the scrutinising, suspicious gaze of the intimidating mother cast over her son's new bride. Or consider the recognition-gaze fired off by Raymond Burr across the courtyard at Stewart where it has to do the opposite of the voyeur's gaze, that is, define its rage instantly at a distance to the viewer. Casting his lead roles, however, was sometimes a matter of chance, as it always is in the film industry. Cary Grant turned down *Rope*, hence James Stewart. Vera Miles was unavailable for *Vertigo*, hence Kim Novak. Grace Kelly turned down *Marnie*, hence Tippi Hedren. Each of these three substitutions raises the question as to how the original choice would have fared. We ask it especially in Hitchcock's case because his second choices have all triumphed: their success dares us to use our imaginations to envisage the 'someone' different for whom the part was intended.

Yet fascinating patterns emerge through serendipity. With Hitchcock's actors two patterns stand out: the diptych and the triptych effect, double and triple folding screens that animate a transformation of the icon, as the actor's image undergoes multiple incarnations in his or her Hitchcock career. Fontaine, Peck, Granger and Hedren are defined by the *diptych* effect, Grant, Bergman, Stewart and Kelly by the *triptych* effect. To say this, of course, is to limit the impact of Grant and Stewart. They had not three but four leading roles in Hitchcock pictures. In their case, however, I would suggest there is an *alternate* triptych effect. The last screen can be substituted, that is, it presents a choice between two pictures, but either way still leaves a triangle of interconnected images, organic and precise. This also points to the difference of emphasis between diptych and triptych. The former hinges more on transformation and substitution; the latter more on connection and coherence. The two films discussed in this chapter, *Notorious* and *Rear Window*, constitute for all four leading actors the middle term in their series. *Notorious* was a second Hitchcock film for Grant and Bergman: *Rear Window* was a second film for Stewart and Kelly. In both cases neither had acted with the other before. So when we return to the triptych effect the acting roles in these two films are pivotal. But first, let us explore the single transformation where Hitchcock subtly alters the performance of star actor from one film to the next.

The diptych series works through quick succession. With Fontaine *Suspicion* follows quickly from *Rebecca*, for Peck *The Paradine Case* is three years after *Spellbound*, for Granger *Rope* is soon matched by *Strangers on a Train* and for Hedren *Marnie* succeeds *The Birds*. The time-intervals are all short: one year, three years, three years and one year. Like Stewart moving from *Rear Window* into *Vertigo*, there is a continuation here of line and look but also transformation. In the diptych effect there is a following on matched by a moving away. The acting role is refined a second time around with reference to its predecessor in order to show its difference. In *Rebecca* Fontaine plays a young woman who marries to escape a domineering employer but we know nothing of her own family and background. In *Suspicion*, though, we begin with her, as Lina, at home at church, with family and friends, before her relationship with Johnny (Grant) grows serious. The restraint is known, the home, the friends, the village she has outgrown. In her first picture she grows into a new domestic life she cannot fully accept; in her second she grows out of a familiar domestic life, which is holding her back, into a strange kind of void where she has the trappings of the good life but no substance to go with it. The household at Manderley is structured but forbidding. In *Suspicion*'s lush country home there is no real household since Johnny comes and goes at will and she has no idea where or even who he is. She trades her gauche ignorance of the present household (*Rebecca*) for a fearful ignorance of her absent husband (*Suspicion*). In the former she is being watched and judged by others from a position of strength she does not have, in the latter she is forced by circumstance into watching and judging, but not from any position of strength. Is her husband a confidence man, or a thief, or even a murderer? Fontaine responds to the alternations of Grant's presence and absence, the uncertainties that both constantly bring. Hitchcock seems less interested in the answer to the riddle – even though he wanted to flout studio wishes and turn Grant into a murderer – than he is in the uncertainties registered on the face of his leading actress. Anxieties of disappointment, looks of suspicion, thoughts of complicity, anticipation of violence, fear of poisoning: such dramatic registers are the ones he seeks from Fontaine. In truth, he gets them, for she delivers. Acting here means acting out the ordeal of impending disasters that may well turn out to be real. It is a prelude to Bergman's great performance in *Gaslight* (1944) and to Joan Bennett's in *Secret Beyond the Door* where Lang casts her to reprise Fontaine's Hitchcock persona.

Unlike Fontaine, Farley Granger was not Hitchcock's acting invention. He had just played as a romantic outlaw on the run in Nicholas Ray's *They Live By Night* (1948) before Hitchcock cast him in *Rope* and *Strangers on a Train*. With his alternation of roles, he produces a diptych effect of constraint followed by release. In *Rope* Granger is trapped in a single apartment with co-murderer John Dall and their hidden corpse, convinced at first in the power of their audacity then panicking as the noose (metaphorically) tightens and their ruse is rumbled. Both here and in *Strangers on a Train*, his role is reactive. Dall is the prime mover in the murder Granger helps commit in the film's opening sequence. In the film made from the Highsmith novel, Granger reacts ambiguously to the bold proposition of Robert Walker to exchange murders and then turns it down when it is too late. The predatory Walker makes the running; frantically Granger comes running after to pick up the pieces. Yet his final rejection of the villainous Walker also compensates for his reluctant complicity with Dall. He is not only making up for his mistakes in *this* film, but also for those in his *preceding* Hitchcock film. Seeing the movies back to back, one gets the sense of a double atonement in which Granger's instant guilt from the start of his chance train encounter with Walker contains within it the buried agenda of his abject obedience to Dall in the previous film. It seems he is determined not to make the same mistake twice. But his weakness for being used by others also repeats itself. He does allow his wife to be murdered: he does consider fulfilling his side of the bargain. In *Rope* Granger struts and frets anxiously around the tight confines of the apartment. In *Strangers on a Train* he is literally and metaphorically all over the place, in trains, on tennis courts, on Washington streets, at the house of Walker's father and finally at the funfair that ends in disaster. The villain sets the pace; our ambiguous hero is obliged to follow.

With Hedren there is a different crossover effect, a mirror image of that in Fontaine who starts in her first film as a servile, low-status companion and in the second as the daughter of an eminent army general. Hedren begins in *The Birds* as a rich and leisured woman working for worthy charities; in *Marnie* she starts off as a transient office-worker and a compulsive thief. Dressed by Edith Head she has a model's look in both films, a continuation of look from one film to the other. Yet in the second film the social insecurity shows through. Her lesser outfits disguise status rather than expressing it. In *The Birds* the experience of catastrophe shatters Hedren's identity. At the start of *Marnie* it is already fraying at the edges. In *The Birds* she confidently flirts with Rod Taylor by teasing and taunting him. In *Marnie* she is a 'specimen' to be tamed in the eyes of Sean Connery. As with nearly all his lead actors Hitchcock makes no great attempt to disguise their look or their voice in transferring them from one film to the next. There are instantly recognisable the second time around, just as Kelly and Bergman are the third time around and Grant and Stewart are the fourth time around. He builds on the star system and feeds it but that motive is secondary. The prime motive is a wish for his audience to bear witness to the shift, the transfiguration. The icon moves from one screen to the other in altered form as if the fold in the screen imprints the first image upon the blank surface but in doing so changes it miraculously, going with our expectation but then subtly altering the end-product.

Just as the Stewart fear-look is the link between the end of *Rear Window* and the opening of *Vertigo*, so Grace Kelly's Riviera romance with Cary Grant in *To Catch a Thief* comes straight out the pages of *Harper's Bazaar*, the journal she secretly reads as Stewart – now totally encased in plaster – dozes in his wheelchair. One senses the *Rear Window* relationship cannot last. Hitchcock, after all, had sprung Kelly loose across the courtyard, and when she arrives in Nice accompanied by her mother she is almost a continuation of the same character, Lisa Fremont as Frances Stevens. The mother might well be the companion to give consolation after one intimacy has ended but also a mildly scolding chaperone while she is searching for another. Hitchcock here gets the chance to reverse an earlier Riviera link of Americans abroad, the tight starchy link between *Rebecca*'s Fontaine, ever the cowering companion, and her overbearing dowager, Mrs Van Stratten. The comic banter between mother and daughter, their stubborn conflicts, equals them up in a freer age. And the mother, played by Jessie Royce Landis, is also transferable. Here she plays Kelly's mother who helps deliver her daughter unto the handsome ageing rogue that is jewel thief Grant. In *North by Northwest*, however, Hitchcock casts her to play Grant's *mother*, though in life she was of the same age: a sly diptych effect for a superb supporting actor.

With Kelly, however, we are into the deeper realm of triptych effect. In her first film she is the pale-faced victim of spousal conspiracy, trapped in her Maida Vale flat until arrested, whereupon she is trapped off-screen in her prison cell. Then in *Rear Window* Kelly's animated performance of self comes from *not* being trapped in Stewart's apartment or through marriage, following his obsession yet holding a distance from him, coming and going physically at will, above all perfecting her dramatic exits and entrances. Hitchcock of course plays on the irony of another arrest, this time for secretly entering Thorwald's apartment, which is squashed in the nick of time. In *To Catch a Thief* she is no thief but a self-possessed tourist on the Côte d'Azur whom Hitchcock unleashes into forms of dangerous and elegant motion. The predatory kiss of *Rear Window* is repeated here but in long shot in a hotel corridor, without slow-motion. Grant the lucky recipient matches her mobile self with his instinctive fluency. They drive dangerously together down the Corniches with Kelly at the wheel. They dance elegantly together, though at the masked ball Grant is long gone showing his agility instead on the rooftops as he stalks the real 'Cat' to clear his name. The ease of mobility is a perfect match enhanced by the smooth innuendo of Hayes' dialogue in which they both gladly share. As a comedy-adventure where nothing is really at stake, it creates an effortless intimacy of equals. Indeed the triangular effect of the film, where Kelly's rival for Grant is the agile Brigitte Auber, is a visual treat that hinges on different forms of fluency in movement against Mediterranean landscapes and settings.

In the Bergman triptych more was at stake. Thematically the range is greater; morally the trajectory is downward, a steep emotional descent. Bergman moves from self-confident doctor to remorseful daughter of a traitor and finally in *Under Capricorn* to a concealed killer whose husband-cousin, Joseph Cotten, has secretly appropriated her crime. As a triptych effect the descent is palpable, but at each stage with Bergman there is redemption. She 'falls' in order to be redeemed: in the first two films she is redeemed by passion, in the last by confession, a long eight-minute sequence that Hitchcock filmed in a single shot. In the first two films Hitchcock decentres her lovers. Peck is amnesiac and traumatised with no clear agenda: Grant is a secret agent with a collective agenda that is not his own. In the third her lover is an old-fashioned Anglo-Irishman (Michael Wilding) who fails to break the ties that bind, the ties of family complicity. In the first two films, Bergman is a modern single-minded woman whose weakness is a sudden passion. In the latter two she is a disturbed victim, a would-be alcoholic who survives worse forms of poison that are not self-inflicted. One suspects Hitchcock ran the poisonings across because Bergman was so convincing the first time around. With Kelly things start off darkly then become lighter and transparent; finally they sparkle with diamonds and sunlight on the Côte d'Azur. But Bergman remains for Hitchcock a figure entrenched in the realm of the Gothic. Each house she inhabits is a trap from which she must be sprung – the scientific madhouse of Green Manors, the Nazi safe house in Rio, the newly-built mansion in *Under Capricorn* where Milly the housekeeper is trying to poison her. And the predicament gets darker as it rolls back into history. Yet because the darkness intensifies the power of redemption does likewise: against all odds of character and chance Bergman has to radiate that power, to make it come from within. In the first two films redemption is romantic, but in the last her murderous secret makes such a resolution impossible. Redemption comes through the sacrificing of romance, where she rejects her would-be lover to stay with her ex-convict husband. It was savage irony that Bergman at that moment in her troubled life was about to reject husband and family in favour of Rossellini.

With Cary Grant in 1941, Hitchcock inherited an actor who had excelled in comic roles for Howard Hawks, an actor who had used his great timing, downbeat manner and physical fluency to create memorable roles in *Bringing up Baby* (1938) and *His Girl Friday* (1940). Both directors placed him memorably in role reversal. With Hawks it was audacious and funny – witness a churlish Grant stuck in the sidecar as GI Anne Baxter drives the motorbike in *I Was a Male War Bride* (1949). With Hitchcock it was erotic – witness the ambivalent charge of fear and fire in Grant's eyes as Kelly swerves her car around the hairpin bends of the Corniches. If Hawks had made him take his share of pratfalls Hitchcock made him altogether more sinister, a figure whom you could never read closely. Three films pose questions of character that impinge upon criminal intent: in *Suspicion* is he a charming and manipulative killer?; in *Notorious* is he a cool sadist abusing his political power?; in *To Catch a Thief* is he the ex-thief gone back to old habits who needs to be caught? The fourth, *North by Northwest*, is very different yet engages an issue following on from the other three. If they all ask questions of Grant's characters, of how others might read them, this film poses the opposite question: how does Grant's character *read himself?*

If we follow the pattern of a *Suspicion/ Notorious/ North by Northwest* triptych we move from a position where Grant is facing us as we try to figure him out, to one where he is on our side also trying to figure out who he is. He moves from being mysterious to being, quite literally, vacuous. In the first two figures of the triptych there is the convention of something and someone to find out, but in the last the puzzle of whether there is anything to find out at all. You could say that Hitchcock had brought him in from the cold, but also that he has emptied him of enigma. Yet the absence of enigma creates further enigma! How can someone be so bleached out that all their senses are there but they somehow act like an amnesiac with a foolproof memory? Moreover, if Roger O. Thornhill is a complete nobody he is definitely played by somebody, namely Grant at the height of his fame. Hitchcock plays triumphantly on the idea of a man without qualities performed by a star with exquisite qualities. For Eve Kendall, the figure of Grant is both a stranger on a train and a stranger to no one who has been anywhere near a cinema.

In the first three films the quality Hitchcock ensures that Grant brings to his roles is what Graham McCann has termed his 'intimate strangeness' (1997: 142). In his repertory of glance, gesture and reaction Grant can turn on or turn off in the flicker of an eyelid. He can be the perfect lover or the perfect stranger. And in *North by Northwest* he does it again. As an intimate stranger on the Chicago train he shows Eva Marie Saint his full seduction repertoire that includes, of course, leaving himself open to seduction. So if these things are constants, where is the triptych effect? It is Grant's relation to the Law, the outsider becoming insider and then being forced out again. In *Suspicion* he hovered tantalisingly on the wrong side of legality, the confidence trickster who may well be planning murder. In *Notorious* he is back in the fold of the Law but within an organisation, the FBI, which seems a law unto itself. In *To Catch a Thief* and *North by Northwest* he is wrongfully cast out again, made peripheral or peripatetic. In the former instance there is a contained and circular flight, which returns to origin and exoneration. After all this is romantic comedy. In the latter, however, he is in free fall, a cipher of Cold War conspiracy that Hitchcock turns into a Cold War comedy of errors with echoes of Hamlet in his title. The title intimates the vague direction in which he is heading, New York to Chicago to North Dakota, yet he in truth is everywhere and nowhere. The identity-makeover he had inflicted on Bergman is now inflicted on him. The organisation may have changed from FBI to CIA, but the principle is the same. This is role-reversal and he now is the bait.

With Stewart the movement is, as mentioned earlier, rather different. It is also easier to plot, from the Kammerspiel closeness of the first two films to what Rohmer called the open 'architectural' qualities of *Vertigo* and *The Man Who Knew Too Much* (1989: 168). These, if you like, are the alternate third where Stewart is sprung loose from the confines of a single room. The remake movie, which came first, is a tale of two cities, Marrakech and London. *Vertigo* is Northern Californian and circulates from city to country. Marrakech is bustling and full of life, but utterly foreign in culture. London, for Hitchcock, is home but hardly reassuring. For Stewart it is even more unnerving, a ghost city of empty streets. Colonial Marrakech is expectedly strange and disconcerting under Western eyes – Islamic, traditional, steeped in poverty. But London, instead of being reassuring, is unexpectedly bizarre as the famous taxidermist and chapel sequences show us. In London, Stewart feels he is chasing the ghost of his kidnapped son. Later in *Vertigo* he is also chasing a ghost, but a visible apparition – Madeleine Elster. Thus the alternate third of the triptych sets Stewart in motion on a 'quest-following' whose outcome is uncertain. But that is set against iconic solidity. With Stewart we always feel, to start with, that we know where we are. Grant is protean, labile and easily slips our grasp. At the same time he is always a survivor who escapes permanent damage. The same cannot be said for Stewart. In *Vertigo* Hitchcock casts him as someone who disintegrates in front of our eyes.

Novak and Perkins: three in one

The final word on the triptych rests with Kim Novak and Anthony Perkins. For in *Vertigo* and *Psycho* Hitchcock created two distinct variations on three-screen effect. Critics may have ignored it but the effect is extraordinary. The triadic image appears within the *same picture*. Conventionally the two actors are seen as doubles, Novak as Madeleine and Judy, Perkins as Bates and Mother. Yet in each case a third term is forged out of the contrast, again a complex Hitchcock variation on montage. Madeleine, the impersonation, is transformed into Judy, the original, only to be transferred back again at

Scottie's insistence into Madeleine, a perfect imitation of the first imperson-ation. With Perkins the transformation is more direct but also more macabre. Having been caught *in flagrante* dressed as his knife-wielding mother, Nor-man ends the picture in his prison cell where Hitchcock superimposes on his seated image the face of his mother's skeleton that we have just seen in the final mansion sequence. As the mother's voice takes over the silent body of the accused, so her skull grins out from beneath his flesh and skin. In the final shot of the picture he has segued into his composite schizoid image. Montage dialectic without politics, and pure tongue in cheek; or it would be, if it didn't send a shiver up the spine

In *Vertigo* the composite image has a degree of subtlety that tests not only our visual imagination but the whole range of our mental powers. We see the process of doubling backwards, the copy before the original, and only then the original changed back once more into the prototype. Poised and balanced perfectly between its three moments, it is the greatest triptych ever created in a single film. As for the last transformation, Hitchcock stretches it out slowly, agonisingly: the couple's power-struggle, the visit to the shoe store, the dress store, the dyeing of the hair and the changing of the hair-style, the pony tail transformed back into the spiral knot. It is also a change in the rhythms of voice and movement. Judy is so *unalike* the only giveaway are the eyebrows, and on a first viewing most spectators do not spot it. She looks and talks in the way that Hitchcock wants: earthbound, street-wise, an ordinary working girl come to town from the Midwest, living up to the data on the driving licence she shows Stewart to convince him of her true name. Thus Hitchcock was right to place the flashback where he does. For then we have to endure the backward transition and share the couple's anguish in the fullness of knowledge.

There are no concessions and no short cuts. Only in slow-motion, meta-phorically speaking, does Novak finally turn back into the ghost that *does* move and talk in slow motion. She endows Madeleine with the precise voice and physical rhythms of a trance. She glides rather than walks: her voice sings rather than talks. It is one of the great accomplishments of film acting anywhere in cinema history, the delivery of a spectral style and a manicured body punctuated by the switch to Judy's loose walk and loose body and then the return down the corridor and into the hotel room as Madeleine reborn. Novak is exactly the same in look, identical to the first time around. The dif-ference is external. She is bathed in artifice that has a real source – the sea green of the neon sign for the Empire Hotel that casts upon her face and her body the ghastly shadow of death. This is the second coming as prelude to extinction. And it is the third screen of the triptych that differs from the first purely through the colour of the light. But the colour of the light is enough, the clinching detail that generates perfection.

chapter 6

PERVERSE MIRACLES: HITCHCOCK AND THE FRENCH NEW WAVE

French cinema presents us with a special case of Hitchcock's legacy. Not only did the French New Wave make many films that reveal Hitchcock's imprint, doubling as critics their directors had also revealed his work to their readers in a new light. Truffaut's extensive series of 1960s interviews, later updated, are probably the best interviews that Hitchcock ever gave. The 1957 Rohmer-Chabrol study remains the best critical book on his work in any language. As noted, it also crops up, self-referentially, in the hands of a bookshop customer in Chabrol's first Paris feature, *Les Cousins*. Though most of the book was written by Rohmer, Chabrol proves his perspicacity elsewhere. A review of *Rear Window* for *Cahiers du Cinéma* in April 1953 remains one of the best short pieces on a Hitchcock film. Four years later in *Cahiers du Cinéma* Jean-Luc Godard wrote his review-essay of *The Wrong Man* and it remains the best critical piece on that film (1986: 48–55). Since then French director-critics have carried on the tradition. Among others, Jacques Rivette, Jean Douchet, Alain Resnais, Chris Marker, Jean-Claude Brisseau, Pascal Bonitzer and Gilles Mimouni have added praise and insight in telling contributions.

Back in the 1950s it had been difficult to claim that Hitchcock was the equal of the great European filmmakers like Carl Theodor Dreyer, Sergei Eisenstein, Jean Renoir and Roberto Rossellini. André Bazin, founding father of French criticism, was initially sceptical about Hitchcock worship among the young cinephiles of *Cahiers du Cinéma* but after interviewing Hitchcock on the Côte d'Azur during the shoot of *The Man Who Knew Too Much*, his attitude mellowed. And just before he died in 1958 he paid due tribute to the power of the Rohmer-Chabrol study (1982: 171–80). The French critique is there to be seen and savoured: yet Hitchcock's artistic impact on French film is often undervalued, and remains strongest in the two figures who analysed him the most, Claude Chabrol and Eric Rohmer. To see the effect of Hitchcock on both directors is not to lessen their originality, but to enhance it, and to see their work in a different light. Yet historically it also poses a fascinating question. Is the Hitchcock factor a key feature of the New Wave or does it only kick in after the New Wave movement is over? Is it part of the modernist advance of the 1960s or a reactive feature of more conservative ex-New Wave figures after 1968?

Let us take a brief look at the history. The New Wave originated in *Cahiers du Cinéma*, founded in 1951, and edited by Bazin and Jacques Doniol-Valcroze as a continuation of the *Revue du Cinéma* (1946–49). It gave rise to a new generation of critics who then became filmmakers within the space of a single decade. By 1959 Doniol-Valcroze, Godard, Truffaut, Chabrol, Rohmer, Rivette and Pierre Kast were all making feature films. Of these the big five of the New Wave made key debuts in which the city of Paris, at the end of the 1950s, also becomes a central character, Truffaut with *Les Quatre Cents Coups* (1959), Chabrol with *Les Cousins* (1959), Godard with *A bout de souffle* (1959), Rohmer with *Le Signe du Lion* (1959) and Rivette with *Paris nous appartient* (1960). Indeed the title of Rivette's film – Paris belongs to us – aptly sums up the group's collective achievement in the early years. Paris *was* their centre of gravity. Between 1958 and 1964, the *Cahiers* group transformed itself into the core of the French New Wave, a much broader movement that captured the city's nature in a way that has been done by filmmakers with no other city, before or since. In addition here we can also cite Truffaut's *Tirez sur le pianiste* (1960), Godard's *Vivre sa vie* (1962), *Bande à part* (1964) and *Alphaville* (1965), Agnès Varda's *Cléo de 5 à 7* (1961), Jean Rouch's *Chronique d'un été* (1961), Chabrol's *Les bonnes femmes* (1960) and Rohmer's short films *La Boulangère du Monceau* (1960) and *Place de l'Étoile* (1965). This starburst of energy owes much to four key predecessors: Jean Renoir for humour, depth of field and lyricism; Roberto Rossellini for bold locations coupled with a feel for the fate of ordinary people; Fritz Lang for his paranoid, political edge; Orson Welles for his vision of modernity's injustice and corruption and for his camera's kinetic powers. Hitchcock's influence, at first, was in a minor key.

The New Wave explosion, astonishing in its own right, was an oblique forerunner of the events of May 1968 in Paris. Though some critics have now come to see the movement as a cinematic wave cresting and breaking by 1964 (see Marie 2003: 141–6), in 1967 Truffaut still saw the New Wave as a living force (1986a: 103–15). Arguments over dating echo those over Italian neo-realism after the war. Some critics opt for the short and pure burst of artistry, others for the longer haul. A case can be made for the key date, the true cut-off point, as 1967–68. To pirate the title of Bertolucci's 1964 film the New Wave is a movement that flourishes 'before the revolution', but not after since it is overwhelmed by a monster wave that makes a bigger splash. True the 'Events of May' and their aftermath were more uprising than revolution. Though their militancy did lead to reforms and helped to precipitate the eventual resignation of President De Gaulle, it failed to overthrow the Fifth Republic or hinder the renewed Gaullist tradition that emerged all the stronger in a countrywide reaction against 'the events' and their turbulent aftermath.

Any direct link between May 1968 and the New Wave seemed unlikely but there was one nonetheless. A few months earlier the Parisian film community, lead by the *Cahiers* group, had its own mini-uprising when it protested on the streets of Paris against the dismissal of Henri Langlois, director of the Cinémathèque, by Culture Minister André Malraux, and then organised a boycott of Cinémathèque films. The protest ended violently (see McCabe 2003: 201–3). But the wider politics then generated by the events of May forced the New Wave into a stark choice – to draw back or to go with the flow. As a result Godard, the most political of the movement by the time of *Weekend* (1967), became even more radical and Maoist, soon distancing himself from Truffaut whose initial enthusiasm for change quickly faded. *Cahiers* earlier did go with the flow under Jacques Rivette as its editor: it then responded to May 1968 through a new generation of film critics who absorbed revolutionary rhetoric, took up the discourses of Marxism and semiology and attacked the cult of authorship, the means through which earlier *Cahiers* had rhapsodised about their favourite American directors. Along with Truffaut, two of the old guard who drew back and remained less involved were Chabrol and Rohmer. Of the new world of 1968 their cinema showed only indirect signs. Yet, it could be argued, both directors did find inspiration in the turbulence of the time – Rohmer in his encounters with ideology and the younger generation, Chabrol with his deconstructions of bourgeois life-style and the bourgeois family.

Despite this they were criticised for their apolitical turn, out of Paris and towards provincial bourgeois life, and were then berated for their 'old-fashioned' movies. The move out of Paris is true enough. In 1967 Chabrol's *Les Biches* moves in setting from Paris to Saint Tropez in winter. In the same year Rohmer's *La Collectioneuse*, deemed the fourth (though filmed third) of his Six Moral Tales, also begins in Paris but quickly moves to Saint Tropez in summer. During 1968, Chabrol was in Brittany to make *Que la bête meure* and then during 1969 in the Dordogne for *Le Boucher*. In the same year Rohmer went to Clermont-Ferrand for *Ma nuit chez Maud*, then in the following year to Lake Annecy near the Swiss border to film *Le Genou de Claire*. Truffaut also shot his most Hitchcockian films in the late 1960s, using greenbelt London suburbs as a setting for the futuristic *Fahrenheit 451* (1966) then following it with *La Mariée était en noir* (1967) and *La Sirène du Mississipi* (1969), which was partly filmed on the African island of Réunion. Both were bourgeois revenge-thrillers, modelled on a combination of Hitchcock and film noir. Through American Hitchcock these three directors had found a different source of renewal at a critical time. One wing of the post-New Wave owed much, therefore, to a figure for whom revolutionary rhetoric meant very little at all. Indeed Hitchcock's career at this time suffered its worst dip since the early 1930s. He filmed two sterile Cold War thrillers, *Torn Curtain* and *Topaz*, both deeply anti-communist in tone. *Topaz*, badly acted, anti-Cuban and Francophobe, is one of his most forgettable features.

Yet Hitchcock remained an icon on the basis on his films up to *Marnie*. In location shooting, he had been revered by *Cahiers* for two things. The first was the vivid documentary quality of *The Wrong Man*, filmed in the Queens borough of New York City. Gaining a mixed reception elsewhere it had been a special *Cahiers* favourite (fourth in their 1957 Top Ten) and its authentic documentary flavour was clearly a spur to the New Wave vision of contemporary Paris. But it was also more and that 'more' haunts the later work of Rohmer and Chabrol as a transforming vision of the world. In his review-essay Godard claimed the film had shown cinema was 'better fitted than either philosophy or the novel to convey the basic data of consciousness' (1986: 50). It is this view of cinema that played such a large part in New Wave evolution and beyond. The second source of inspiration was a more lasting one, the idea of a rigorous location topography that apart from *The Wrong Man* can be seen in the Québec of *I Confess* and Hitchcock's Northern California triangle: Santa Rosa for *Shadow of a Doubt*, San Francisco, the Redwoods State Park and San Juan Bautista for *Vertigo*, plus San Francisco and Bodega Bay for *The Birds*. These are all key location films for the 'bourgeois' turn of Truffaut, Rohmer and Chabrol, for all had strong and stringent identities of place their films duly try to match. He thus helped the 'bourgeois' wing of the New Wave to outlive itself and gain a second lease of life during the crisis of Cultural Revolution, Paris-style.

Hitchcock: Resnais and Marker

At the same time French engagement with Hitchcock went wider than the *Cahiers* group. Close to Chabrol in spirit and ambition was Jean-Pierre Melville, best known for his gangster thrillers and attacked by *Cahiers* in the late 1960s for his genre obsessions and Gaullist sympathies. After *Le Samouraï* (1967) Melville, as already mentioned, made his memory film of the French Resistance, *L'Armée des ombres*, whose intricate patterns of duplicity, transfer of guilt and double-cross contain strong echoes of Hitchcock's wartime Resistance short *Bon Voyage*. Elsewhere there was a deeper connection. Within the wider rubric of the New Wave, Alain Resnais was usually seen as part of the Left Bank group comprising Chris Marker, Agnès Varda and Jean Rouch, politically committed filmmakers of the Left who did not particularly share the *Cahiers* enthusiasm for Hollywood. Yet Resnais had taken Hitchcock's themes of memory and guilt and his fascination with bourgeois life into a Francophile dimension that was at once more abstract, formal and experimental than any of the *Cahiers* group. If Hitchcock's sporadic use of the flashback often raises the question of duplicity, in Resnais its constant use and vision of the past becomes a fundamental issue of epistemology. Hitchcock's philosophical shadow was Hume: Resnais' shadow was the French philosopher of time and memory, Henri Bergson, who had compared the complex operations of the mind to forms of temporal succession in the workings of the cinematographic frame. There are explicit clues to the Hitchcock connection. In the middle of Resnais' most formal and abstract film, *L'Année dernière à Marienbad* (1961), a cardboard silhouette of Hitch appears by the hotel lift, a tongue-in-cheek tribute in what for the most part is a solemn film but one in which Delphine Seyrig's role is also Resnais' subtle play upon the haunting, and haunted heroine of late Hitchcock: for sure upon the ghostly presence of Madeleine in *Vertigo*. In Seyrig's rape scene, there is a prefiguring of the harrowing fate of Marnie. The question we are prompted to ask as Resnais shifts the elegant, statuesque Seyrig through time and space (and endless hotel corridors) in a delirium of metempsychosis is whether or not she, like Madeleine, is a ghost come back to haunt an imperfect world. Since Hitchcock was an avid viewer of the European modernists, the figure of Seyrig may in turn have influenced the iconography of Tippi Hedren in *The Birds* and *Marnie*.

In Resnais' most difficult memory film, *Muriel* (1963), not only does he explore the complex relationship between past and present but he also uses forms of montage in intimate settings that are, as Truffaut noted, reminiscent of Hitchcock's technique and a homage to his use of suspense (1994: 327–8). But it was not just montage-effects in the exceptional sequence that link the two. In general the *mise-en-scène* in the Boulogne family apartment, with its sharp, dovetailed editing of static shots, recalls *Dial 'M' for Murder* with Hitchcock's exact dispersal of static shots in the living-room of the Maida Vale flat. Scorsese claims that Hitchcock's editing here is a form of rhythmic visual composition out of minimal sources, a magical something-out-of-nothing that never does the obvious; watching it is 'like listening to a fugue by Bach, trying to figure out where the next phrase is beginning and where it ends' (1997: 98). A similar claim can be made about the complex interiors of *Muriel*, creating mystery out of its abstract mosaic of shots, and its use of memory as trauma in which the hero cannot escape the constant repetition of images of torture of a girl, Muriel, whom he had met during the Algerian war. The haunting of the past rooted in war that Hitchcock had used in *Spellbound* and which he would reprise, obliquely, in *The Birds* pervades the atmosphere of Resnais' film, which came out in the same year. We might also see a parallel in film chronology, self-conscious on Resnais' part. He would have known that in Hitchcock's career the sharp static montage of *Dial 'M' for Murder* had followed on from the opposite effect, the moving shots within the long takes of *Rope* and *Under Capricorn*. His early career then repeats that effect. The endless tracking shots and long takes in

Hiroshima, mon amour (1959) and *L' Année dernière à Marienbad* are replaced by the short sharp staccato shots of *Muriel* that clearly unnerved yet also disappointed his audience of the 1960s. Again Resnais had taken Hitchcock into greater realms of abstraction, but this time had not taken his audience with him.

In 1976 his first English-language film, *Providence*, succeeded. It proved popular both in France and elsewhere, and is set in an indeterminate future in an unnamed country with East Coast American locations that have strong echoes of Hitchcock's California. The look of the empty streets is eerie and menacing, the fog filters – shades of *Vertigo* – give a sense of darkness at noon, while the isolated family mansion has a Gothic quality present from *Rebecca* right through to *Psycho* and *The Birds*. The family relations are as fraught as they are in any Hitchcock film yet displayed in a formal, pseudo-elegant manner that is comic and mocking in tone. Resnais, we might say, turns Hitchcock into modernist science fiction. If *The Birds* signified catastrophe, *Providence* signifies its aftermath. The film, perhaps, is more like a composite of Hitchcock and Welles: the family mansion has strong echoes of Xanadu and the totalitarian future even stronger echoes of *The Trial*. But the elegant formalism of the bourgeois family comically but also sadly tearing itself apart is one stage on from Hitchcock, a virtual re-visiting of earlier sites and themes *after* the catastrophe of *The Birds*. The family in David Mercer's scintillating screenplay is also a very *English* family with its ageing writer played by John Gielgud, who of course had worked for Hitchcock on his spy thriller *Secret Agent* forty years earlier. Resnais' film may then have been a tongue-in-cheek way of bringing Hitchcock back home to an English reference point very different from the London of *Frenzy*, yet also further on to a dystopian nowhere where all reference points have gone and discontinuity, in editing as well as life, is the order of the day.

Left Bank compatriot Chris Marker paid more direct homage to *Vertigo* than Resnais in two of his key films, the short *photo-roman*, *La Jetée* (1962), and later in his full-length documentary essay *Sans Soleil* (1985). The later film, which moves back and forth between Japan and Guinea-Bissau, contains an excursus to San Francisco to follow a Japanese video-artist obsessed by Hitchcock's film. We follow the route of his obsessive journey through the film's city settings in a way that repeats the obsession of Scottie Ferguson revisiting all the city haunts where he had seen the dead Madeleine in the search for her ghost. It also cues the spectator into the *Vertigo* reference of *La Jetée* – now a cult artwork – where the time-traveller of a post-nuclear world returns to the time of his childhood as a grown man to seek out the woman he had glimpsed at Orly airport shortly before catastrophe strikes. They go to the Jardin des Plantes in Paris to look at the trees, where the voice-over narrator recounts the Man's words to the Woman that almost replicate Madeleine's to Scottie as she points to the dated rings on the Sequoia tree: 'This is where I was born and this is where I shall die.' The Woman then tells the Man he is a ghost and we realise that Marker has created a gender-reversal in the identity of the ghost but not in the nature of the quest. The Man's return to childhood is a metaphysical version of 'the second chance' that Scottie imagines he has when he returns to the tower with Judy to conquer his vertigo, a second chance that is a perverse miracle, an illusory moment of transcendence that time will then destroy as it proves impossible to reverse history and, in *La Jetée*, to prevent apocalypse.

As Left Bank figures with their own agenda, neither Resnais nor Marker were part of the cresting of the New Wave in 1968 when *Cahiers* solidarity started to unravel. The radical post-New Wave of the 1970s that inherited the city film departed from the tragicomic sensibility in early Godard and Truffaut, and it had little interest in Hitchcock at all. Its intense existential feel was foreshadowed by Rivette's four-hour rumination on the theatrical and the real, *L'Amour fou*, and then renewed in the work of Jean Eustache, Philippe Garrel, Chantal Akerman and Jacques Doillon, a generation soon to be followed by the more studied naturalism of Maurice Pialat. The New Wave thus went in two directions – one developing as a more abstract, radical modernism with a new stress on intimacy and the body that was more immanent than transcendent (Deleuze 1989: 193–203). This entailed a rejection of rapid camera movement as self-conscious distraction and often entailed a preference for the static shot. In contrast the Chabrol/Rohmer alternative was a revised cinema of bourgeois life, material and mysterious at the same time; largely mimetic in form but briefly transcendental in its mysteries. It can be called neo-Hitchcockian, and leads to a cinema of perverse miracles that is foreshadowed by *La Jetée*. Here though, there is no science fiction but rather a material or mundane narrative with a miraculous ending where the 'miracle' is always shadowed by a question mark, and hovers between scepticism and belief, between utter disbelief and utter conviction.

Hitchcock: Chabrol, Rohmer and Truffaut

For Chabrol and Rohmer, 1967 had been a year of lift-off in the new form, after hitting the doldrums in Paris. Both temporarily abandoned the city as a film site after suffering box-office flops for innovating work – *Le Signe du Lion* (1959) for Rohmer and *Les bonnes femmes* (1960) for Chabrol. They went regional, a realm of the imaginary where Hitchcock's legacy looms large in their new form of bourgeois chronicle. Where Resnais' use of Hitchcock had been oblique and abstract, and Truffaut's romantic and lyrical, theirs was more sharply attuned to the life and mores of the times. It is a register that changes right through until the turn of the century, as they grow old but remain astonishingly productive. With Chabrol it is a stylised register of bourgeois mores often told through the medium of the thriller, using techniques of menace and suspense and also using many of the best French actors of the period. With Rohmer it is usually a discourse-register of life in a *younger generation*, in city or country or just by the sea; a favourite Rohmer setting is the summer vacation. After the *Moral Tales* (1962–72) Rohmer was to make two more decade-long series, the 1980s *Comedies and Proverbs* and for the 1990s *The Four Seasons*, where this changing world is seen increasingly through the eyes of loquacious but vulnerable women searching for a voice that strengthens their uncertain selfhood. While Rohmer focused on talk as a key medium of emotion and meaning and favoured static takes, Chabrol's film language was more fluid and visual, his dialogue often spare and oblique.

Thematic contrasts in the Hitchcock legacy are even starker than the differences in style. Rohmer's fables stress the importance of redemption in small ways with no overt violence while Chabrol plays on the suspense of momentous downfall that pivots around the act of killing. Rohmer's production values, of course, are scarcely those of Hitchcock at all. The budgets are modest, the acting often done by non-professionals; meticulous rehearsals are used to reduce the length of shooting and the expense of film stock. Yet like Hitchcock, Rohmer has a low shooting ratio because he planned his films so thoroughly in advance. Moreover Hitchcock's flair for publicity and general shrewdness come through in both directors. While Chabrol cunningly refined the bourgeois murder for French viewing tastes of the period, Rohmer's plan for the *Six Moral Tales*, an idea which he sold to public and critics alike, works as an artistic package, a coherent series to be viewed one after the other. He then followed it with two further 'packages'. The co-authors of Hitchcock thus push him in two opposing directions, yet two elements of his work are vital to both: *narrative suspense*, which is constant and the *miracle ending*, which is periodic and but even more significant.

We shall see this shortly in two films indebted to *Shadow of a Doubt* but as different as day and night – Chabrol's *Le Boucher* (1969) and the fifth of Rohmer's *Moral Tales*, *Le Genou de Claire* (1970). But first let us look elsewhere as the Hitchcock connection reverberates in ways vivid and uncanny. In his bold lesbian psychodrama *Les Biches* (1967) Chabrol harnessed hybrid strands of the sex-power relations in *Rebecca*, *Rope* and *Strangers on a Train* to charge up a plot based on identity-transfer and betrayal. In Rohmer's complex portrait of philosophy and desire, *Ma nuit chez Maud*, Hitchcock's *Vertigo* serves as a template for key themes: the topography of a city and its surrounding countryside matched by dilemmas of sexual choice, guilt and obsession. In general the Rohmer/Chabrol films subtly make over themes of doubling and obsession they had analysed so well in *Rear Window* and *Ver-*

tigo. Recently, they have also gone back to the face and figure of Hitchcock's Ingrid Bergman whose acting both as critics had praised so much. Certainly Bergman is the beautiful ghost that haunts recent themes of fallen-ness and redemption in Chabrol's more recent *Betty* (1992) themes that are matched by Rohmer's 2001 French Revolution drama *L'Anglaise et le duc* which strongly echoes *Under Capricorn*. Their two heroines in question, Marie Trintignant and Lucy Russell, were, we might say, very opposite transformations of the image of Hitchcock's Bergman.

The key to Hitchcock transformation, here and elsewhere, is to move beyond generic format. This is precisely what Chabrol and Rohmer did and what Truffaut had failed to do. Whereas 1960s Godard had boldly turned Hollywood genre inside out, after *La Peau douce* Truffaut starts to capitulate to it. Because he thinks in terms of the thriller and very consciously of suspense techniques he starts to run aground on the reef of pastiche. Consequently he pays lip service and homage to Hitch when he thinks he is reinventing him. In addition he often tries and fails to match Hitchcock motifs to noir narratives. *Fahrenheit 451* and *La Sirène du Mississippi* are rapid responses to the films that *Cahiers* critics most admired in 1960s Hitchcock, *The Birds* and *Marnie*. Yet their very rapidity is an indication of shallowness: a skirting over the surface of things, a failure to achieve the emotional complexity that marks out later Hitchcock and makes his films such a challenge.

Sadly, these are killer comparisons that show up Truffaut's limits and draw out the daring of the Hitchcock originals. In his science fiction film *Fahrenheit 451*, adapted from Ray Bradbury's tale and set in leafy English suburbs, Truffaut tries to intimate the power of love amidst catastrophe. His fire-fighters are indoctrinated arsonists, paid to root out all books and burn them, but are then let down by Oskar Werner's cryptic love affair with Julie Christie. The paid pyromaniac becomes turncoat and doggedly protects his book-loving lover while still married to a happy robotic wife. In a strategy that echoes *Vertigo* the talented Julie Christie doubles up as wife Linda and lover Clarisse while Bernard Herrmann provides Truffaut with a musical score which, as in that film, pitches romance at breaking point. But even this homage cannot conceal Truffaut's flaws. Instead of state-of-the-art special effects to help us envisage a tyrant future he relies on a handful of awkward props: a bizarre Toytown fire engine and fire station, silly uniforms and a strange monorail stretching across green fields. Design-wise Truffaut is caught between the bold naturalism of Godard who concocts out of Paris suburbs the future city of Alphaville and the sophisticated special effects that Hitchcock developed to intimate terror on a grand scale in *The Birds*. For Truffaut the romantic, love must conquer all. For Hitchcock the visionary, it was catastrophe that had conquered all – catastrophe not as tin-pot technology but in *The Birds* as primal force of nature.

Yet Truffaut's film triumphs in its last sequence, which remains one of his most powerful; he does so by giving us the first miracle ending after *La Jetée* to enter the realm of the perverse. First he prefigures it with a *Wrong Man* shot, in which Werner as Montag has at last abandoned one image of Christie for another, the uncaring spouse for the sympathetic lover. After a nightmare connected to the book burning in his own house, Montag's distraught face is superimposed on that of Clarisse, which then takes it over (see Insdorf 1994: 54). But this conscious homage is later followed by something deeper as Montag escapes from book-burning tyranny. The last sequence that so moved Bradbury ushers us into a rural hideaway of 'book people' who keep famous texts alive by reciting them word for word, knowing them by heart. Memory thus preserves what fire has consumed. The miracle is perverse because there is an exchange, a trade-off that changes things utterly. In order to keep great art alive, the book people become autistic figures on a forlorn winter landscape, where snow has replaced the fire of the book burning. Criss-crossing paths as they recite without noticing one another, they seem intent on reducing themselves to walking texts. In one scene on the riverbank, a dying man verbally bequeaths the text of *Weir of Hermiston* to his son who tries frantically to memorise it before his father expires; in another twin brothers introduce themselves as Parts 1 and 2 of *Sense and Sensibility*. The survivors literally are what they read, sacrificing their own humanity to the future restoration of the book.

Truffaut's ending exemplifies the New Wave rewriting of Hitchcock. For every miracle that occurs there is always a price to be paid, questions to be answered about the nature of chance and necessity, and within the Catholic framework that Hitchcock's French admirers shared with him, the tantalising possibilities of Grace. In *The Wrong Man* do we take the sudden outburst of the inept juror that leads to a mistrial as a sign of God's intervention on the side of Manny Balestrero? On the side of the man wrongly accused, the side of the just? Is it just Manny's good fortune that comes through, pure luck that arises out of pure chance? Or is it a harsh trial of endurance forced by a harsh God upon his weak subjects? Whatever it is, in cinema it is a reflexive question too, like the one Chabrol knew had been posed by the resolution of *Rear Window*. For the fact that Thorwald is a murderer not only exonerates Jeff's dubious antics but also gives Hitchcock, playing God, a neat closure to his plot. The MacGuffin somehow ends up as a perverse miracle but the film's ending leaves us with no doubt that the division between the two is on a razor's edge. After all, Jeff starts the film with one broken leg and ends it with two, still sitting in his wheelchair. That too had been a perverse trade-off. Jeff's snooping may have 'miraculously' caught his man but has also left him permanently in plaster.

Hitchcock and Chabrol: murder and miracle

From *Les Biches* onward, meaning and emotion in Chabrol nearly always hover around the act, or the fact, of killing. Sometimes the killing has yet to come and sometimes it has come and gone without us witnessing it. Yet it remains ubiquitous in its powers of menace and is the source of the suspense at the heart of his narrative. Here, and in his chronicle of the darker side of bourgeois life, he is Hitchcock's truest successor while the strong sense of destiny his films display is something both he and Hitchcock had inherited from the early films of Fritz Lang. Indeed Chabrol, in interview, has claimed that Lang is more important to his work than Hitchcock for that reason (Magny 1987: 213–14). Within his use of suspense there always resides an air of fatality, of impending death. Expressionist motifs echo throughout the Hélène cycle. At the end of *Le Boucher* we have a 'Mabuse' car shot of onrushing trees at night as Hélène rushes the dying killer to hospital. *Les Biches* can be seen as a modulated vampire film in which the *femme fatale* passes on her dubious gift of seduction to her female lover who then becomes her vengeful double, while *La Rupture* (1970) uses motifs of dream enchantment, such as the tram ride, that are taken from Murnau's *Sunrise* (see Austin 1999: 46). Yet the juxtaposition of terror and suspense always links Chabrol back to Hitchcock as do the surface formalities of bourgeois life, and as does the perverse miracle hinting that Grace may yet triumph over chance. The relationship between murder and miracle is at its strongest in the films of the so-called Hélène cycle and revolves around the pivotal role of Stéphane Audran, the Hélène figure in *La Femme infidèle* (1968), *Le Boucher* and *La Rupture*. As in Hitchcock, the mix of meaning and emotion here revolves around the precise manufacture of stardom. Audran is to Chabrol what Bergman, Kelly and Hedren had been to Hitchcock.

In a decade and a continent that provided him with greater freedom of cinematic expression than Hitchcock had under the studio system, Chabrol could afford to be more explicit. Where *Strangers on a Train* and *Rope* had relied on sexual subtext, *Les Biches* was upfront about same-sex relationships. Audran seduces Jacqueline Sassard within the first ten minutes. Likewise *La Femme infidèle* supplies adultery with a mundane daily routine that *Dial 'M' for Murder* could only hint at fifteen years earlier. No Hitchcock film had ever shown the terrorising of one's own children that opens *La Rupture*. And Hitchcock was only ever more explicit than Chabrol in his portrait of serial killing in *Frenzy*, a film made three years after *Le Boucher*. While *Shadow of a Doubt* seems to haunt much of Chabrol's work, his Canadian thriller *Blood Relatives* (1978) took the teen/adult relationship of family life – that Hitchcock hints at – to new levels of candour. Sexual precocity, incest and paedophilia: all are intimated here in stark and disturbing ways. This boldness is sharpened by Chabrol's preference for precise locations, his strong sense of place and season. Yet the expressive moments that Hitchcock had culled from Weimar cinema, where the interplay of artifice and reality are paramount, are equally fore-grounded within the framework of Chabrol's greater naturalism. There are ghosting moments where his characters, like Hitchcock's, seem to operate in a parallel world. The capacity to intimate that world while action is rooted firmly in the world of the senses is often down to the performances of Audran.

In her Chabrol persona of the Hélène cycle, the fair-haired heroine combines the features of key Hitchcock blondes. There is a blend of Grace Kelly's cool sophistication and Tippi Hedren's neurasthenia with the ghost-like tread of Kim Novak's Madeleine. It is a cultural translation – American to French – that crosses the Atlantic. And it is a cultivated image: witness the immense difference between her acting in *La Femme infidèle* and *Les bonnes femmes* or *Les Cousins* a decade earlier. Thus it is also a difference between New Wave Chabrol and Chabrol of the bourgeois (Hitchcockian) turn. Even in *La Rupture*, where she plays a working woman (barmaid and ex-striptease artist) who has married into a bourgeois family she does not totally revert to her earlier acting style and the class differential seems uncanny. The rage of her failed writer-husband appears as proletarian, the wife's reaction as bourgeois rather than vice versa. Like Kelly, Audran is equally adept at the role of the single or the married woman: she combines Kelly's lithe sensuality with Hedren's glacial retraction in the same role, and does it twice over, the first time in *La Femme infidèle*, the second in *Le Boucher*. Hence she provides two different versions of the blend for the two films: the marital – unfaithful in the former; the single – traumatised in the latter. Her differing roles in *Le Boucher* and *La Rupture* recall Hedren's ability to shift easily between high social status in *The Birds* and low status in *Marnie*. Her conspicuous performing in the role of discontented spouse in *La Femme infidèle*, especially at home, recalls Kelly at her performative best in *Rear Window* yet also contains some of the trance-like elements that Novak displays in *Vertigo*'s Madeleine. All are bona fide variations of the woman Chabrol calls Hélène in all three films and equally of the acting power of Audran herself.

La Femme infidèle works as a neo-Hitchcockian inversion of noir narration. We do not see the adulterous couple in action, but rather the ambiguous and seductive poise of Audran's Hélène at *home* and the impact it still has on her betrayed husband Charles (Michel Bouquet), who is loving but suspicious and possibly impotent. Her affair, tracked by a private investigator, seems banal but the seductive withholding of her body in marital intimacy, where she invites desire but then withdraws from it, gives us a very domestic *femme fatale*. Rather than a noir conspiracy of passion where the lovers plot to murder the husband, we have the husband's murder of the lover Victor

(Maurice Ronet) that is condoned, if not induced, by Hélène herself and a renewed love for him when she finally guesses the truth of Victor's disappearance. As if to round off the intertextuality of the motif, we can refer back to the film Chabrol had wished to make from Patricia Highsmith's *The Talented Mr Ripley* but which he ceded in 1959 to René Clement – *Plein Soleil* (see Austin 2000: 50). There too a jealous rival Ripley (Alain Delon) kills a would-be male lover, Dickie, played by Ronet; his sudden disappearance is never explained. And Highsmith of course was already a Hitchcock author. Yet this is no straight copy by Chabrol of other film sources, and the intimacy goes beyond what Hitchcock had previously done. The film is about the rediscovery of love through the necessity of death. In his own restrained way Charles is as obsessed by Hélène as Scottie was by Madeleine in *Vertigo*, and yet here they are comfortably married with a young son and Audran ghosts unnervingly through their pleasant bourgeois home in Versailles. Chabrol later repeats the theme of marital obsession in his 1994 film *L'Enfer* where the tone is more frantic and phantasmagorical. Emmanuelle Béart is the beautiful ethereal wife (and mother), François Cluzet the paranoid husband whose suspicions gradually become hallucinatory and deranged. Here and in *L'Enfer* Chabrol gives us two very different versions of marital vertigo, clearly inspired in both by the film of that name, and in *L'Enfer*, two different endings.

Chabrol's earlier film, however, is the variant that remains the more compelling, working through understatement and not through excess, and containing against all odds its miracle of redemption. It is of course a perverse miracle. In the final sequence, just before the police return to arrest Bouquet for murder, Audran finds her lover's photograph in her husband's jacket pocket and burns it when she realises what he has done. Before he leaves with the police, the couple exchange love vows on the path outside the house. Then a reverse-angle shot from Charles' point-of-view, clear homage to Hitchcock, seals the tryst. Chabrol echoes the Tower shot in *Vertigo* with its reverse track and forward zoom, but does so in a specific way. The tracking POV shot, as Charles leaves, is more lateral then backward. As Hélène's image comes closer to him through the zoom, his movement back and sideways camouflages her magnifying image with tree branches that come suddenly to block his view. The further away she gets in reality, the nearer she becomes in his imagination, yet the image is always blocked, withheld. It is the combination of murder and loss, therefore, that perversely sets the seal upon a renewed love. Marriage, that battered fragile institution in all Chabrol, triumphs in its moment of perishing.

Marriage, however, perishes in the very first sequence of *La Rupture*, an opening as violent as any in the French director's work. Victor, an addicted young husband (Jean-Claude Drouot) viciously attacks wife and son in the aftermath of a bad narcotic trip and her counter-assault on her attacker marks her out in the eyes of his bourgeois family as a fallen woman who must be divorced not only from her deranged spouse but also from their hapless child. This is a 'wrong-woman' movie that foregoes the documentary style of *The Wrong Man* for left-field Gothic as Audran's Hélène retreats to an eccentric boarding house to battle her scheming in-laws and their sleazy investigator Paul (Jean-Pierre Cassel), who tries in vain to frame her on a pornography rap. (Here the Brussels locations give the film a genuinely surreal edge.) The illness of the husband, seemingly incurable, echoes in its own way the ill-ness of Vera Miles, Fonda's disintegrating spouse in *The Wrong Man*. Here too there is a redeeming miracle for the wrongly accused but none for the mad spouse. Paul, who may be the drugs supplier for her deranged husband, spikes Hélène's orange juice in a last desperate attempt to frame her. But even under psychedelic influence Audran's Hélène refuses to be a fallen woman. Her 'trip' becomes a rapture trip, not a bad trip, as she goes out in a trance to meet the local balloon seller whom she identifies as God and whose bal-loons she liberates because she sees them as imprisoned angels. The balloons are framed against the deep blue sky in a POV shot of psychedelic colour negatives, accompanied on the soundtrack by eerie electronic harmonies. The joyous sight of the freed balloons prompts her to return to the hospital to reclaim her injured son. In Chabrol's ironic coda, her virtue is unassailable and 'the miracle' is almost complete.

Yet an antiphonal movement is needed to complete the miracle in full. Paul's killing of the deranged husband provides it. The corrupt investiga-tor is attacked by Victor but then retaliates in repetition of the violence that opens the film. While Helene had fought back with a frying pan, Paul grabs a knife and delivers a fatal blow. The final struggle descends dangerously close to farce, the mode into which Cassell's character is often forced by Chabrol's uneven narrative, but it is part of the trade-off, the exchange signifying the sacrifice that perverse miracle entails. In her psychedelic state Hélène fails to realise the meaning of Victor's death even as she witnesses it. The irony, as Chabrol heavily stresses, is that it finally frees her from all responsibility. In both films we might say Hélène's miracle is only accomplished through the loss of the husband, in one the murdered Victor she pities, in the other the accused Charles whom she still loves. Yet the two films highlight the differ-ence between psychodrama and melodrama in the Chabrol oeuvre. The ear-lier film views adultery and its consequences in a way that is controlled, aus-tere, but also compassionate. The later film displays marital grief through the lens of a black comedy where shock and menace are sporadically brilliant but farce is often played to excess.

Unlike *La Rupture*, the thriller preceding it, *Le Boucher*, had clearly built more upon the strengths of *La Femme infidèle*. It is controlled, austere, haunting. Yet it is also more menacing and finally tragic. Chabrol's adultery drama had been based upon a disaffection out which disaster springs. *Le Boucher* digs deeper: violation springs obliquely out of trauma as does the poignant complicity that accompanies it. In the small Perigord town of Tremolat – whose inhabitants play themselves in the film – Popaul the butcher (Jean Yanne) is a war veteran who has witnessed atrocities in Algeria and Indochina, and cannot control his continuing impulse to kill. Teacher Hélène's trauma is the lesser one of a love destroyed years earlier, but with its stringent vow of celibacy it shares Popaul's sense of a life lost and senses in him too, despite the yawning gap in status between butcher and headmistress, a kindred spirit. The solitary figure of the schoolmistress living at the school in which she teaches, echoes another solitary figure in the Hitchcock canon, smalltown schoolteacher Annie Hayworth in *The Birds*, discarded by Mitch Brenner and now leading a lonely life in a house next to the isolated Bodega Bay school. Intriguingly, Audran's Hélène combines the forlorn predicament of Annie with the glamorous look of her new rival, Melanie Daniels. Yet, unlike Annie, Chabrol's Hélène is given a new, ambivalent intimacy, which poses more questions than it solves. Why does Hélène continue to insist on the company of a butcher with whom she has no wish to be physically intimate, and thus torture him? Chabrol lets the question linger in the mind of the spectator, the more so by making this Hélène composed and assured, not compulsive or neurotic in any obvious way at all. Yet celibacy for this beautiful and sophisticated woman is clearly an embrace of the perverse. (Here Chabrol plays on the French double meaning of *l'allumeuse* in the role that the lighter plays as a gift from Hélène to Popaul, a form of flirtation on her part in which she ends up unwittingly playing with fire.) Yet there is no sign of neurosis in her daily life, just as there is no sign of the butchery perpetrated by the friendly local butcher.

Juxtapositions deftly pose ominous questions. Hélène and Popaul meet at the wedding of her teaching assistant to a local woman and it is clear that Hélène finds him attractive in a sweet and harmless way. Yet the brutal killing of the teacher's wife, whose funeral she attends with Popaul the killer, is one at which she shows little emotion and no grief. It is almost – almost but not quite – as if Popaul's action could clear the way for her own future opportunity. Yet the film does not even hint at this. It merely shows, but then it has to. Without this discreet hint of a wish-dream come true we can make little sense of Hélène's lack of compassion for the victim and subsequently, her excess of compassion for the man she believes to be the killer. It is of course excess accompanied by fear for if Popaul is a killer of women she, as a woman who has rejected him, could be next. Her desperate wish for him *not* to be the killer is clinched by the affair – Hitchcock-style – of the significant object. At the site of the second body she discovers near the Cro-Magnon caves as she picnics with her pupils, she also finds a cigarette lighter she takes as the one she has previously given Popaul as a present. (This echoes the incriminating lighter we recall from *Strangers on a Train* by which Bruno intends to frame Guy for Bruno's murder of his wife.) She takes it back and hides it away, assuming it to be his, yet cries with relief on his next visit when he uses an identical lighter. Through the device of the lighter we see her relief at Popaul's 'innocence' as a greater emotion than grief for the teacher's murdered wife. Yet the lighter is more. It is an object that has a central function in all the mechanics of their emotional exchange – flirtation, seduction, guilt, complicity, suspicion and betrayal. Its image crystallises that fatal network of interconnection.

The film's tension follows the format of *Shadow of a Doubt*: female suspicion of the male killer shadowed by guilt and by love. Here the love is not, on Hélène's part, desire but if anything guilt which is more deep-rooted. The criminal guilt of the guilt-free murderer sullies the legal innocence of the suspecting female, and the lighter in Chabrol serves the same metonymic function as the ring in *Shadow of a Doubt*. It signifies pure guilt. Chabrol of course reverses the direction of the gift-exchange. Uncle Charlie has given the ring of a murder-victim to niece Charlie as a gift and by doing so, manages to incriminate himself: Popaul receives the lighter as a gift from Hélène yet by first leaving it at the murder-scene for her, fortuitously, to find and then buying another to replace it equally incriminates himself. Popaul, looking for a cleaning rag as he redecorates her room, comes upon the lighter hidden in her desk drawer. Suspicion is reciprocated. He does not trust her to be complicit, even though we know she already has been. Exchange of suspicion, mediated by the object, leads to breakdown. For him, rather than for her. The dramatic irony in Popaul's repossession of his lighter is that it *releases Hélène from complicity*. It is the object alone that seals the relationship. Once taken back, the complicit bond is broken. The exchange, where Hélène has shown all the signs of anguish and guilt, and Popaul has revealed none, is abrogated. When she realises the lighter has gone compassion and guilt turn to fear and desperation. Alone at night, she locks all the doors of the schoolhouse only to find he has already gained entry. The fusion of menace and suspense recall *Dial 'M' for Murder* where we know in advance the would-be murderer will enter furtively through the French windows, yet we still do not know the outcome of his intrusion. It is the same with Popaul. We suspect he will gain entry but cannot second-guess the outcome. What we find out in due course, however, is that the knife he draws is not intended for Hélène. Her very inaccessibility, her air of being untouchable that makes 'Mlle Hélène' perversely pure, also saves her life.

The point of encounter when the knife has been drawn is a pure Hitchcock moment. Hélène faints – one thinks of Scottie Ferguson and of Marnie here, not to mention *Spellbound*'s John Ballantyne – and the image fades out to black: when she comes to, the knife handle is pointing out of Popaul's stomach in which the blade is embedded. We can also think here of the knife sequence between the Verlocs that Hitchcock had filmed in *Sabotage*. The suspense proceeds from our uncertainty. Who will be stabbed? Who will die? In Hitchcock's film, the ambiguity hinges on the sharply edited movement of the couple around the dinner table. Did the wife actively stab the husband and or does he, complicit, draw himself onto the knife? Hitchcock uses montage here not to clarify things but to make them perennially ambiguous. In his simple reverse-angle shots Chabrol attempts the same. Does Hélène's fainting save her life, immobilise her as (no longer) a live and reactive woman who could then be a compelling victim? Is it his shame or her immobility that prompts Popaul to turn the knife upon himself? Or is it a deadly mix of both at the same time?

Whichever way we look at it, the consequence defines the first phase of the perverse miracle. He has taken his own life, and not hers. In the second phase she drives him to hospital in a doomed attempt to save him. Chabrol makes of it an eerie, unending journey, expressively lit, that takes in Popaul's last faltering confession. In the onrushing headlights where the trees are like petrified ghosts, Popaul himself is already a ghost. Ashen-faced yet always adoring her, he starts to fade away. At the entrance to the hospital lift as he is stretchered in, Hélène accedes to his last request. She kisses him moments before he enters the ascending lift, and then dies. The kiss is the final exchange, the act of compassion on the edge of life, a version of the last rites perhaps, that is still a substitute for a passion that never existed. Or is it? It broaches the question the audience must answer. If Hélène had loved him, would he have been otherwise? Would he never have killed? Yet the answer, clinically, has to be no. Chabrol refuses the romantic trap that has two traumatised people curing each other of their past nightmares. For this an impossible passion and shows the desperate and failed attempt of the couple to help each other *in its absence*. It is probably the greatest onscreen moment in Chabrol's career, a brilliant climax to an astonishing film. Yet it is also a completion of Hitchcock, a refinement of his themes and obsessions, done with boldness and daring that Hitchcock, after *Marnie*, no longer possessed. We might say that Chabrol, on his own terms, had completed Hitchcock's vision in a way that Hitchcock himself was no longer capable of doing. Yet this was also Chabrol's vision, and in 1969 the makeover was complete.

Hitchcock and Rohmer: small miracles

The difference between Rohmer and Chabrol's makeover of Hitchcock can be stated in a simple formula: Chabrol reworked the menace and the suspense while Rohmer jettisoned the menace and transformed the suspense. Menace is always related to the potential of the violent act. But in Rohmer's contemporary films, violence is conspicuous by its absence. Suspense, meanwhile, is redirected to the outcome of relationships, the end-point of intimacy. Rohmer's cinema thus remains microcosmic in scale, no politics, no espionage and no psychosis. There are no chases, no fugitives and no wrong man. But there is obsession and there is voyeurism. There is guilt and there is confession. Their practical consequences can be highly expressive but they are never conveyed by expressionistic means. In that respect Rohmer is the heir of Renoir and Rossellini and also of the whole tradition of French impressionism, an elegant lightness of touch rooted firmly in precise cityscapes or landscapes. For he always embeds his fiction in an actual world. Hitchcock's stylistic interplay of artifice and reality never enters his vision of contemporary life. If he uses studio interiors, as in Maud's apartment for *Ma nuit chez Maud*, the detail is always lifelike, true to scale and to the culture and décor of place and time. In low-budget films like *Pauline à la plage* (1983) he is happy to use recorded sound on location and dispense with artificial lighting for interiors altogether (see Almendros 1985: 267). For moving shots he is happier using a wheelchair or to have his crew push a soundless car than he is in laying actual tracks. In that respect Rohmer is a forerunner of low-budget film and digital video at the century's end, and ends up as an eighty-year-old veteran still making films about the young at heart.

If suspense revolves around intimacy rather than the chase or the killing, Rohmer nonetheless follows Hitchcock at times in focusing on encounters in transit. People not only meet and talk in rooms and cafes but at train stations, in buses and on trains. They meet on their travels, and especially on vacations to which they travel – witness Marie Rivière in *Le Rayon vert* (1986) whose summer vacation is a series of abortive and disconsolate journeys. There is also amid Rohmer's voyeurism, an intricate poetics of following. In *Ma nuit chez Maud*, Jean-Louis Trintignant uses his car to track down Marie-Christine Barrault on her bicycle where he meets her 'by chance' at least three times. In *Le Genou de Claire* Jean-Claude Brialy drives his flashy red speedboat across Lake Annecy to keep tabs on the teenage half-sisters whose life he is trying to control. And if talk in Rohmer seems so lengthy and confessional at times, it is also a key element of exchange which means the listener is often as important as the speaker. Like Hitchcock, Rohmer employs shot/countershot techniques to balance out the conversational exchange and generate the to-and-fro of filmic rhythm. Unlike Hitchcock, he eschews close-up and adheres strictly to the eye-level shot. He thus naturalises the conventions of talk and listening, as a thing of daily life, and places us next to his characters as witnesses to exchange.

The dynamics of exchange are founded not so much as in Hitchcock on lost identities as upon the existential seeking out of connection that links Rohmer back to the philosophical lineage of Sartre, De Beauvoir and Camus. Yet Rohmer's films do observe, like Hitchcock, the rhythmic counterpoint of stasis and motion. Although Rohmer has a preference for the static shot and the couple seated in conversation, mobility is crucial to his film poetics. From early on his vision of Paris in fact gives motion a peripatetic quality that is grimly comic and absurd; in *Le Signe du Lion* the abject journey of his bohemian American through the hot August of a deserted Paris is an existential journey into lost identity. Elsewhere, in his short films, the city lends itself to peripatetic madness – witness the obsessive stalking of two contrasting women by his dubious hero in *La Boulangère de Monceau*, or the daily commuter negotiating the pedestrian nightmare of *Place de l'Étoile* like a scared rabbit. Later *Les Nuits de la pleine lune* (1984) hones topography to a fine art as Pascale Ogier attempts to live a double life, single in the city centre and living with an architect in the new suburb of Marne La Vallée. The train commute plus the double life are a recipe for disaster as is the flaky marriage strategy of Béatrice Romand shuttling back and forth between Paris and Le Mans in *Le Beau marriage* (1982). Meanwhile the vacation is always the sign of going or being somewhere else. In Hitchcock, narrative change is a dramatic and sudden wrench out of the normal, a plunge into the unexpected: in Rohmer it means a trip that everyone takes in their own fashion at least once a year, often to be more normal by escaping from the abnormality of the city. Both directors use opposing means to generate suspense via the openness to encounter: Hitchcock through the extraordinary and Rohmer through the ordinary. In the films of the former we also expect something out of the ordinary, while in those of the latter we always expect the clinching detail within the ordinary.

On the subject of Rohmer's perverse miracle two key points can be made. Yes, *The Wrong Man* was one of his favourite miracle endings but so were those in two other films of the period, Dreyer's *Ordet* (1954) and Rossellini's *Voyage to Italy* (1953), where the religiosity of the miracle is much more explicit. At the same time there is a clear debt to Hitchcock and to Murnau's *Sunrise*. From Hitchcock can be derived Rohmer's miracles of *transit*, chance romance in train or bus that end *Le Beau mariage* (1982) and *Conte d'hiver* (1992), and from *Sunrise* the *miracle* of nature that ends *Le Rayon vert* and is spoofed a year later with the misfiring 'blue hour' in *Quatre aventures de Reinette et Mirabelle* (1987). In *Le Genou de Claire* there is a fluent combining of Hitchcock and Murnau: the speedboat journey across the lake followed by the storm during which Claire breaks down in tears and Jerome ambiguously comforts her. But then so is the ending of *Le Rayon vert* a seductive blend of the two sources. In its penultimate sequence the magical appearance of the green ray during Marie's last sunset in Biarritz (nature) lends the film's first note of enchantment to our tortuous heroine's sad summer. The following morning at the railway station en route for Paris (transit) she meets a handsome carpenter reading Dostoevsky. Is it a miracle that sad tearful heroines find true love at the last gasp or it more of a miracle that French carpenters read Dostoevsky in railway stations? Against the odds, Rohmer persuades us it is both at the same time. There is a tactile quality of the image, a naturalness in the meeting in the humdrum bustle of the station, a gentle facticity of encounter that wards off all temptation to dismiss it as romantic fantasy. And for those who insist on it, though it really does not matter, Jesus was a carpenter too.

Rohmer's perverse miracle is at first sight the intervention of chance, but at second sight it is the triumph of Grace over Chance that is shadowed but never overshadowed by Rohmer's irony. It contains too, Rohmer's fond but ironic take on Hitchcock's 'wrong man'. Until the railway station routing her back home every man she meets on holiday has been a version of the 'wrong man': the miracle of the carpenter is the miracle of the 'right man'. In Hitchcock the 'right man' is often the real culprit, the evasive criminal; in Rohmer he is the true lover, the last-ditch redeemer. (Rohmer replays the motif precisely with the romantic bus encounter that ends *Conte d'hiver*). The existence of Grace is like Pascal's wager on the existence of God, a theme that occupies the discussion in Maud's apartment near the start of the Clermont-Ferrand film, in a city after all, that was Pascal's birthplace. In the very making of the film certainly, there is a strong case for Grace. Did God intervene and provide with sweet timing the early December snows that make the black and white exteriors so beautiful to watch? In the film itself, does God intervene to firm up the chance meetings between the Jean-Louis Trintignant and Françoise (Marie-Christine Barrault), between the unnamed narrator and his blonde Catholic object of desire? The narrator shares with Vidal, his Marxist friend and ex-lover of Maud, a common love of Pascal, and both claim him as their own. Post-1968, Vidal claims him as the classic '*philo*' who tells us to wager on chance and by our actions give meaning to History. Defensively the narrator reclaims him as a Jansenist who tells us to wager on chance as a sign of Grace. The dark-haired Maud, divorced mother of the title, listens late at night to the thrust and counter-thrust of the argument, then brings it down from a realm of abstraction to a realm of erotic possibility. She has turned her living room into a bedroom salon where settled down in a white nightdress under a shiny white cover, she listens to them both. Finally she chooses Grace over History not because the narrator is more persuasive but because he is a sober new face and Vidal is an old drunken one.

Yet just as Maud 'chooses' the narrator, he has 'chosen' someone else and Rohmer makes of his film a crossover between Pascal's dilemma and

Hitchcock's *Vertigo*. The male dilemma of choosing between two females, yet still being indecisive, had been at the heart of his early work and short films. The inspiration of *Vertigo* now gives it a new edge, but with a Catholic blonde rather than a Hitchcock blonde and a reworked formula. The figure of Maud – intelligent, self-assured yet highly sensual – seems a composite of the shrewd observant Midge with the sexy working girl, Judy Barton. She is, like Midge, a figure largely confined to interiors while Françoise is an outdoor girl, a woman of locations like Madeleine Elster. Rohmer also replicates patterns of ascent and descent. At the start Trintignant stalks Barrault's moped in his car up the narrow winding streets of the city, while the pattern of stalking in *Vertigo* is largely down. Yet Clermont-Ferrand and San Francisco are cities of heights and Rohmer plays in addition on the narrator's commute from high in the hills, near where Françoise also lives. Thus he drives her back up to her student residence in the hills through the snow and stays when the snow closes in and forces him to abandon his car. Like Madeleine's jump into the water at Fort Point and Scottie's rescue that entails returning her 'unconscious' body to his apartment, this is a key moment of suspense where 'chance' draws the couple together. Both films share the suspense of the adjoining room where the desired woman is in bed, and of course in *Vertigo* Stewart has clearly undressed Novak to remove her wet clothes. In Hitchcock, suspense derives from the extraordinary; in Rohmer, of course, it is part of the 'ordinary' event. Trintignant merely enters the bedroom in the middle of the night for matches to light his cigarette. Barrault obliges and he duly returns to his own room. Yet the body language of mutual hesitation says it all. In both instances of 'chance' we realise there are strong elements of male design and female complicity.

Dénouement adds to the pattern. In *Vertigo* Madeleine turns out to be Judy, different altogether. In Rohmer's film Françoise seems a virtuous blonde but one of her previous lovers turns out to be Maud's ex-husband, a secret the narrator never discovers. Here Rohmer's irony disallows the chance that obsession will be fatal as it was with Scottie Ferguson. Unwittingly Trintingant, having rejected Maud retreads the path of Maud's husband who had also rejected Maud for Françoise. The key difference is knowledge. That Scottie should rumble Judy's dissembling leads to the film's tragic ending. Yet Maud's withholding of vital revelation from Rohmer's narrator saves his marriage though her voice-over, like Judy's flashback, informs the spectator of her rival's true past. Not being told, he is happy not to know, as is Françoise herself who is happy to listen to all his confessions of past loves, including Maud, and forgive him as long he knows nothing of her own fatal attraction.

A key moment here is the hillside sequence of the couple, the narrator and Françoise, perched high over the city as they talk and tussle in the driving snow. The shot recalls the sequences in *Suspicion* where Johnny Aysgarth roughly courts and reassures the resisting Lina at the cliff edge. Both are suspicious of what they do not know yet; Françoise, like Aysgarth, is more fearful of what the other may yet come to know. Unusually Rohmer's camera zooms in on each lover in turn, stressing the frailty of his or her trust amidst the hostile elements. It is a defining moment, the overcoming of suspicion in the midst of suspicion; and redemptive too, setting the tone for the climate change of the summer beach scene five years later where the narrator, now married and a doting father, bumps into Maud once more. The setting is idyllic as long as Maud holds her tongue, and it is clear the 'virtuous' blonde has become what the narrator wants her to be, a faithful spouse and devoted mother. The ideal has come down to earth. The 'miracle' as parents and child dash out into the sea is mundane, a joy in nature and life made possible by what is impossible for Scottie Ferguson, a forgetting and suppression of a painful past. But it is also perverse, since it depends entirely on the discretion of the very lover the narrator has rejected. Moreover, and very conveniently, life provides no Hitchcock suspense convention. There is no incriminating object of exchange: no ring, no necklace, no lighter, no front door key. Life can go on. The meaning is then clear. Life itself *is* the immediate source of the perverse miracle and unlike a traumatised Scottie, our naïve hero does not need a second chance.

chapter 7

INSIDE OUT: HITCHCOCK, FILM NOIR AND DAVID LYNCH

In the realm of film noir, vital truisms connect Hitchcock to contemporaries and successors. First, Hitchcock is *not* film noir but his 1940s films run parallel in fascinating ways. Second, his end-of-century legacy is one where a new generation – the figure of David Lynch looms large – has run Hitchcock and noir together, blending them with surprising results. The blend is down, in part, to matching Hitchcock's parallel work like *Shadow of a Doubt* or *Spellbound* with the post-noir greatness of the next decade – *Rear Window*, *Vertigo*, *Psycho* and *Marnie*. Of these *Vertigo* stands out on its own as a model for noir alternatives to stale Hollywood remakes of Hitchcock, for a diverse 'post-Hitchcock noir'. This rebirth, however, leads us back to a question many critics have failed to answer and which is the kernel of the first part of this chapter. Why were 1940s Hitchcock and 1940s noir not the same in the first place? Why, instead, were they running on parallel tracks? To flesh out the answer we can go literal and map out three variations on a theme, eleven features in two variants of the noir canon to match a Hitchcock XI; that is to say, a Classical noir XI of the 1940s and a Post-Hitchcock noir XI to complete the filmic triangle:

Hitchcock XI (1940–53)	Classic Film Noir XI (1941–50)
Rebecca	*The Maltese Falcon* (John Huston, 1941)
Suspicion	*Double Indemnity* (Billy Wilder, 1944)
Saboteur	*Fallen Angel* (Otto Preminger, 1945)
Shadow of a Doubt	*The Woman in the Window* (Fritz Lang, 1945)
Spellbound	*The Postman Always Rings Twice* (Tay Garnett, 1946)
Notorious	*The Big Sleep* (Howard Hawks, 1946)
The Paradine Case	*Out of the Past* (Jacques Tourneur, 1947)
Rope	*The Lady from Shanghai* (Orson Welles, 1948)
Stage Fright	*Criss Cross* (Robert Siodmak, 1949)
Strangers on a Train	*In a Lonely Place* (Nicholas Ray, 1950)
I Confess	*Sunset Boulevard* (Billy Wilder, 1950)

After Hitchcock's death in 1980 two films defined the transition to neo-noir: Lawrence Kasdan's *Body Heat* (1981) and David Lynch's *Blue Velvet* (1986). While Kasdan absorbed the power and legacy of *Vertigo* into his loose remake of *Double Indemnity*, Lynch used elements of *Shadow of a Doubt*, *Rear Window* and *Psycho* to fire the style and story of *Blue Velvet*. Hence *Body Heat* and *Blue Velvet* in turn moulded a loose genre of rich variation that includes the following, where Lynch's name dominates:

Post-Hitchcock Noir XI (1989–2001)

Kill Me Again (John Dahl, 1989)
Wild at Heart (David Lynch, 1990)
After Dark, My Sweet (James Foley, 1990)
Liebestraum (Mike Figgis, 1991)
One False Move (Carl Franklin, 1995)
The Underneath (Steven Soderbergh, 1995)
Le Confessionnal (Robert Lepage, 1996)
Lost Highway (David Lynch, 1997)
Memento (Christopher Nolan, 2000)
The Man Who Wasn't There (Joel and Ethan Coen, 2001)
Mulholland Dr. (David Lynch, 2001)

Comparing box-office figures across the three lists we could say that 1940s Hitchcock had won handsomely. Only a handful of 1940s noirs like *Gilda* (1947) with a sensual Rita Hayworth or *The Postman Always Rings Twice* from the James M. Cain novel with John Garfield and Lana Turner, matched the profits for *Rebecca*, *Saboteur*, *Spellbound*, *Notorious* or *Strangers on a Train*. Much of 1940s noir remained a B-movie genre. Likewise, post-Hitchcock noir has been on the margins of movie commerce, some of it comparable function-wise in the era of home viewing to the B-movie. (Neo-noir becomes cultish, that is, mainly through the media of art-house cinemas, video and now DVD.) Of course, *Blue Velvet*, *Memento* and *Mulholland Dr.* were also modest box-office successes. But they follow the neo-noir pattern: most have come from independent production with modest budgets, few big stars and low studio involvement. The mythic power of their narratives, and their audience appeal, derive from new explorations of the underside of American life and a continuing obsession with the roller coaster ride that is the American Dream. Yet they also absorb key elements of the Hitchcock narrative formula: a dynamics of exchange based on guilt, sexuality and memory. True, they represent only one strand of neo-noir in the period and there are others. We can think for a start of *comedy* noir with its dumb fall-guys and upfront femmes fatales that embraces *The Hot Spot* (1989), *Red Rock West* (1992), *The*

Last Seduction (1993), *Delusion* (1990), *U-Turn* (1997), *Palmetto* (1998) and the big hit of comedy noir (yet style-wise marginal since it is shot in garish 1950s Technicolor), *Pulp Fiction* (1994). The appeal of comedy noir is the appeal of chump fiction, the noir fall guy as a cartoon cut out, seemingly cool and loaded with irony yet doltish and heading for a fall. In contrast, post-Hitchcock variants go against the surface structure of the cartoon. They deepen noir ambiguities, glossing through their special take on male identity the shifting ambivalence of the embattled fall guy. And now that noir is identified as a special genre (which it was not in the 1940s) its attractions are much more self-conscious. Yet in 1940s and 1990s noir, one point of connection is clear. Talented directors float in and out of the genre so that it never completely defines them: in the 1940s Hawks, Welles, Wilder, Siodmak, Lang and Ray and in the 1990s Lynch, Dahl, Franklin, the Coens, Figgis, Tarantino and Soderbergh. Back in the 1940s Hitchcock, however, never moved in and out of anything. He was always at a precise tangent to noir in constructing his own vision, and never felt tempted to be part of it.

Hitchcock and 1940s noir

Usually film noir means all things to all people. Yet to label any crime thriller with dark menace and atmospheric lighting as 'noir' is not only misleading, it is so wide as to be vacuous. Classic noir is not just a style-legacy of Weimar cinema. It adds to Weimar considerably, making a virtue of necessity in its wartime economies of filming. This then is what we have been used to: low-key lighting and high-contrast photography in rooms with cross-hatched blinds, extreme camera angles, subjective distortion in the shot or in the ambience of city streets with mist and rain, seedy bars and diners, glistening sidewalks and neon light. The first thing to be said is that Hitchcock is a world apart from many elements of noir style. He will use distortion in the shot only if that shot is clearly subjective and a feature of altered states, like the hangover POV shot of Bergman watching Grant's morning entry into the bedroom in *Notorious*. Elsewhere he opts in most of his shots for 50mm lenses that mimic the field of human perception and also where possible, a more even lighting that would correspond to what his subjects might normally see. He thus dispenses with the extreme lighting economy of B noir set-ups, the excessive use of deep-focus or wide-angle, or the premeditated derangements of Orson Welles that evoke 1920s expressionism (see Naremore 1999: 269–70). And by the late 1940s he is already into colour with *Under Capricorn* and *Rope*, where he adds a new (anti-noir) dimension to the look of his cinema.

If Hitchcock differs stylistically from noir, this is only half the story. For noir house style does not define noir itself. All its style features can be run into a general conception of the genre and usually are. But they are not enough in themselves; we need to look for something deeper in the realm of plot and narration. The essence of noir is *thematic* in the tangent it takes to the nature of crime in the American way of life. Crime alone is not the subject. Noir is much more specific, highlighting the intent to kill and the consequences that result from a *financial conspiracy of passion.* Here the legacy of European *Kammerspiel* shows itself in the foregrounding of a triangular intimacy at the centre of criminal intent, where passion bursts into life and is then betrayed. Yet noir turns into American *Kammerspiel* and then opens it out, objectively, into the world of the city where it is chamber drama no more. Noir always conjoins two kinds of plots, the plotting of its filmmakers with the plotting of its lovers. Here the intimate noir triangle (two plotters, one victim) is usually of *two* kinds, *bourgeois* as in *Double Indemnity* or *Sunset Boulevard,* or *criminal* as in *The Killers* (1946) or *Criss Cross*: in *Double Indemnity* wife, bourgeois husband and wife's lover and in *Criss Cross,* gangster, gangster's girl and girl's lover. Typically the class difference shows in the different LA locations of Billy Wilder and Robert Siodmak. Wilder's bourgeois ambience leads him to shoot in the plush suburbs of Bel Air, Glendale and West Hollywood while in *Criss Cross* Siodmak opts for the downtown area around Union Station and the blue-collar apartments of Bunker Hill, later shooting the robbery at a Terminal Island factory: all working-class locations, ignoring the suburbs entirely (see Davis 2001: 38–40). In *Criss Cross* Burt Lancaster and Yvonne de Carlo meet up in the steamy La Rondo cabaret bar. In *Double Indemnity* Fred MacMurray and Barbara Stanwyck conspire in a bright new supermarket. (In contrast to both, Hitchcock may have lived in Bel Air but *Saboteur* apart, he never set any of his films in Los Angeles, and never filmed there substantially outside the studio until *Family Plot.*)

Whatever its class ambience, noir narration broadens out the fatal triangle of fall guy, *femme fatale* and victim by adding on financial *exchange* to its conspiracy of passion. Money translates into imaginary success – as wealth for Phyllis Dietrichson or as fame for Norma Desmond in *Sunset Boulevard* who buys in debt-ridden screenwriter Joe Gillis as a gigolo and a kept man. But money also involves murder, the ultimate crime: a conspiracy of passion where crime and success, usually as murder and money, are brought into play as offshoots of desire. A murderous fate thus binds the ties of erotic and monetary exchange then rips them asunder. As fall guy Walter Neff confesses after killing Phyllis's husband in *Double Indemnity* and suffering the double-cross that follows: 'I didn't get the money, and I didn't get the girl.' James Damico has given us the most succinct account of this passion-triangle at the heart of noir narration (1996: 102–4). We can articulate his insights further and be more categorical. The central motif of 1940s noir, affirmed most emphatically by *Double Indemnity,* is this: Eros makes no sense without the desire for wealth or fame, which means nothing in turn without criminal ambition, through which desire translates itself into a willingness to kill. In noir narration *Double Indemnity* set the standard in 1944 for all to come, right up to its dreamlike, turn-of-the-century apotheosis in David Lynch's *Mulholland Dr.*

Three interconnected elements come to define noir conspiracies of passion: ambition, Eros and betrayal. Desire, plotting, blackmail, and often the switch of allegiance followed by the double-cross (victim turns into plotter and plotter into victim): all testify to the brittle nature of trust, to a simmering lust just on the right side of the Studio Code, and to the deep ubiquity of suspicion. The steamy dynamics of exchange intensify as conspiracy moves up a gear in the storyline. The ensuing suspense has much in common with that of Hitchcock. In his work too suspicion, blackmail and double-cross are key modes of exchange. But if comparison with noir easily goes this far, at a certain point it goes no further. There is a barrier, a dividing line that starts with style-differences but then runs deeper. As noted, Hitchcock's aesthetics do provide a key. His camera is much more intimate, more subtly attentive to his subjects and the changing relations between them. It is a close witness to the intense liaison and its deepening ambiguities. There are none of the complex alienation-effects of Welles, few expressionist tricks outside the POV shot, no stereotyping of role or character, no hard-boiled dialogue. It thus seemed predictable that his collaboration with Raymond Chandler on the screenplay for *Strangers on a Train* was doomed to failure. Working together on *Double Indemnity* Wilder and Chandler had had their tensions but co-existed. For Hitchcock, who demanded that dialogue served his images, Chandler's work was judged inadequate and Hitchcock brought in Czenzi Ormonde to produce a new script days before shooting was scheduled to begin (see Krohn 2000: 115–16). In general the hard-boiled idiom creates distancing effects for camera and spectator alike and was unsuited to Hitchcock's vision. Moreover it often gives the spoken word priority over the image, the exact opposite of what Hitchcock had taken from the silent cinema of Weimar.

The Hitchcock/noir impasse has three other key dimensions. The first lies in a reversal of gender roles, the second in the contrast between noir and Hitchcock murders and the third in the Hitchcock element normally missing from noir transactions, the transfer of guilt. Differing plot outcomes between noir and Hitchcock are derived from all three elements and from the contrasting structures of feeling they generate, structures that govern the look and the feel of the picture. At origin, they also spring out of contrasting legacies. Despite Weimar sourcing common to both, noir adds on the heritage of popular American fiction, the hard-boiled thriller of Dashiell Hammett, Raymond Chandler and James M. Cain, while Hitchcock's literary ties are elsewhere, with adventure-flight narration, romantic irony and the Gothic turn of late-romanticism. The results are clear. Hitchcock has no tough-talking private eyes, no cynical gangsters, no brassy *femme fatales*. Noir has no poetics of redemption, no transfer of guilt and no intimation of miracles. Noir boldly features upfront its tough-talking grotesques, its gangsters and low-lives. Hitchcock spins out evil in unlikely places, often in a web of bourgeois corruption where decorum and formality still reside in everyday life. Here those who escape the web may be flawed and complicit in deed but can yet rediscover purity of heart. Noir's fatal endings destroy such an option and the Good who survive, as they must under the auspices of the Studio Code, are often too good to be true, honest investigators or minor characters of shining virtue that close the film under the watchful eye of the Code, but also threaten to close it off.

Hitchcock/noir gender-reversal holds throughout the period. If noir typically pits the fall guy against his erotic adversary, the *femme fatale*, Hitchcock's terms reverse it and had *preceded* it in *Suspicion*, giving us a different formula: *fall girl* pitched against *homme fatal*. A further difference ensures. The Hitchcock murder victim is usually female, the culprit usually male: the noir victim is usually male, the culprits usually male and female in joint conspiracy. American Hitchcock set the standard in 1941. In *Suspicion* fall girl Joan Fontaine marries the charming Cary Grant who turns out to be the perfect *homme fatal*, even though the Studio Code forbids him to poison her and forces Hitchcock to change the film's original ending. Moreover Fontaine not only feels fearful and suspicious but also guilty, as if there is something she may have done to provoke Grant's unpredictability. Teresa Wright duly follows suit in *Shadow of a Doubt*, guilty that she has fallen in love with a serial widow murderer who is also her uncle. The world of noir is entirely different. It may be a 'bright, guilty world' as Mike O'Hara's voice-over tells us in *The Lady from Shanghai*, but no one in that film ever feels truly guilty, and if they appear to, as Hayworth's Elsa Bannister does when it suits her, they are faking it. It is a guiltless genre. In *Double Indemnity* fall guy Walter Neff feels stupid and bitter for having been fooled by Phyllis Dietrichson, but hardly guilty. His Dictaphone confesses mistakes of judgement and strategy but no real lapses of conscience, though Wilder clearly meant his censors to confuse the former with the latter. There is a line, of course, that has to be crossed at the start. Few fall guys, who often start off as regular guys, are willing to risk murder if they know they are going to be double-crossed afterwards. For the Walter Neffs of this world there is no lingering guilt; the feeling of stupidity outweighs remorse for they have simply gambled and made the wrong move.

The nature of the calculated murder must differ too. In Hitchcock it is an amoral absolute: comic at times, perhaps macabre, always ambiguous but always signifying the existence of a clear evil. In noir all values are relative.

Murder starts off as a means to an end, to that blend of success and desire in which unwanted spouse or rival is dispatched, freeing up a heady blend of wealth and passion as the ultimate American Dream. For if you get away with the murder you free up your own future and need transgress no further. Or so the rationale goes. Noir conspiracy is notionally one-off transgression, enabling lovers in their daydreams to be absorbed by a vast open society where they can reinvent themselves. Except that conspiracy to murder itself corrupts and double-cross duly follows as night follows day. There are of course variations. In *The Big Sleep* it looks at one point as if Vivian Sternwood (Lauren Bacall) will double-cross Marlowe (Humphrey Bogart) by going back to Eddie Mars. But she never does, knowing on which side her bread is now buttered. If she has been complicit in the blackmailing of her younger sister and the mayhem that follows, we never know for sure, and Marlowe has his own reasons for turning a blind eye, hoping to claim her as his prize when he closes the case. He knows, shrewdly, when to ask questions and when not to. Thus convenient for the film's happy ending is the fact that the ex-lover to be dispatched is gangster and blackmailer Eddie Mars who gets his comeuppance in line with the Code. Yet in classic gangster noir it usually works the other way round. In *Out of the Past* cold-blooded killer Kathy (Jane Greer) betrays ex-lover Jeff Bailey (Robert Mitchum) because she is still hooked into gangster-villain Whit Sterling (Kirk Douglas). Likewise in *Criss Cross*, the double-cross comes during the robbery when co-plotter and *femme fatale* Yvonne de Carlo betrays ex-husband Burt Lancaster to whom she has returned, only for her gangster boyfriend Dan Duryea to take revenge on both of them. Siodmak here repeats the fatalistic patterns of betrayal and double-cross he had already fashioned a year earlier in *The Killers* where fall guy Lancaster is obsessed by Ava Gardner as Kitty Collins, the sensual *femme fatale* who then ditches him to go back to her gangster-husband. The film unreels in multiple flashbacks after Lancaster calmly awaits and receives the fate of assassination for his own double-cross over the robbery in which all had conspired. Siodmak, often seen with Lang as the true embodiment of the German legacy in Hollywood, seems closer in tone and mood to the dark poetic realism of Marcel Carné where Lancaster is his Jean Gabin and fate is given new existential qualities.

Noir thus reverses the Hitchcock point of view premised on the woman, whose sharp nuances made such stars of Joan Fontaine and Ingrid Bergman. It is the noir fall guy who has the voice-over, the flashback and the POV shots embracing his treacherous object of desire. Or, if he does not, it is investigators like Edmund O'Brien in *The Killers* whose quest homes in on the life and fate of the doomed Lancaster, eliciting in the style of *Citizen Kane* multiple flashbacks from those who knew him. The gender oppositions of classic noir and Hitchcock pave the way for oppositions of surface and depth. In noir the first-person voice-over is terse, hard-boiled, the flashback dreamy but functional; the *femme fatale* ends up more often a figure of transparency than of mystery, a woman who clearly dissembles and not a woman of guilt, remorse, dilemma and hesitation. The noir *femme fatale* is disconcerting because of the *absence* of guilt, the Hitchcock heroine disconcerting because of the *excess* of guilt. The latter are the qualities we find in the Fontaine/Bergman personae of the 1940s, explored by Hitchcock in a way that no Hollywood director of the time except for Max Ophuls, ever did. Meanwhile as ageing *femme fatale* Norma Desmond, Gloria Swanson epitomises the noir opposite in *Sunset Boulevard*'s closing sequence. She displays no remorse for the killing of her young screenwriter/lover (William Holden), misreading the press flashbulbs as signs of fame, not guilt, as she momentously descends her mansion's outer staircase into the arms of the waiting police. In Hitchcock the resistant, suspicious heroine faces off the *homme fatal*: personified by Grant in *Suspicion* and *Notorious* as the unreadable face of male intention that is matched by Cotten in *Shadow of a Doubt*, by Peck in the opening of *Spellbound* and at a fascinating tangent, by Montgomery Clift in *I Confess*. Yet Hitchcock's *homme fatal* is a case study in ambivalence – witness *Suspicion*. When Lina tumbles from the car during the famous coastal ride, does Johnny push her or try to prevent her falling? In noir only Rita Hayworth in *The Lady from Shanghai* matches the enigma and mystery of Hitchcock's Grant but Welles is so concerned to deconstruct her star icon and plunge her into one farce after another that Hayworth becomes enigmatic *in spite of* everything that happens to her. Grant, on the contrary, is enigmatic *because* of everything that happens, and Hitchcock plays on the constant hiatus between intention and action, where every act he performs can be read in at least two ways.

Gender-reversal has its knock-on effect in the arena of killing. The Hitchcock woman is a redeeming force, a way out of the impasse of transgression. In contrast the Hitchcock murder has a male perpetrator, who in the 1940s films is usually an outsider, a fascinating yet distanced figure for the audience. The exception of course is *The Paradine Case*, with the enigmatic Valli as his guilty murderess; the closest Hitchcock ever came to noir. But this is courtroom drama with a murder based on a passion (for husband's valet Latour) that is never shown, a solitary crime of passion bereft of financial motive and conspiracy. Its transgression lies elsewhere and also, under the watchful eye of the Studio Code, discreetly veiled: it is murder borne out of heterosexual desire for a gay lover. Elsewhere the Hitchcock murder has a distinctly male profile. It is a hovering threat that turns into a chilling, enigmatic deed and at times it bears a precise ideological freight that arises from the Nazi catastrophe. It is, primarily, the deed of the pseudo-Nietzschean *Übermensch*, of perpetrators who consider themselves above humanity. In different films it takes different forms but always this is the common denominator. In the spy narratives, of course, the intending killers are Nazis and Hitchcock makes sure we see them on the surface as stock characters, as normal as the neighbour next door in some ways but in other ways as cold, calculating figures who consider themselves beyond morality. At first sight this achievement might seem all too easy. Yet the dull banality with which the talented Welles treats the same theme in *The Stranger* (1946) shows just how effective Hitchcock is. If Hitchcock offers us a Langian version of murderers amongst us, it is also a bourgeois one with no low-life psychopaths in sight. Most of his murderers have impeccable bourgeois credentials, and if they do not, their confederates do. Both *Saboteur* and *Notorious* feature elegant parties run by Nazi murderers in large studio mansions. The fanatic proto-Nietzschean killers of *Rope*, both preppy young men, hold their elegant apartment soirée with refreshments offered on the chest containing their victim's corpse. In *Shadow of a Doubt* wealthy widow-slayer Joseph Cotten is a fastidious and elegant dandy with excellent manners. In *Spellbound* fastidious asylum director Leo Carroll finally confesses to killing his rival with the clinical air by which he might dissect the actions of a deranged patient. In *Strangers on a Train* Bruno is a spoilt rich brat full of contempt for humans, and his perverse exchange-agenda shows him quite happy to kill someone he has never met if it furthers his own aims.

Hitchcock's male killers are respectable psychotics who wish to alter the world to conform to their own perverted vision of what it might become. They can be part of a collective madness or simply menacing loners: Nazi, Nietzschean or seriously schizophrenic like Norman Bates. By contrast, noir conspirators might be edgy or neurotic in the face of suspicion but they do what they do because they like the world as it is, and want more of it than they normally get. Wealth, success, fame, beauty – these are the goals, selfish no doubt but also a sign of desired autonomy, to go outside the fabric of conformity and routine in collective Fordist America, to be someone standing out from the crowd, not in order to be superhuman but to enjoy the good life to the full. In *Double Indemnity* Barbara Stanwyck's discontented housewife, Phyllis Dietrichson, is the Ur-sign of noir's blonde ambition. If only He (the husband) was out of the way, if only we could collect on the insurance policy, if only the other He who is part of the We (fall-guy lover) was also disposable, the world would open up, as it never has before. The logic of this reasoning heads out in the end towards self-destruction but the premise is clear. America is the dreamland of opportunity, where all possibilities can be considered and soon you can lose sight of all contexts and all limit in your delirium. Hard-boiled is the fleeting illusion of an arrow's trajectory that never falls or comes to rest; noir endings are the shattering of that illusion.

The Hitchcock/noir opposition can also be seen in a different light, as contrasting European visions of America, its promise and its danger. But

Fig. 10 Two into three won't go: Farley Granger, Robert Walker and Ruth Roman in *Strangers on a Train*

then the United States from its very inception has been a land of incom-
ers. In our classic noir XI five listed directors are European. Three of these
– Lang, Wilder, Preminger – are Austrians with Berlin experience (to which
in the noir canon could be added their Viennese associate Edgar Ulmer with
his low-budget gem *Detour* (1945) made in six days) while the fourth, Robert
Siodmak, a Berlin colleague of Wilder and Ullmer, grew up in Leipzig. The
fifth is Frenchman Jacques Tourneur, whose *Out of the Past* has a dreamier,

more poetic style that in contrast links him to the pre-war cinema of French Impressionism. Yet this too is equally distant from American hard-boiled. Of the four American directors three – Huston, Hawks and Garnett – are directing versions of popular novels, known commodities brought to the screen. The exception is Nicholas Ray, a genuine American romantic who goes beyond the hard-boiled style his films embrace. At the end of the 1940s *In a Lonely Place* is the key film to bridge the divide between noir and Hitchcock since it oscillates between fingering each of its lovers, Humphrey Bogart and Gloria Grahame (like Hitchcock's Valli), as figures of unreadable intent whose motives engender mutual suspicion and destroy a short-lived passion. Neither proves to be a fatal figure in the order of things – there is no killing other than the murder Bogart did not commit – but both are figures of ambivalence. The film insinuates that under the right circumstances either could be deadly in their actions. Is the violent Bogart homicidal in nature despite his innocence of the murder where he is wrongly suspected? Is Grahame by nature perfidious by having an affair with an older woman (her masseuse) despite her pleas of heterosexual loyalty? The alternation between male and female suspicion is balanced, ambiguous and fascinating. There is no noir fall-out, but neither is there female redemption.

Outside of Ray, much of noir originality comes from the work of recent émigrés casting a fresh eye on the American experience but also, like Hitchcock, bringing something of their own with them. Noir narrative taps indirectly into the horrors of a European war whose horrors are often unspeakable. The process is oblique yet the legacy is there. Lang and Preminger's studio films show clear traces of the clinical vision of the New Objectivity. *Fallen Angel*, however, Preminger's taut drama of smalltown California with long mobile takes that echoes *Shadow of a Doubt*, is much closer to Siodmak's narratives, to the atmospherics of a dark fatalism, prefacing death and destruction. Wilder's two great renderings of noir *folie à deux*, *Double Indemnity* and *Sunset Boulevard*, start off with fall guys who want to exit the corporate order of the new America; Walter Neff from the soulless factory-style office of Pacific All Risk Insurance modelled, quite possibly, on Paramount's New York office (Naremore 1998: 86), while Joe Gillis (William Holden) finally opts for the Renaissance style mansion of the demented Norma Desmond (Gloria Swanson) where he becomes Norma's kept man, in preference to the screenwriting offices at Paramount where he had been a hireling at the heart of the studio machine. The *folie à deux* is thus a way out of the soulless organisation, images of which permeate most of Wilder's work up to *The Apartment* (1960). It touches base with the dark culture critique of the new industrial age brought west by German critics like Siegfried Kracauer and Theodor Adorno and which is rendered here with much intelligence but little concession to intellect. It is intuitive, and triumphantly so, a necessary foil to the myth of individualism that prompts its noir couples along the road to self-destruction.

In contrast Hitchcock, who came from a country fortunate enough to escape Nazi occupation, shows us a redemptive power in human nature amidst the forces of darkness. Here the special case of *Strangers on a Train* deserves closer scrutiny. Patricia Highsmith's 1950 debut novel with its fateful train encounter had been read in galley form by Hitchcock, Alma and Whitfield Cook (who did the film treatment) while travelling back on a train to California from the East Coast (McGilligan 2003: 441–2). Through it Hitchcock was able to filter many of the homosexual elements in *Rope* but here the obsession of one man for another that is covertly reciprocal, is made much more complex. Indeed, Highsmith could well have been inspired by *Rope* in her crossover tale about two men who meet on a train and then exchange murders, one man's wife traded in death for the other man's father. For her enigmatic detective, Gerard, who suspects Guy and Bruno (in the novel Anthony Bruno, in the film Bruno Anthony) then finally tracks Guy down after Bruno's drowning, is reminiscent of *Rope*'s Rupert Cadell not only in his full tenacity, but also in his prior and complicit acquaintance with Bruno. Significantly, Hitchcock's film removes Gerard from the plot and more significantly rescues Guy – with one eye no doubt on the Studio Code – from malice aforethought and murder most foul. Unlike Highsmith's Guy, Hitchcock's Guy refuses his side of the murder bargain and escapes the web of complicity through which Bruno tries to blackmail him, to fulfil his ambition and marry the Senator's daughter. But Hitchcock leaves enough clues to suggest the power of guilt-transfer and the subterranean workings of desire. As in the novel, Bruno goes ahead unilaterally and murders Guy's wife, thus setting his new 'friend' free to remarry Anne (Ruth Roman), but also makes Guy indebted to him.

Hitchcock then plays on the ambiguity of Guy's visit to Bruno's father. The script dialogue tells us that Guy intends to warn the father of his son's murderous intent. Yet visually Hitchcock tells a different story. The furtive late-night visit with the pistol, the stealthy entrance into the family mansion by the front door key that Bruno has given him, the tiptoeing up the dark unlit staircase past the family dog to the father's bedroom; all suggest Guy may well have wished to carry out the murder Bruno has suggested. When Bruno is discovered in his absent father's bed, Guy of course protests his real intent and leaves in disgust. But there is more than a hint in his contrary state that he had thought of murder: in addition a sly insinuation on Hitchcock's part of his latent desire when he discovers his foe, the object of his love-hate, between the sheets. Is this an overt nightmare transformed into a covert daydream? (The fact that Guy is dressed in a tuxedo and not pyjamas would satisfy the censors that this was not the intended meaning.) Yet Bruno plays a double role that goes beyond the heterosexual premise of noir conspiracy. At the funfair he lures Guy's wife away from her pals by a desiring look, which she readily reciprocates, as a prelude to strangling her. He now casts the same desiring gaze on Guy, guilty with knowledge of Bruno's murderous act and himself suspected of it by the police.

Hitchcock here turns the noir formula inside out, with Bruno as insane *homme fatal* and Guy as his bait. Instead of the lover killing the husband because he desires the wife, we have the lover killing the wife because he desires the husband. Usually the cuckolded noir spouse is the source of the loot to be transferred into the lovers' hands, but here Guy is the source of something else too. As a big tennis star he is bathed in celebrity, and Bruno's desire is clearly narcissistic, desire not only for the handsome body of the male Other he wishes to possess but for the stardom that goes with it. As ever Hitchcock confounds us through his casting, his homosexual rogue played by a straight Robert Walker and his girl-romancing tennis star played by a gay Farley Granger. After *The Manxman, Murder!, Rebecca, The Paradine Case* and *Rope* the film contains his sixth variation, we might say, on a covert queer aesthetic. Yet Hitchcock was not finished. For in his next film, the religious psychodrama *I Confess*, he used gay actors Montgomery Clift and O. E. Hasse for the key roles of the wrongly accused priest and his murderer double, the sacristan (Spoto 1983: 340). Like *Strangers on a Train* this film plays off ambiguous sexuality against complex guilt transfers, but buries it away from the Code – as we shall see – in a patchwork of half-truths and duplicity.

Vertigo and after

If classical Hitchcock turns noir inside out, his boldest ever film turns it completely upside down. How in fact did *Vertigo* achieve this? The motion is two-fold. First the film appears to construct a noir *femme fatale* as a figure of mystery, following Rita Hayworth's role in *The Lady from Shanghai*, but then it deconstructs that mystery by giving us the secret of Madeleine's true identity two-thirds of the way through Judy's flashback. By turning Madeleine back to Judy, Hitchcock transforms his would-be *femme fatale* into a nervous fall-girl, manipulated then abandoned. In the background Gavin Elster hovers as the ruthless male of unreadable intention, the *homme fatal* whose true motive Scottie fails to decipher. Boldly Hitchcock also plays with the sexual identity of his male protagonist, feminising Scottie in his obsession with a ghost-woman who *embodies as beautiful* his own secret obsession with death. Yet in the second part of the film Scottie's desperation makes him ruthless. His makeover of Judy is a fanatic strategy for making love to her in the image of Madeleine, fulfilling his desire to lay a beautiful ghost. When he twigs her true identity, however, the return to the Mission tower is

Fig. 11 Beseeching a beautiful ghost: James Stewart and Kim Novak in *Vertigo*

neatly poised through its ambiguity. We can never truly read his intention. Is he dragging her up the staircase to punish her for deceit, to cure his vertigo, to consummate their passion the second time around or to lead her to her death? Or is it a mixture of all of these things that Scottie simultaneously desires? His nightmare journey is a tale of two instalments, the first in the role of feminised fall-guy and the second in the guise of ruthless *homme fatal*, while Novak's is the same journey in reverse. In the first instalment she is the *femme fatale* as beautiful ghost and in the second the nervous fall-girl as palpable flesh and blood.

A key transformation of noir, inconceivable without *Vertigo*, is to be found at the start of the 1980s in Lawrence Kasdan's *Body Heat* with its clear elements of pastiche. Yet Kasdan's film is set in the present with a critical edge to its view of contemporary mores that echoes Wilder at his best. The film's passionate intimacy, however, is closer in tone to *Notorious* or *Vertigo* than it is to *Double Indemnity* or *The Killers*. Moreover as a film of the post-Studio Code era it is sexually explicit and morally unbound. *Femme fatale* Matty Walker (Kathleen Turner) ghosts through the hot humid summer of an atmospheric smalltown Florida, eluding the law, explicitly sampling the body of fall-guy lawyer Ned Racine (William Hurt) and escaping with the inheritance gained from her husband's murder, for which Racine takes the rap. Turner is a post-*Vertigo femme fatale* in dress, in manner, in movement, in mystery. Kasdan has remarked that his noir fall-guy was someone of his own generation 'who just happens to be the film noir world, but ... is really a 1960s character' (Fuller 1994: 125). Yet Hurt is also one stage on from the 1970s anti-hero, possessing the existential, maverick qualities of New American Cinema but now seduced in the age of Ronald Reagan by the ease of abundant sex, by monetary ambition and the big financial score, all values of Self over Other, ego over moral worth. Kasdan's film is post-Hitchcock noir as the dream of the counter-culture gone sour, or at best uneasily absorbed into the older American Dream that is now even more amoral than ever, and in which women now have a more equal part. After the boathouse fire at the film's climax, Matty disappears from Ned's life as a nighttime ghost exactly, we might add, in the same languid manner in which she had appeared, ghosting suddenly out of an open-air concert and across Ned's sightline on the waterfront. The spirit of late Hitchcock thus inflects neo-noir intimacy in surprising ways, an inflection that takes different forms right up to the turn of century.

Hitchcock and Lynch: American Gothic and second chances

After *Body Heat*, with its languid pacing and sensuous retro-style, post-Hitchcock noir divides into two connected categories, the *memory noir* and David Lynch. Both press at the metaphysical boundaries of the genre but if the former is neatly original, then Lynch is truly formidable. If Hitchcock had turned classic noir inside out, we could say that Lynch turns Hitchcock outside in with four memorable films: *Blue Velvet, Wild at Heart, Lost Highway* and *Mulholland Dr.* While *Body Heat* had forged a revolution in style that revived the caustic noir observation of contemporary mores, it was still a remake of *Double Indemnity.* Lynch creates new dimensions altogether. His four features set up a cinematic universe to rival the key quartet of neo-modern Hitchcock – *Rear Window, Vertigo, North by Northwest* and *Psycho.* The compression in Hitchcock is remarkable, six years from 1954 to 1960. In Lynch it is spread out, diffused through all of sixteen years. And yet the match is uncanny, three very dark, complex pictures, offset in each case by a fugitive-romance. Although the chronology is different – Lynch's adventure-romance is second in his quartet, Hitchcock's third in his – there is parity in the aesthetics of evil, and in the balance of light and darkness. Like *Rear Window* and *North by Northwest, Blue Velvet* and *Wild at Heart* are fables of nail-biting redemption; like *Vertigo* and *Psycho, Lost Highway* and *Mulholland Dr.* are fables of intimate catastrophe. The jury is still out on whether or not Lynch's vision matches in scale and power that of later Hitchcock. Critics are divided; judgement may be premature. What cannot be denied are the closeness and continuity, the *affinity*, even though Lynch is a filmmaker for a different generation with altered obsessions, sometimes so bold in his attraction to risk that he fails to take his audience with him.

Blue Velvet has been compared to *Psycho* in its stark treatment of psychotic evil, but the deeper link is surely with *Rear Window*, a film Lynch has acknowledged as a Hitchcock favourite (see Lynch 1997: 57). Its premise is curiosity, an investigation that draws others in and proceeds against the odds to a battered triumph. It entails overstepping the mark in a precise way. At a key point, curiosity shades into voyeurism with its own addictions that become irreversible. Yet again an implausible story of evil turns out to be entirely plausible. Like Jeff in *Rear Window*, Jeffrey (Kyle MacLauchlan) in *Blue Velvet* becomes a driven Peeping Tom, nosing out vital evidence by dubious means and with all the moral ambiguity that entails. Of course he is also, unlike the disabled Jeff, physically active in his search for danger and courting disaster; more reminiscent in that respect of Melanie Daniels' foray into the Brenner attic in *The Birds* when she invites horrifying attack. Certainly when Jeffrey breaks into Dorothy Vallens' apartment using Sandy (Laura Dern), a detective's daughter, as his foil, he gets more than he bargained for. We see here a reprise of the Stewart-Kelly relation in Hitchcock's film with the roles reversed. Jeffrey initiates and enters with Sandy as innocent accomplice. Unlike Hitchcock's camera, which stays in Jeff's room, Lynch's camera follows Jeffrey's nightmare into the Tall River Apartments, a dark city hulk looming out of Lumberton's pleasant smalltown architecture. If Lynch upends the investigative premise of *Rear Window* based on remote control, he also reverses the smalltown premise in *Shadow of a Doubt*, where evil intrudes from the outside in the form of Uncle Charlie. Here it is firmly embedded at the centre of things, in the plotting between the psychotic Frank Booth (Dennis Hopper) and a corrupt local cop, and it has deep roots. The American late-century smalltown is no longer in Lynch's vision of things a haven from anything corrupt and certainly not from the narcotics trade and the killings that surround it.

Like Hitchcock, Lynch takes his visual sense of place into the realm of the Gothic while retaining his clear sense of the realm of the ordinary. It is a similar talent for distilling menace out of the look of the everyday and the normal, and it also means taking Gothic out of its primal realm of design and ruin. Unlike Hitchcock, Lynch's Gothic at times *overpowers* the ordinary. Any building, any place, any shape can be endowed with menacing qualities, above all the sense of a lived-in place that bears the threat of death – isolated, claustrophobic, gone to ruin or decay. Lynch thus turns a cliché of schlock-horror into a truism of pure cinema. After all, every edifice contains within it the future seeds of its decay and in Lynch that imminence of decay seeps through its very walls. In his own period Hitchcock could turn any building into a theatrical set that exudes Gothic chill. But he also set the future standard in *Psycho* where the sense of menace is balanced out between the Bates mansion and the flat modernistic structure of the Bates motel. One murder takes place in each; neither can act as sanctuary from the other. If some people nowadays are still scared by Gothic mansions, others are scared by motels in the middle of nowhere. That is down in part to a fear of rootlessness in a mobile wide-open society, but in part also to the notoriety of Hitchcock's films. The edifice as part ruin, part trap and always drenched in neglect is a Gothic trope the cinema can transform in different ways and no one does this better in late century than Lynch. There are so many variations. The Texas motel in *Wild at Heart*, the dingy trailer at Deer Meadow but also Laura's sweet suburban home in *Twin Peaks: Fire Walk with Me* (1992), the modernistic fortress of *Lost Highway*'s Hollywood hideaway, the decayed Spanish-colonial apartments 'Betty' and 'Rita' check out in *Mulholland Dr.* all suffer ineffable haunting. In Lynch as in Hitchcock any home or resting-place can turn a sanctuary into a prison.

The casting of Isabella Rossellini as singer Dorothy Vallens positions her persona intriguingly between Hitchcock and classic noir as a woman whose unstable image shifts back and forth between *femme fatale* and abject victim, so much so it defies obvious labelling. With her screen voice uncannily a dead ringer for that of mother Ingrid in Hitchcock's 1940s films, Rossellini's role oscillates between wishing to seduce and punish with Jeffrey as victim, and wishing to be violated and punished with Frank as tormentor. It is a masochistic desire that goes beyond her tactical submission to Frank's blackmail in order to save her kidnapped family. Here when Rossellini's Dorothy finally springs the Gothic trap and escapes bruised and naked from her tormentors she recalls her mother's close escapes from poisoning at the end of *Notorious* and *Under Capricorn*. But she is out in the open, fleeing across suburban lawns, vulnerable and exposed. Meanwhile Lynch's villains are more firmly in the noir lowlife tradition, which they duly update. Their simmering menace, their singular and unpredictable natures enable him to avoid cliché. They are his exemplars of unreadable evil, existential sociopaths that elude definition and take gangsterism beyond the confines of genre. Cinematically Lynch *reinvents* evil for the late twentieth century. Coppola or Scorsese this is not, nor is it either when Lynch shifts focus from drugs to pornography in *Lost Highway*.

In this film, unreadable male and female purposes co-exist: both spring from unreadable identity. The doubling of identity here indicates something new in Lynch, a form of *meta-noir* where the parameters of sense-experience are broken and violated. In *Blue Velvet*, of course, there is only one Frank Booth but in *Lost Highway* Mr Eddy is also Dick Laurant. Instead of one Jeffrey there is Fred Madison (Bill Pullman) and Pete Dayton (Balthazar Getty) as matching formations of the same persona; instead of one Sandy there is Patricia Arquette as the dark-haired Renée *and* the blonde Alice. At Andy's party for hedonistic LA wannabes, Fred meets the Mystery Man (Robert

Blake), who then persuades Fred to phone him at Fred's home, thus contacting his voice-double over a cell phone. Identities multiply, are lost, found and then lost again; in *Mulholland Dr.* they go even further into a delirious circulation of names in continual transfer. Here Lynch clearly outbids Hitchcock in his ambition to juxtapose and to intermingle life and dream. He makes of the two modalities a simultaneous happening. In Hitchcock there is a clear empirical line to narrative that will, however, also be dreamlike in its residues. That is to say narration is nearly always an instance of a dream-inflected waking life. In Lynch there is something more extreme: a constant oscillation between life and dream, difficult, dense, obliquely coded. In *Lost Highway* and *Mulholland Dr.* there is a crossing and re-crossing of the metaphysical divide that Hitchcock avoided, and places Lynch even closer than Hitchcock to their great American predecessor, Edgar Allan Poe.

Despite this there are two key points of contact between Hitchcock and later Lynch: first the transformation of the central subject out of noir fixities and then the Lynch glossing of the *metaphysics of the second chance* contained with the complex narration of *Vertigo*. We could argue the most complex and troubling figures in the Lynch canon are those played by Bill Pullman in *Lost Highway* and Naomi Watts in *Mulholland Dr.* In noir terms they are fall-guy and fall-girl in their respective narratives, both seeing themselves as betrayed and taking deadly revenge. Yet there is a key departure in Lynch from noir narration. Pullman and Watts undergo dramatically altered identities that illustrate the metaphysics of the second chance and whose outcome, as in *Vertigo*, is equally doomed, *a redemption that cannot take place*. Chris Marker (1995) has ingeniously outlined *Vertigo*'s second chance poetics in his comparison with the second part of the film to the mechanics of a 'free replay' in a video game. He points out the exact process of repetition that ends with the return of Scottie and of Judy once more playing Madeleine to the tower at the Mission, the re-enactment that could be cathartic but instead turns tragic. Yet he also looks at the key absences in part two of the narration after Scottie's 'recovery' from catatonic breakdown. There is no Midge and no Gavin Elster; there is no return to the mooring interiors of the first narrative, Elster's club, or the respective apartments of Midge and Scottie. In fact there are no real signs of recovery at all. All the empirical signs of the normal that are *independent* of the figure of Madeleine are gone. Instead we have two phases, the first being the mistaken sightings of Madeleine in old familiar places – for which Hitchcock used both Novak in long shot *and* her various body doubles (Krohn 2000: 194) – and the second comprising the chance meeting with Judy and the use of Judy's hotel room as a sole interior. Judy Barton could then be read as the *hallucinated double* of the ghostly Madeleine who is not fake but real. Having failed to find her likeness in other wealthy women who resemble her, Scottie embarks on a different and desperate attempt to flesh Madeleine out as an ordinary working girl – different clothes, lipstick, walk, voice, demeanour – but whom *he* then transforms into his ideal woman, a power that finally gives him the impetus to make love. Madeleine can be redeemed and loved, that is, only if she is *his* creation, formed out of someone else as (initially) *unlike* substitute for the Madeleine who has died.

Yet paradoxically this omnipotent fantasy points to its very opposite, the total absence of power. In recreating Judy as Madeleine, Scottie discovers for himself what Judy's flashback has already told us, that Elster got there first and that he is simply repeating the pattern of his rival's creation – so that for Judy this is also the second time around. The dream then turns to nightmare and Judy Barton suffers the same fate as the original Madeleine whose corpse Elster had thrown from the tower above. Marker's reading suggests an inversion of this material world where Judy first appears as the flesh-and-blood variant of the ghostly Madeleine, for on second sight everything could be the exact opposite. Judy could well be the hallucinated embodiment of a 'ghost' with a real body, which of course Scottie has already seen naked after the 'drowning' incident, a body real in every sense. On this reading, after all, there is no murder or conspiracy. Novak's Madeleine is Elster's real wife, genuinely possessed of a death wish and obsessed with her ancestor Carlotta Valdez, whose suicide she repeats. It is, on the contrary, Judy who is invented by Scottie during the continuation of his breakdown, from which he does not truly recover. If we do not wish to follow Marker's interpretation, at least it shows us the enduring power of a double reading where the second reading (his) clearly reverses the other (majority) reading, though both equally stress the poetics of repetition as the key to the film's mystery. It highlights too the mutually excusive nature of the doubling: either it is Madeleine-Judy that is real and Carlotta's ancestry that is invented, or else it *is* Carlotta-Madeleine that is the true lineage and Judy who is Scottie's invention (flashback included) after the fact.

This conceptual openness in *Vertigo* may well be the source of Lynch's later free-ranging across metaphysical boundaries. And he does leave one tantalising clue. In early treatments for the *Vertigo* script worked on by Angus MacPhail and Maxwell Anderson, 'Judy' features under the name used in the screenplay's literary source, that of Renée in Pierre Boileau and Thomas Narcejac's *D'entre les morts*. In their novella, she was the woman whom the hero, Roger, meets in Marseilles after the death of Madeleine and then attempts to make over in Madeleine's image. The name 'Renée' lasts in the Hitchcock metamorphosis well into first complete draft of Alec Coppel before she is later renamed Judy when the screenplay is entrusted to Samuel Taylor (see Auiler 1998: 44–53). 'Judy/Renée' acts as a version of the original woman of whom Madeleine is a copy, an impersonation and Lynch perhaps in oblique homage names Patricia Arquette 'Renée' in her first, dark-haired incarnation in *Lost Highway* before she is transformed into 'Alice' in the film's second section. Here the doubling is a puzzle never fully resolved. In one photo, seen by Balthazar Getty, Arquette is present in her two incarnations, dark and blonde, with her alternate lovers, Andy and Mr Eddy. When the same photo is next seen in exactly the same place by the police investigating Andy's gruesome death, Alice has disappeared, or been airbrushed out. After Pete (Getty) makes love to Alice in the desert in the 'Song for the Siren' sequence, he suddenly 'turns back' into Fred (Pullman) who then searches, naked, for his disappearing lover only to be cautioned by the menacing Mystery Man in his cabin that: 'Her name is Renée. If she told you she was Alice she was lying.'

Lynch's Renée would then have the same function as Hitchcock's Judy (previously Renée) has on the common reading of *Vertigo*, the real woman whom the hero sees in a different guise (impersonation in Hitchcock, hallucination in Lynch) as the blonde, and ideal object of desire. Yet Lynch has also taken *Vertigo* as a source for the enigma of the *insoluble* double reading. Who says one character is more real than the other, if they are both embodied in the same actor? Who can say that one is the copy of the other? Who can say for sure whether they are the same woman or different women? After all, this does look like second-chance poetics. If Fred had murdered Renée because he suspects her of betrayal, he may have hallucinated a double metamorphosis on Death Row, his own persona as the younger virile Pete and hers (Renée) as the voluptuous blonde Alice. This may then repeat their love affair, giving desire a second chance where it has petrified the first time around. But as in Hitchcock, the pitfalls of the second chance outweigh the advantages. Fred is suspicious of his wife's infidelities (a variant on the bourgeois variant of noir: Fred possesses her but then loses her) yet Pete knows that Alice whom he covets is the girl of his porn-baron patron Mr Eddy (a variant on the gangster variant of noir: Pete can possess her briefly but only by proxy). As Alice tells him in the desert night, making love to him and then deserting him, 'You'll *never* have me'. Last words as she wanders off leaving him to be reincarnated in the glare of the car headlights as a naked Fred Madison. Aided by the Mystery Man, Fred tracks Mr Eddy, alias Dick Laurant, to the Lost Highway Hotel where he discovers him *in flagrante* with Renée, not Alice (who never returns in the film). The final disappearance is that of the Mystery Man who vanishes after 'aiding' Fred to kill Mr Eddy. Yet even this hallucination merely takes us through its feedback loop to the start of the picture when a voice has intoned on Fred's intercom the demise of Mr Eddy's double: 'Dick Laurant is dead.' The 'free replay', instead of being the redemptive second chance, is simply a repetition of the fatal, prior enactment the hero wishes in vain to rewrite through virtual history. It will not stop him murdering his wife because he has already done so.

Lynch's dark aesthetic is the very opposite of the utopian time-travelling in Steven Spielberg's *Minority Report* (2002) where Tom Cruise can predict future murders using the latest scientific aids and then prevent them before they happen. In *Vertigo* and *Lost Highway*, the actual and the virtual both return to a common source; personal histories cannot be rewritten and both Lynch and Hitchcock present this as a source of enduring pain. *Lost Highway* has an oblique chronology made difficult through its feedback looping but at least it is *there* in space and time with a point of departure, the forlorn marital home and a point of transition, the death cell where Pullman disappears and is replaced by Getty. *Mulholland Dr.* is different altogether. It appears to begin with a dream that takes up three-quarters of the narrative before it segues into the actual world the dreaming brain has scrambled through elided events, identity-transfers and thwarted desires. Or at least that is one reading among many in which Naomi Watts as Betty/Diane tries to replay her life with Rita/Camilla (Laura Elena Herring) to give it a rather different outcome to the doomed one it has. In 'free replay' readings of *Vertigo* the replay, chronologically, is a version of the second time around. Yet in Lynch the chronology is reversed. The dream replay is presented on screen *prior* to the events it refracts. The second time around comes *first* when, from the credits sequence onward, Diane dreams an alternate scenario to the killing she had already contracted on her lover, Camilla, who has betrayed her with lovers of both sexes. Moreover, Diane's dream, where Camilla escapes a car crash before she is murdered and then falls in love with the bright-eyed Betty (Diane's innocent double) who discovers her hiding in her 'aunt's apartment', is inflected with forms of narcotic delirium. It is a delirium that seems to continue in her waking life after the dream is over. For the drugged Diane, on waking, still hallucinates the return of ex-lover, a semi-naked Camilla, for sexual foreplay on her sofa before the latter disappears without trace. For Betty/Diane persona demarcation is made clear – shades of *Vertigo* – through clothes, look, voice, body language and, finally, moral value when Betty the rosy-cheeked idealist turns back into Diane, the pallid cynic. And of course the dream has already ended, as many dreams do, with the inexplicable disappearance of the lover, the winding down of the dream-work before Diane's rude awakening into a seedy and disordered life.

If Betty is an idealised fiction, a naïve enthusiast out of a time-warp, of the age of the perky Hitchcock blonde pitched somewhere between Anne Baxter, Doris Day and Tippi Hedren, Diane is a grunge figure straight out of low-budget American 'Indies', part-time junkie, part-time prostitute, pale and anorexic, a good-looking wannabe actor gone to seed. By contrast the love-object Rita/Camilla looks the same voluptuous, well-tended woman under both names. She looks and acts, that is, like a movie star in both her 'lives'. Only her invented amnesia, another Hitchcock trope, in Diane's dream sequence obliterates her Camilla role as narcissistic betrayer. Yet *femme fatale* she is, and knowingly so. If Betty could be mistaken for Hedren, Rita is a dead ringer for Ava Gardner in *The Killers*. For Lynch this is a hybrid first, a same-sex synthesis; in short, Hitchcock heroine falls for noir *femme fatale*. The parallel worlds of 1940s noir and 1940s Hitchcock with their distinct gender constructions are here confounded, but only by breaking with the heterosexual code that dominates both in main text (though not always in subtext). Thus the men are all sidelined from the emotional core of the picture as neo-noir rogues or chumps of one kind or another – vanity auteur, Mafia producer, Mafia thug, Clark Gable clone (in Betty's audition sequence), cowboy pimp, grunge agent, errant hit-man and so on. Except intriguingly the two sensitive male souls at Twinkie's diner who discover on waste-ground the same corpse Betty and Rita will later discover in Diane's apartment. One way to read the quest-intimacy of the delicate diner-guys – they could well be lovers – is to see them as the *male* doubles of Betty and Rita and thus given key cameos as male reflections of Lynch's troubled duo.

But the point is taken. The delirium of doubling and identity-transfer seems endless, yet it does have a finite point when (nearly) all the dream personae are unscrambled at Adam and Camilla's engagement party on Mulholland Drive and Diane's humiliation becomes complete. Unlike Judy Barton, Diane Eastman is not made over the second time around: she has already failed and is out of the loop. Having embarked in her dream in a quest to find out who Rita really is – a makeover quest that glosses innocence by starting from zero – she can only accede to the point she has already reached. For her love-hate object Rita/Camilla is an empty canvas on which anything can be painted – there is simply nothing to discover – whereas Betty simply ends up discovering herself as Diane in her decaying apartment in the same way that reworking *Vertigo*, Madeleine might make the journey from the luxury Brocklebank apartments on Nob Hill to discover herself as Judy in the seedy Empire hotel on Sutter. We feel that starting with Mulholland Drive, near the summit of the Hollywood Hills, Lynch is making us witness the same downward journey in a different city. And in terms of the American film empire it is much closer to home.

Hitchcock's legacy: meta-noir and memory noir

Vertigo is thus a primal source for a *meta-noir* that overlaps the physical and metaphysical, the actual and the virtual. For it raises the question through the persona of Madeline of key relations: past and present, the origin and the copy, cause and effect, and the question too of parallel worlds. If they do exist, which do we privilege? Marker's reversal of the conventional reading is thus a fruitful quandary. On one interpretation, a fabrication is substituted by an actuality and on Marker's reading an actuality is transformed into a fantasy. In *Lost Highway* and *Mulholland Dr.*, where we are confronted by two distinctive worlds that seem to parallel one another, both these readings, mutually exclusive, are also possible. In contemporary film the pursuit of parallel worlds can be seen not only in Lynch's features but also in many others that mark the end of millennium. *The Double Life of Véronique* (1991), *In the Mood for Love*, *Code Unknown* (2000) and *21 Grams* (2003) are among many that spring to mind. In addition there are the ghost stories of M. Night Shyamalan – *The Sixth Sense* (2000) – and Alejandro Amenábar – *The Others* (2001) – that run together colliding worlds of humans and of ghosts and then, as thrillers, abruptly reverse our sense of which is which.

In memory noir, the mark of Lynch may not be so strong but is still there. The central subject remains male, and problematic; if anything the *femme fatale* is even more on the periphery. The tough guy, fatalistic perhaps but ever hard-boiled in classic noir, has become a more ambivalent figure through murky intersections of the objective past and subjective memory. Not only ambivalent, but also devious. The roles are varied: Jason Patric as gullible punch-drunk boxer become devious drifter in *After Dark, My Sweet*; Val Kilmer as fall-guy private eye still grieving – or is he? – after his wife's mysterious death in *Kill Me Again*; Bill Paxton as local sheriff who has secretly fathered the son of a psychotic gangster's black lover in *One False Move*; Kevin Anderson as the diffident traumatised architect of *Liebestraum* whose affair with his buddy's wife threatens, through his repetition-compulsion, to trigger the repeat of murders in his family's previous generation (though in a clear nod to *Vertigo*, it is the architect's dying mother, played by Kim Novak, who is the real *femme fatale*); the gullible Peter Gallagher updated by Soderbergh's *The Underneath* as Burt Lancaster's security guard from *Criss Cross* but so fixated on his past failures, financial and romantic, he fatally repeats them in his present life; Guy Pearce as Lenny, the manipulated (or manipulating?) short-term amnesiac of *Memento* seeking revenge (or seemingly) in the featureless edge cities of Southern California for the traumatic motel rape and murder of his wife, yet who could well be the killer himself.

All of the new fall-guys are damaged goods, emblems of a male identity crisis in late-century America, dysfunctional figures haunted by their past, who may be victims and may yet be monsters. Over all of them hovers the ghostly ambivalence of Johnny Aysgarth in *Suspicion* working a double shift with that classic amnesiac, John Ballantyne of *Spellbound*. It is a pure Hitchcock legacy, a Jekyll and Hyde act often stretched out on a plane of greater relativity by filmmakers who have also absorbed Alain Resnais' abstract modernism and his inventive variations of subjective memory on Hitchcock themes (and equally the modernist LA makeover of Resnais by John Boorman in his 1967 gangster parable, *Point Blank*). Yet the legacy remains. The unreadable Hitchcock male hero, now reinvented in neo-noir, is dogged by the ambivalence he did not have in classic noir. While appearing as the victim, he may yet want others to suffer. Unsure of his own identity he has a secret destructiveness that goes against the grain of any fatal attraction. He may be a drifter in the physical and geographical sense but he is also drifting through an uncertain state of mind, often physically strong but always mentally weak. He is a compendium of opposites: weak and strong, feeble and ruthless, macho and feminine. Anything but hard-boiled coda

I CONFESS, OR I'M GIVING NOTHING AWAY

At a tangent to post-Hitchcock noir but with many of its features is *Le Confessionnal*, the 1995 film debut of Canadian theatre director Robert Lepage. While other forms of memory noir echo *Spellbound* and *Marnie*, Lepage's Francophone film is firmly and reflexively anchored in *I Confess*, a film property it takes as object in its own narrative with sequences that feature the casting, filming and first night of Hitchcock's film in Québec City. It was a bold and audacious move by Lepage, yet *I Confess* was indispensable as a springboard for the dramatic events in his own film, which then serves as an ironic sequel forty years on. Lepage had a triple incentive for turning around Hitchcock's narrative. Unconstrained by a Studio Code he could be much more explicit about darker issues of religion and sexuality. He could also experiment in the 1990s more boldly with time-sequence, and finally he could invert the Anglophone conceit of Hitchcock's Warner Bros. film by restoring Québec as a truly French-Canadian city, making the English-speaking characters marginal, rather than the other way around. Yet his film-within-a-film sequences that make the making of *I Confess* the fulcrum of his own narrative are at times naïve and disingenuous. In his undoubtedly scintillating film are happenings, of course, that would never have passed Hitchcock's double set of censors, front office back in Hollywood and Hitchcock's panel of clerical advisers in Québec. Yet it may be that Lepage is too facile in celebrating his artistic freedom so simply, and contrasting it with the straightjacket of its source. For Hitchcock's film has an abrupt sting in its tail, a dark subtext at total variance from its official plotting. In *I Confess* there is an upfront transfer of guilt that provides the film's through-line. Father Michael Logan (Montgomery Clift) is accused of the murder committed by his Parish's refugee gardener Keller (O. E. Hasse) of a shadowy lawyer Villette, and confided by Keller to Logan in the confessional. Unable to share his confessional secrets Logan must stand trial, for Villette, it transpires, was also blackmailing him and his childhood sweetheart Ruth (Anne Baxter), now married, over an alleged affair before he entered the priesthood.

In Lepage's meta-text the secrets of the confessional relate to sex, parentage and suicide, not murder. In family terms, they go deeper. In 1952 a taxi driver, Paul-Emile (François Papineau), on the periphery of Hitchcock's film set, impregnates his teenage sister-in-law, Rachel (Marie Gignac), who commits suicide after the birth. He confesses his secret to his local priest, Father Massicotte, who, unable to name the true father is then accused of being the father and dismissed from the priesthood in disgrace. The illegitimate son Marc (Patrick Goyette) is adopted by the taxi driver and his wife and the story is reconstructed in 1989 by Paul-Emile's legitimate son Pierre (Lothaire Bluteau) who seeks out his half-brother and finds that while Marc now has his own lover (a striptease dancer) and young son living in dire straits, he is also having an affair with Massicotte, now a wealthy Quebecois businessman and politician. On first sight a viewer might take Massicotte as Marc's true father, and the story one of tragic incest, but Lepage wants to repeat Hitchcock's wrong man motif in a different context. As a priest sworn to the secrets of the confessional, Massicotte had hidden the identity of the true father (who has passed on diabetes to Marc and his own son) and paid the price. Pierre is subsequently unable to prevent Marc's suicide, where, emotionally and sexually torn in his loyalties between very different male and female lovers, he repeats the family tragedy of his mother's fate.

Lepage exposes the genealogy of an unhinged family over two generations as an open wound that cannot heal, and in the process contrasts the tight austere and censorious Catholic culture of the 1950s to the corrupt secular hedonism of his own age. An anti-Hitchcock style invigorates his narrative. As opposed to the black-and-white naturalism of the location shooting in *I Confess* Lepage offers a sumptuous visual palette of primary colours dominated by deep saturated reds. Against the famous '*direction*' montage that ushers in the murder at the start of *I Confess*, Aleksandar Dundjerovic has noted the extensive use here of sequence-shot aesthetics, long following takes that edit the action within the frame as they move through separate social spaces (2003: 62). The sequence-shot echoes the time-travelling of Theo Angelopoulos in the tracking movement done both externally and then internally in one shot that begins in the hallway of the family house in 1952 and ends in the living-room in 1989 as Pierre starts to paint the walls red. The film is a meta-text that not only takes from the culture of its own age but the film stylistics of its own time, neither of which are familiar to us from the work of Hitchcock. Lepage's meta-text is thus a cinematic style that embodies precise social and historical observations. But its starting point is also reflexive, an amalgam of fact and fiction in the renewed topography of a city. Meta-text clearly has the advantage of hindsight in its transcendent form, but it also has a duty to the original. And this is where Lepage is clearly ambivalent.

The ambivalence works on two levels. As a gay director now seen as part of New Queer Cinema, he would have known that Hitchcock's casting of two gay actors, Montgomery Clift and O. E. Hasse, might well intimate a hidden agenda. Yet his placing of Hitchcock in his film suggests a narrow, old-fashioned auteur protected from the real world of Québec by his person-al assistant, an iconic ice-cool blonde (Kristin Scott-Thomas) who mediates abrasively between the master and the locals. Lepage highlights Hitchcock's collusion with the Québecois clerical establishment, without, however, men-tioning the censorious force of Warner Bros. that was much, much stron-ger. After the film premiere he manufactures a scene in which Paul-Emile is chauffeuring Hitchcock away from the cinema and offers him as fiction a thinly-veiled version of his own secret life, to which Lepage's Hitchcock retorts, 'that's not a suspense story … It's a Greek tragedy'. This not only short-changes the original, it demeans Hitchcock as a director. For *I Confess* is not purely a suspense-story and a dilemma ensues that can never be resolved. Lepage's meta-text purports to transcend a constrained film hedged in by the pincer movement of Hollywood and clerical censorship. Yet it could be argued that his own storyline could have been stronger if he had sustained the incest theme into the present. (Unlike Hitchcock he certainly did not have the same levels of censorship to contend with.) Moreover, Hitchcock had his own strategies of evasion that *Le Confessionnal* overlooks. His 'monolithic' text, where all seems obvious, has an underground sub-text where nothing is obvious. The more this film is watched, the more it eludes us.

The film, too, had been a truncated project. Warner Bros., not the reli-gious authorities in Québec, had forced Hitchcock to take out those elements of judicial and heterosexual drama that attracted him and were present in the early drafts of screenwriter George Tabori. Here the falsely accused priest has fathered an illegitimate child after an affair with a married woman and then is powerless to prevent a guilty verdict that results in his execution for a murder he did not commit (see McGilligan 2003: 457–8). Hitchcock not only lost the minor violation of a censorious moral code; he also lost his wrong-man miscarriage of justice. In the film the priest, anglicised as Michael Lo-gan, is not yet a priest when he has the 'affair', a truly brief encounter, and is finally *acquitted* of the murder he did not commit. The outcome was tame and Hitchcock knew it. Forced away by censorship from themes of justice and heterosexuality he wished to confront, it is possible to speculate that his reworking of an intensely personal project took on a new, subterranean dimension. Or perhaps it was that a sub-text he wished to embed in his plot anyway suddenly enlarged itself and acquired a new significance altogether. For *I Confess*, like *Spellbound* before it and *Marnie* after it, becomes a flawed and fascinating film by first stating the obvious and then evaporating into something else that is completely elusive.

Deborah Thomas (1996) points out many plot details that render it 'an enigmatic text'. Here are some of them: Keller confesses to Logan and later to his wife Alma (Dolly Haas) that as a poor man he had robbed Villette (Ovila Legare) but not intended to kill him, yet Villette's money is found untouched in his room after the murder. At breakfast Logan's colleague, Father Benoit, asks housekeeper Alma if her husband is free to mend the flat tyre on his bicycle. Keller then tells Alma, after the murder is discovered, that Benoit's tyre had not been flat after all. Logan's testimony during interrogation and later in court – like that of André Latour in *The Paradine Case* – never produces a straight answer. Logan always answers ambiguously: 'I can't say', for example, stands in for either 'I don't know' or 'I refuse to say'. Beyond that Hitchcock uses enigmatic repetitions. Following the opening montage sequence the camera discovers Villette's murder by tracking in through an open window from the street and finding him spread eagled on his back, dressed all in white, before it pulls back to reveal the murderer disappearing down the street in a priest's cassock. Later in the flashback sequence where Ruth claims to have stayed the night on the island with Logan because the last ferry has already left, she is filmed in a similar posture to Villette next morning in the open summerhouse, and also dressed in white – though shot in medium close-up to avoid trouble with the censors. There are many other details; a series of anomalies that unsettle any obvious reading of the film and prompt the attentive viewer to ask questions of a narrative that had seemed lamely cut-and-dried but on close inspection disperses all certainty to the wind. One detail we might well add to the list is in the confession itself. Hitchcock fades out in the middle of the confession where Keller is pleading poverty as murder motive to Logan and fades in to an identical moment in his later confession to Alma, his wife. Thus we never witness everything Keller confesses. What is it, then, that Hitchcock omits?

A composite picture starts to emerge suggesting an alternate reading, not a reading to displace the obvious one but to run in counterpoint to it, and keep us guessing. This, however, is just one possible reading; it does not resolve the film's enigma but at least indicates something so deeply embedded the film cannot be dismissed as tame melodrama. This reading sees *I Confess* with its casting of gay actors in the two main roles, as a continuation of the queer aesthetic inherent in *Rebecca*, *The Paradine Case*, *Rope* and *Strangers on a Train* but because of its religious subject-matter, more covert than ever. Intriguingly, Anne Baxter had told Donald Spoto about her difficulties in working with Montgomery Clift because of his alcohol problem on set; in key scenes like the ferry sequence, his eyes would just glaze over as her character bared her soul to him (Spoto 1983: 339). Yet this fits perfectly with what Hitchcock wanted, and it certainly raises questions about the intensity of Logan's attraction to Ruth when he is longer making eye contact with her. Hitchcock wanted blankness visible in the face of Logan, a mask to blot out all personal secrets and emotions as being *too much* to reveal. Despite the director's reported difficulties with Clift, his acting coach and his Method background, his lead actor does deliver the mask, the peremptory blankness that conceals so much. Let us look more closely at what the mask might conceal. Logan is a figure who seems most comfortable in the company of men and above all of men in uniform. For the duration of the film we hardly see him in civilian clothes – at one point before turning himself in to Larrue (Karl Malden), the investigating cop, he looks longingly into the window of a men's clothes shop. He is either in military uniform, with Ruth before and after the war, or in clerical garb. When dancing with Ruth on their last night before leaving for the war in Europe, his full uniform seems like a barrier to her pressing body. When painting a room with Keller the morning after Villette's murder we see him in the same khaki shirt with shoulder straps that he later wears in flashback, years earlier, in the summerhouse scene with Ruth, part of his returning uniform. The war is not a barrier out of their control. Logan chooses it as an escape. 'He was one of the first to volunteer', Ruth claims, 'I hated him for that.' After being discovered by Villette with Ruth, now married to Grandfort, in the summerhouse he chooses the company of men the second time around but this time in the priesthood.

Hitchcock gives us a number of sly clues, visual and verbal, to exemplify Logan's 'manliness' and imply homosexual ambience. When Ruth explains her concealment of Villette's blackmail she lets slip that she fears Michael 'would be unfrocked'. Unfrocked, not defrocked. When Keller and Logan (in army khaki shirt splashed with paint) are busy decorating together, Alma complains vociferously about the odour (of the paint) their joint activity is producing. When the effete Villette and the manly Michael clash outside the summerhouse in Ruth's flashback, there is more than a flicker of mutual recognition as an irate Logan hurls his adversary to the ground. Since the flashback is shot through Ruth's voice-over but with no dialogue audible we never know what they say to one another. At the trial, moreover, when the prosecutor questions the motive for Logan's anger he immediately puts his own answer into a grateful Logan's mouth, suggesting that Villette had made disparaging remarks about Ruth. Logan gratefully agrees. The question of happenstance also arises. Is it purely by chance that Logan takes Ruth to that part of the island where Villette has a house? The man-in-white, lady-in-white repetition of Villette (murdered) and then Ruth (seduced?) suggests erotic abandonment in both cases. The hint of Eros is echoed again in the pieta framing of the final chase sequence when the distressed Logan holds the dying Keller in his arms having just ignored the dead body of poor Alma after Keller has shot her. Intriguingly the enigma extends to politician Pierre Grandfort whom Ruth has married without conviction in Logan's wartime absence. Called to the phone by Ruth to be informed of Villette's murder, he is first seen in a recumbent position on the floor (echoes of Ruth and of Villette) but comically, balancing a glass of water on his forehead for the entertainment of dinner guests. He is yet another of Hitchcock's middle-aged husbands, who, like Maxim de Winter, shows no flicker of interest in a lovely younger wife.

Yet such clues are premised on two key plot-elements, the truth-status of Ruth's flashback scene and the nature of Villette himself. For who or *what* is Villette? The feminised naming may well echo the strategy of Proust (Gilberte, Albertine and so forth) and the same signalled cover-up. And the two plot elements that are so elusive are almost inseparable. It is only through Ruth's flashback that we have any real notion of who Villette might be, since after his murder no one voluntarily claims to know him well. Initially, a wall of silence confronts the police. Yet why do we take that flashback as a key to truth, a confession to the police that reveals all? The confession is idyllic and romantic, overlaid by lush orchestral strings. Hitchcock for once shoots it almost entirely on location and when the couple are caught in a storm on the island, they are soaked in a deluge of real rain. There is no chiaroscuro; no dark shadows. The flashback thus invokes documentary veracity, a transparency of the image in which we feel ourselves to be truly there.

Yet we must remember that in *Stage Fright* three years previously Hitchcock had deceived his audience by giving them through the first-hand account of Richard Todd a duplicitous flashback that masks the true nature of the film's murder. Earlier still, in *Bon Voyage* he had juxtaposed two conflicting flashback versions of the same clandestine events. If the first-persona flashback had become a filmic signifier of confessional truth (used regularly of course in film noir) then Hitchcock is clearly challenging the convention, not only in *Stage Fright* but here too. Could Ruth be an unreliable narrator? We need to look not only at the content but the setting of her confession. After the murder she is interrogated by Larrue, who has first seen her with Michael in the crowd outside the dead man's house then assigned agents to watch the couple on the local ferry, where they discuss their blackmail dilemma. Yet Larrue is in a long line of clueless cops stretching back to *Sabotage* and beyond, that are part of Hitchcock's trademark. He stupidly interrogates Ruth while Logan is present in the room. Thus Logan is wrongly allowed to witness her 'confession' and adjust his own story accordingly when his interrogation, and trial, follows shortly after. In fact he is forced to adhere to Ruth's version, and not contradict it, whether it is true or not. Ruth claims the night spent in the summerhouse had been innocent and that she had first seen Villette once before when he turned up uninvited at her wedding, where Grandfort seemed not to know him. This also plants the link with her husband and suggests a wider conspiracy of silence where the motif of heterosexual blackmail could indeed seem lame beside *other secrets* that Villette holds in his keep. We could well be in *Murder on the Orient Express* mode where everyone does it or where, adapted to Hitchcock's more subtle style, everyone would be happy to see Villette dead. But these are for reasons

Fig. 12 Unreliable confessions: Montgomery Clift and Anne Baxter in *I Confess*

other than those specified. The blackmail would be over something unspoken rather than something obvious, and unspoken because homosexual acts at the time were not only 'immoral' but criminal, a different realm of danger altogether.

Villette then acts as the signifier of an alternate circuit of desire whose full nature the film never reveals (and never can reveal) to us. There is no point at which we can say reductively that such and such a liaison occurred and that is the real 'reason' for the murder. Instead there is a sense in which Villette dies because he was a man who knew too much: more, indeed, than that we shall never know. At some level all the characters seem implicated, including Hitchcock himself who resembles Keller in two key respects. Like Keller, he also walks away from the murder during his cameo in the *direction* montage that opens the picture and in real life his wife shares the same name as Keller's wife – Alma. Indeed the *direction* montage acts as a visual metaphor of plot deception too. It seems to indicate that the plot itself is pointing us away from the scene of the crime and therefore its motive, which is more likely to lie in *homosexual* blackmail. After all, Pierre Grandfort gives the impression of someone who could not get insanely jealous over a brief encounter where nothing could be ever shown to have taken place. Who is blackmailing whom therefore, and why, we shall never know but what Villette knows and we do not is crucial to the nature of the picture.

Moreover, the opacity of subtext does not weaken or invalidate the doubling motif that lies at the heart of narration. In fact it strengthens it. Logan and Keller are each torn between a loyalty to a woman they revere and a hatred of Villette whom they would like to see disappear. Both implicitly share, therefore, a dilemma of sexual loyalty, and both women, Alma and Ruth, may well be struggling, however tacitly, to keep their loved ones straight when their desires are leading them in the opposite direction. The dilemma, formally a 'bisexual' dilemma, does not therefore go away. Indeed it cannot be truly resolved. But though it leads to resemblance, Hitchcock also plays cruelly on its inherent difference. Keller may be like Logan and may well like him – we never know what their relationship truly is – but he is also a refugee thrust down into the service class with no status and little money while those he serves, the priesthood, would clearly have considerable status in 1952 Québec. The resentment and distrust he feels towards Villette is felt towards Logan too, where ambivalence is rife, and it has a class basis. Here Keller, not Logan, is the odd man out and even though a murderer who has been made corrupt and paranoid by his killing, he is still a refugee victim of a dark system of circulation that is never brought to light, and never can be.

We have a precedent for the tight and secretive tone of the film in *The Paradine Case*. There too Latour, like Michael Logan, is more than economical with the truth during his trial interrogation (and also a brave Canadian soldier in the war). There lurks a queer subtext too in Keane's sudden visit to Latour at the country house of the murdered Colonel Paradine. Louis Jourdan's Latour ('a pretty-pretty boy' as Hitch called him) was not only Paradine's faithful valet and ex-military subordinate but also, most likely, his clandestine lover, even after the colonel's marriage. His surprise visit to Keane's room at the inn late at night after hiding out during the day is never explained, despite Keane's demand for an explanation. The most obvious motive is seduction. Keane is being offered what he secretly wants, a chance to replace the colonel, but definitely not in the way he imagined. Later in her dramatic courtroom confession of her husband's murder, and of her love for Latour after hearing of his suicide, Maddalene Paradine's anguished words, 'I wanted us to be free', are a near precedent for Ruth's exclamation to Michael after Villette's death: 'At last we are free.' The 'freedom' envisaged by both women entails a final transfer from one sexual identity to another.

Hence the alternate title of *I Confess* could well be *I'm Giving Nothing Away*. Boxed into a corner by his censors, Hitchcock had responded by climbing out of the ring while leaving his ghost behind. In his 'straightforward' melodrama he fades out in the middle of a true confession and then mimics it with a confessional romantic flashback that is as duplicitous as anything in the film. The Québec island locations with the locked, deserted farmhouse, the late summer sun, the violent storm with real rain and the fortuitous summerhouse somehow clinch the flashback for us. The real feel and pleasure of it force suspension of disbelief. We believe in it for it is somehow Edenic, a Garden of Eden in the middle of nowhere in which true love is briefly consummated. But Villette, the dawn intruder, may then either be one of two things, the hovering serpent who destroys true love, or alternately God's witness (or avenging angel) who has discovered Original Sin in the Garden. In either case we must surely pose the critical question: what, then, is Original Sin? Is it, God forbid, *heterosexuality*? And is that why our loving couple are banished forever?

conclusion

HITCH IN THE TWENTY-FIRST CENTURY

At the start of the twenty-first century Hitchcock's influence on ambitious filmmaking across the world is as strong as ever. We have noted his impact on Asian cinema in films like *Audition, In the Mood for Love* and *Suzhou River.* That is reinforced by Lou Ye's most recent feature *Purple Butterfly* (2003), a spy thriller set atmospherically in 1930s Shanghai about the disintegration of Sino-Japanese relations and the horrors that result. The 1930s, of course, was the first decade of Hitchcock's own spy thrillers, yet this film is more strongly influenced in its sensuous labyrinth of doomed passion and betrayal by later pictures, especially by *Notorious* and *Vertigo.* Looking elsewhere, we have seen in France Hitchcock's enduring legacy throughout the latter part of the last century. It continues unabated. While new directors like Dominik Moll can echo his black humour with scarcely a false note in *Harry, He's Here to Help* (2000), veteran directors seem more indebted to Hitchcock the older they get. Chantal Akerman, for example, crosses Hitchcockian obsession with Bressonian poise in her filming of Proust, *La Captive* (2000) in a way that echoes the enduring theme of sexual transgression always downplayed but always pervading the Englishman's work – a love that dare not speak its name. As a master of dialogue, not action, Eric Rohmer has recently performed a surprising about-face in *Triple Agent* (2003), giving us an intricate 1930s spy thriller that partly pays homage to Hitch but is politically explicit in a way that Hitchcock at that time, could never be. Not to be outdone Jacques Rivette has become more Hitchcockian than ever in his old age. In his oblique but intriguing fable about death and 'crossing back from the other side' in *Histoire de Marie et Julien* (2003) he has arguably made in his own spectral and Parisian style the delicate haunting ghost story that Hitchcock wanted to make towards the end of his life. But never did. At the same time this is a film that could never have been made without *Vertigo.* It is almost, one could argue, its true sequel.

While in the UK Hitchcock's influence and status seems now to have gone down to zero, much to the detriment of British cinema, in the United States, his adopted homeland, it persists and prevails. We have already seen how Lynch, like Rivette, delves more and more into Hitchcock obsessions the more ambitious his films become, but we can also note the American debut of the young English director Christopher Nolan, *Memento*, a film of Hitchcockian proportions – thematically bold, stylistically daring, a fable of lost

y for a younger generation that builds on Hitchcock's legacy and that
nfrontation in the New World with things American. We have also
noted that after the debacle of his *Psycho* remake Gus Van Sant rivals the
sense of menace and impending doom we find in Hitchcock's *Psycho* with his
fictional take on the Columbine high school killings, *Elephant.* The sense of
fatality here is as strong as it is in Hitchcock's classic, our sense and dread
that innocents will be slaughtered for no good reason and die. This is what
his film displays: the sudden switch between the normal and the abnormal,
the inevitability of a fate that can never be replayed or exorcised.

Unsurprisingly, styles change in the age of the hand-held camera and
digital editing. The Hitchcock style of filmmaking is like that of any great
director, a function of its own age and technologies. Van Sant's film seems
stylistically to owe more to Angelopoulos or Béla Tarr in his use of long
takes and following shots. Lou Ye's persistent use of hand-held camera
might place him closer to Dogme95 than to Hitchcock's formalism. Nolan's
fast tracking shots and dynamic editing mark him out as part of a generation that has followed on from Scorsese. Yet to use the old-fashioned word
that Orson Welles did to describe his love of Jean Renoir – 'sensibility' – we
could say that the Hitchcock sensibility lingers on and does more besides. It
prevails at the start of a new century as something that still diffuses through
the universe of film.

FILMOGRAPHY

Films cited in text by date of release.
P: Producer. Sc: Screenplay. AD: Art Director. M: Musical Score.
DP: Director of Photography.

Silent pictures

The Mountain Eagle (Gainsborough-Emelka, 1926, b/w)
P: Michael Balcon. Sc: Eliot Stannard from story by Charles Lapworth.
DP: Baron Ventimiglia. Cast: Bernard Goetzke, Nita Naldi, Malcolm Keen,
John Hamilton.

The Lodger: A Story of the London Fog (Gainsborough, 1927, b/w)
P: Michael Balcon. Sc: Eliot Stannard from the novel by Marie Belloc
Lowndes. DP: Baron Ventimiglia. Cast: Marie Ault, Arthur Chesney,
June Tripp, Ivor Novello.

The Manxman (British International, 1929, b/w)
P: John Maxwell. Sc: Eliot Stannard from the novel by Hall Caine.
DP: John J. Cox. Cast: Carl Brisson, Malcolm Keen, Anny Ondra, Randle
Ayrton.

Sound pictures

Blackmail (British International, 1929, b/w)
P: John Maxwell. Sc: Alfred Hitchcock from the play by Charles Bennett.
DP: John J. Cox. Cast: Anny Ondra, Sara Allgood, John Longden, Donal
Calthrop.

Murder! (British International, 1930, b/w)
P: John Maxwell. Sc: Alfred Hitchcock, Walter Mycroft and Alma Reville
from the novel *Enter Sir John* by Clemence Dane, Helen Simpson. DP: John
J. Cox. Cast: Norah Baring, Herbert Marshall, Miles Mander, Esme Percy.

The Man Who Knew Too Much (Gaumont-British, 1934, b/w)
P. Michael Balcon. Sc: Edwin Greenwood and A. R. Rawlinson from a story
by Charles Bennett and D. B. Wyndham Lewis. DP: Curt Courant.

AD: Alfred Junge. Cast: Leslie Banks, Edna Best, Nova Pilbeam, Peter Lorre.

The 39 Steps (Gaumont-British, 1935, b/w)
P. Michael Balcon. Adapted by Charles Bennett from the novel *The Thirty-Nine Steps* by John Buchan. Dialogue: Ian Hay. AD: Otto Werndorff. DP: Bernard Knowles. Cast: Robert Donat, Madeleine Carroll, Lucie Mannheim, Godfrey Tearle, John Laurie, Peggy Ashcroft.

Secret Agent (Gaumont-British, 1936, b/w)
P: Michael Balcon. Sc: Charles Bennett from the play by Campbell Dixon, adapted from Somerset Maugham's *Ashenden*. AD: Otto Werndorff. DP: Bernard Knowles. Cast: John Gielgud, Madeleine Carroll, Peter Lorre, Robert Young.

Sabotage (Gaumont-British, 1936, b/w)
P: Michael Balcon. Sc: Charles Bennett from the novel *The Secret Agent* by Joseph Conrad. Dialogue: Ian Hay, Helen Simpson. AD: Otto Werndorff. DP: Bernard Knowles. Cast: Sylvia Sidney, Oscar Homolka, Desmond Tester, John Loder.

Young and Innocent (Gaumont-British, 1938, b/w)
P: Edward Black. Sc: Charles Bennett, Edwin Greenwood and Anthony Armstrong from the novel *A Shilling for Candles* by Josephine Tey. AD: Alfred Junge. DP: Bernard Knowles. Cast: Nova Pilbeam, Derrick de Marney, Percy Marmont, Edward Rigby.

The Lady Vanishes (Gainsborough, 1938, b/w)
P: Edward Black. Sc: Sidney Gilliat and Frank Launder from the novel *The Wheel Spins* by Ethel Lina White. DP: John J. Cox. Cast: Margaret Lockwood, Michael Redgrave, Dame May Whitty, Paul Lukas.

Jamaica Inn (Erich Pommer Productions, 1939, b/w)
P: Erich Pommer. Sc: Sidney Gilliat and Joan Harrison from the novel by Daphne du Maurier. DP: Harry Stradling, Bernard Knowles. Cast: Charles Laughton, Leslie Banks, Marie Ney, Maureen O'Hara.

Rebecca (Selznick Studios, 1940, b/w)
P: David O. Selznick. Sc: Robert Sherwood and Joan Harrison from the novel by Daphne du Maurier. M: Franz Waxman. AD: Lyle Wheeler. DP: George Barnes. Cast: Laurence Olivier, Joan Fontaine, Judith Anderson, George Sanders.

Foreign Correspondent (A Wanger Production, 1940, b/w)
P: Walter Wanger. SC: Charles Bennett, Joan Harrison. M. Alfred Newman.
AD: Alexander Golitzen. DP: Rudolph Maté. Cast: Joel McCrea, Laraine
Day, Herbert Marshall, George Sanders.

Suspicion (RKO, 1941, b/w)
P: Harry E. Eddington. Sc: Samson Raphaelson, Joan Harrison and Alma
Reville from the novel *Before the Fact* by Frances Iles. M: Franz Waxman.
AD: Van Nest Polglase. DP: Harry Stradling. Cast: Joan Fontaine, Cary
Grant, Sir Cedric Hardwicke, Nigel Bruce.

Saboteur (Universal, 1942, b/w)
P: Frank Lloyd. SC: Peter Viertel, Joan Harrison, Dorothy Parker.
M: Frank Skinner. AD: Jack Otterson, Robert Boyle. DP: Joseph
Valentine. Cast: Robert Cummings, Priscilla Lane, Otto Kruger, Norman
Lloyd.

Shadow of a Doubt (Universal, 1943, b/w)
P: Jack H. Skirball. Sc: Thornton Wilder, Sally Benson and Alma Reville
from a story by Gordon McDonnell. M: Dimitri Tiomkin. AD: John B.
Goodman, Robert Boyle. DP: Joseph Valentine. Cast: Joseph Cotten,
Teresa Wright, MacDonald Carey, Patricia Collinge.

Lifeboat (20th Century-Fox, 1944, b/w)
P: Kenneth Macgowan. Sc: Jo Swerling from a story by John Steinbeck.
AD: James Basevi, Maurice Ransford. DP: Glen MacWilliams.
Cast: Tallulah Bankhead, John Hodiak, William Bendix, Walter Slezak.

Bon Voyage (26 mins)/*Aventure Malgache* (31 mins) (Ministry of Informa-
tion/Phoenix Films, 1944, b/w)
P: Sidney Bernstein. SC: *Bon Voyage*: Arthur Calder-Marshall, Angus
MacPhail, *Aventure Malgache*: J.O.C.Orton, Angus MacPhail. DP: Günther
Krampf. M: Benjamin Frankel. Cast: The Molière Players.

Spellbound (Selznick International Pictures, 1945, b/w)
P: David O. Selznick: Sc: Ben Hecht from the novel *The House of Dr
Edwardes* by Francis Beeding. M: Miklos Rozsa. AD: James Basevi. DP:
George Barnes. Cast: Ingrid Bergman, Gregory Peck, Leo G. Carroll,
Michael Chekhov.

Notorious (RKO, 1946, b/w)
P: Alfred Hitchcock. Sc: Ben Hecht. M: Roy Webb. AD: Albert D'Agostino.

DP: Ted Tetzlaff. Cast: Cary Grant, Ingrid Bergman, Claude Rains, Leopoldine Konstantin.

The Paradine Case (David O. Selznick/Vanguard Film, 1947, b/w)
P: David O. Selznick. Sc: David O. Selznick from the novel by Robert Hichens. M: Franz Waxman. AD: Tom Morahan. DP: Lee Garmes. Cast: Alida Valli, Gregory Peck, Ann Todd, Louis Jourdan.

Rope (Transatlantic Pictures, 1948, colour)
P: Alfred Hitchcock, Sidney Bernstein. Sc: Hume Cronyn and Arthur Laurents, based on the play by Patrick Hamilton. M: Francis Poulenc, Leo F. Forbstein. AD: Perry Ferguson. DP: Joseph Valentine. Cast: James Stewart, John Dall, Farley Granger, Sir Cedric Hardwicke.

Under Capricorn (Transatlantic Pictures, 1949, colour)
P: Alfred Hitchcock, Sidney Bernstein. SC: Hume Cronyn, James Bridie from the novel by Helen Simpson. M: Richard Addinsell: AD: Tom Morahan. DP: Jack Cardiff. Cast: Ingrid Bergman, Michael Wilding, Joseph Cotten, Margaret Leighton.

Stage Fright (Warner Bros.-First National, 1950, b/w)
P: Alfred Hitchcock. Sc: Whitfield Cook from the novel by Selwyn Jepson, *Man Running*. AD: Terence Verity. DP: Wilkie Cooper. Cast: Jane Wyman, Marlene Dietrich, Michael Wilding, Richard Todd.

Strangers on a Train (Warner Bros.-First National, 1951, b/w)
P: Alfred Hitchcock. Sc: Raymond Chandler and Czenzi Ormonde from the novel by Patricia Highsmith. M: Dimitri Tiomkin. AD: Edward S. Haworth. DP: Robert Burks. Cast: Robert Walker, Farley Granger, Laura Elliott, Ruth Roman.

I Confess (Warner Bros.-First National, 1953, b/w)
P: Alfred Hitchcock. Sc: George Tabori and William Archibald from the play by Paul Anthelme, *Nos Deux Consciences*. M: Dimitri Tiomkin. AD: Edward S. Haworth. DP: Robert Burks. Cast: Montgomery Clift, Anne Baxter, Karl Malden, O.E. Hasse.

Dial 'M' for Murder (Warner Bros.-First National, 1954, colour)
P: Alfred Hitchcock. Sc: Frederick Knott from his stage play. M: Dimitri Tiomkin. AD: Edward Carrera. DP: Robert Burks. Cast: Ray Milland, Grace Kelly, Anthony Dawson, John Williams.

Rear Window (Paramount, 1954, colour)
P: Alfred Hitchcock. Sc: John Michael Hayes from the story by Cornell Woolrich. M: Franz Waxman. AD: Hal Pereira, Joseph Macmillan Johnson. DP: Robert Burks. Cast: James Stewart, Grace Kelly, Thelma Ritter, Raymond Burr.

To Catch a Thief (Paramount, 1955, colour)
P: Alfred Hitchcock. Sc; John Michael Hayes from the novel by David Dodge. M: Lyn Murray. AD: Hal Pereira, Joseph Macmillan Johnson. DP: Robert Burks. Cast: Cary Grant, Grace Kelly, Jessie Royce Landis, Brigitte Auber.

The Man Who Knew Too Much (Paramount, 1956, colour)
P: Alfred Hitchcock. Sc: John Michael Hayes from a story by Charles Bennett and D. B. Wyndham Lewis. M: Bernard Herrmann. AD: Hal Pereira, Henry Bumstead. DP: Robert Burks. Cast: James Stewart, Doris Day, Bernard Miles, Brenda de Banzie.

The Wrong Man (Warner Brothers-First National, 1956, b/w)
P: Alfred Hitchcock. SC: Maxwell Anderson and Angus MacPhail. M: Bernard Herrmann. AD: Paul Sylbert. DP: Robert Burks. Cast: Henry Fonda, Vera Miles, Anthony Quayle, Harold J. Stone.

Vertigo (Paramount, 1958, colour)
P: Alfred Hitchcock. Sc: Alec Coppel and Samuel Taylor from the novel *D'entre les morts* by Pierre Boileau and Thomas Narcejac. M: Bernard Herrmann. AD: Hal Pereira, Henry Bumstead. DP: Robert Burks. Cast: James Stewart, Kim Novak, Barbara Bel Geddes. Tom Helmore.

North by Northwest (MGM, 1959, colour)
P: Alfred Hitchcock. Sc: Ernest Lehman. M: Bernard Herrmann. AD: Robert Boyle, William A. Horning, Merrill Pye. DP: Robert Burks. Cast: Cary Grant, Eva Marie Saint, James Mason, Leo G. Carroll.

Psycho (Paramount, 1960, b/w)
P: Alfred Hitchcock. Sc: Joseph Stefano from the novel by Robert Bloch. M: Bernard Herrmann. AD: Joseph Hurley, Robert Clatworthy. DP: John L. Russell. Cast: Janet Leigh, Anthony Perkins, Vera Miles, John Gavin.

The Birds (Universal, 1963, colour)
P: Alfred Hitchcock. Sc: Evan Hunter from the story by Daphne du Maurier. AD: Robert Boyle. DP: Robert Burks. Cast: Tippi Hedren, Rod

Taylor, Suzanne Pleshette, Jessica Tandy.

Marnie (Universal, 1964, colour)
P: Alfred Hitchcock. Sc: Jay Presson Allen from the novel by Winston
Graham. M: Bernard Herrmann. AD: Robert Boyle. DP: Robert Burks.
Cast: Tippi Hedren, Sean Connery, Diane Baker, Louise Herrmann Latham.

Torn Curtain (Universal, 1966, colour)
P: Alfred Hitchcock. Sc: Brian Moore. M: John Addison. AD: Hein
Heckroth, Frank Arrigo. DP: John F. Warren. Cast: Paul Newman, Julie
Andrews, Lila Kedrova, Wolfgang Kieling.

Topaz (Universal, 1969, colour)
P: Alfred Hitchcock. Sc: Samuel Taylor from the novel by Leon Uris.
AD: Henry Bumstead. DP: Jack Hildyard. Cast: Frederick Stafford, John
Forsythe, Dany Robin, John Vernon.

Frenzy (Universal, 1972, colour)
P: Alfred Hitchcock. Sc: Anthony Shaffer from the novel *Goodbye Piccadilly,
Farewell Leicester Square* by Arthur La Bern. M: Ron Goodwin. AD: Syd
Cain, Bob Laing. DP: Gil Taylor. Cast: Barry Foster, Jon Finch, Barbara
Leigh-Hunt, Alec McCowen.

Family Plot (Universal, 1976, colour)
P: Alfred Hitchcock. Sc: Ernest Lehman from the novel *The Rainbird Pattern*
by Victor Canning . M: John Williams. AD: Henry Bumstead. DP: Leonard
South. Cast: Karen Black, William Devane, Barbara Harris, Bruce Dern.

BIBLIOGRAPHY

Allen, Richard and Sam Ishii-Gonzalès (eds) (1999) *Alfred Hitchcock: Centenary Essays*. London: British Film Institute.

_____ (eds) (2004) *Hitchcock: Past and Future*. London. Routledge.

Allen, Richard (1999) 'Hitchcock, or the Pleasures of Metascepticism', in Richard Allen and Sam Ishii-Gonzalès (eds) *Alfred Hitchcock: Centenary Essays*. London: British Film Institute, 221–39.

Almendros, Nestor (1985) *A Man with a Camera*. London: Faber and Faber.

Alpi, Deborah Lazarus (1998) *Robert Siodmak: A Biography*. Jefferson, NC: Macfarland.

Auiler, Dan (1998) *Vertigo: The Making of a Hitchcock Classic*. New York: St Martin's Griffin.

_____ (2001) *Hitchcock's Notebooks*. New York: Harper Entertainment.

Austin, Guy (1999) *Claude Chabrol*. Manchester: Manchester University Press.

Barr, Charles (1999) *English Hitchcock*. Moffat: Cameron and Hollis.

_____ (2002) *Vertigo*. London: British Film Institute.

Bazin, André (1982) *The Cinema of Cruelty from Buñuel to Hitchcock*. Edited and introduced by Francois Truffaut. New York: Seaver Books.

Bellour, Raymond (2000) *The Analysis of Film*. Bloomington: Indiana University Press.

_____ (2002) 'Pourquoi Lang pourrait devenir préférable à Hitchcock', *Trafic 41*, Paris: Editions P.O.L.,163–72.

Belton, John (1980) 'Dexterity in a Void: Hitchcock's Formalist Aesthetics', *Cineaste*, 10, 3, 9–13.

Brill, Lesley (1999) 'Redemptive Comedy in the Films of Alfred Hitchcock and Preston Sturges: "Are Snakes Necessary?"', in Richard Allen and Sam Ishii-Gonzalès (eds) *Alfred Hitchcock: Centenary Essays*. London: British Film Institute, 205–20.

Chabrol, Claude (1985 (1953)) 'Serious Things', in Jim Hillier (ed.) *Cahiers du Cinéma Volume 1, the 1950s: Neo-Realism, Hollywood, the New Wave*. London: Routledge, 136–40.

Christie, Ian (2000) *A Matter of Life and Death*. London: British Film Institute.

Coates, Paul (1991) *The Gorgon's Gaze: German Cinema, Expressionism and the Image of Horror*. Cambridge: Cambridge University Press.

Conrad, Peter (2000) *The Hitchcock Murders*. London: Faber and Faber.

Damico, James (1996) 'Film Noir: A Modest Proposal', in Alain Silver and James Ursini (eds) *Film Noir Reader*. New York: Limelight Editions, 95–107.

Davis, Mike (2001) 'Bunker Hill: Hollywood's Dark Shadow', in Mark Shiel and Tony Fitzmaurice (eds) *Cinema and the City*. Oxford: Blackwell, 33–46.

Deleuze, Gilles (1986) *Cinema 1: The Movement-Image*. Translated by Hugh Tomlinson and Barbara Habberjam. London: Athlone Press.

____ (1989) *Cinema 2: The Time-Image*. Translated by Hugh Tomlinson and Robert Galeta. London: Athlone Press.

____ (2001) *Pure Immanence: Essays on a Life*. New York: Zone Books.

Davies, Norman (2000) *The Isles: A History*. London: Pan Macmillan.

DeRosa, Steven (2001) *Working with Hitchcock: The Collaboration of Alfred Hitchcock and John Michael Hayes*. London: Faber and Faber.

Douchet, Jean (1986) 'Hitch and his Audience', in Jim Hillier (ed.) *Cahiers du Cinéma Volume 2, 1960–1968*. London: Routledge, 150–8.

Drazin, Charles (1999) *In Search of the Third Man*. London: Methuen.

du Maurier, Daphne (1951) *'The Birds' in The Apple Tree*. London: Gollancz.

____ (2003) *Rebecca*. London: Virago Press.

Duncan, Paul (2003) *Alfred Hitchcock: Architect of Anxiety, 1899–1980*. Cologne: Taschen.

Dundjerovic, Aleksandar (2003) *The Cinema of Robert Lepage: The Poetics of Memory*. London: Wallflower Press.

Eisner, Lotte H. (1969) *Expressionism in German Cinema and the Influence of Max Reinhardt*. London: Thames and Hudson.

____ (1973) *Murnau*. London: Secker and Warburg.

____ (1976) *Fritz Lang*. New York: Da Capo Press.

Elsaesser, Thomas (2000) *Weimar Cinema and After: Germany's Historical Imaginary*. London: Routledge.

Finler, Joel (1992) *Hitchcock in Hollywood*. New York: Continuum.

Fishgall, Gary (1997) *Pieces of Time: The Life of James Stewart*. New York: Scribner.

Fuller, Graham (ed.) (1994) 'Kasdan on Kasdan', in *Projections 3: Filmmakers on Film-making*. London: Faber and Faber, 111–53.

Girard, René (1979) *Violence and the Sacred*. Translated by Patrick Gregory. Baltimore: Johns Hopkins University Press.

Glancy, Mark (2003) *The 39 Steps*. London: I. B. Tauris.

Godard, Jean-Luc (1986) *Godard on Godard*. Edited by Jean Narboni and Tom Milne with an introduction by Richard Roud. New York: Da Capo Press.

Gottlieb, Sidney (ed.) (1997) *Hitchcock on Hitchcock*. London: Faber and Faber.

Greene, Graham (1972) *The Pleasure Dome: Collected Film Criticism 1935–40*, edited by John Russell Taylor. London: Secker and Warburg.

_____ (1973) *A Gun for Sale*. London: Heinemann.

_____ (1990) 'The Lieutenant Died Last', in *The Last Word and Other Stories*. London: Reinhardt Books, 46–60.

_____ (1999) *Ways of Escape*. London: Vintage.

_____ (2000) *The Ministry of Fear*. London: Vintage.

Gregory, Richard (1997) *Eye and Brain: The Psychology of Seeing* (fifth edition). Oxford: Oxford University Press

Gunning, Tom (2000) *The Films of Fritz Lang: Allegories of Vision and Modernity*. London: British Film Institute.

Hillier, Jim and Peter Wollen (eds) (1996) *Howard Hawks: American Artist*. London: British Film Institute.

Highsmith, Patricia (1999) *Strangers on a Train*. London: Vintage.

Hoskins, Robert (1999) *Graham Greene: An Approach to the Novels*. New York: Garland Publishing.

Houston, Penelope (1992) *Went the Day Well?* London: British Film Institute.

Hume, David (1971) *Hume on Religion*. Selected and introduced by Richard Wollheim. London: Fontana.

_____ (2000 (1739–40)) *A Treatise of Human Nature*. Edited by David Fate Norton and Mary J. Norton. Oxford: Oxford University Press.

Hunter, Evan (1997) *Me and Hitch*. London: Faber and Faber.

Insdorf, Annette (1994) *François Truffaut* (revised and updated edition). Cambridge: Cambridge University Press.

Kaes, Anton (2000) *M*. London: British Film Institute.

Kline, T. Jefferson (2003) 'Recuperating Hitchcock's Doubles: Experiencing *Vertigo* in Garcia's *Place Vendôme*', *Studies in French Cinema*, 3, 1, 35–46.

Krohn, Bill (2000) *Hitchcock at Work*. London: Phaidon Press.

_____ (2003) 'Ambivalence (Suspicion)', in Sidney Gottlieb and Richard Allen (eds) *The Hitchcock Annual, 2002–03*. New York: New York University Press, 67–116.

Leff, Leonard J. (1987) *Hitchcock and Selznick*. New York: Weidenfeld and Nicolson.

Leitch, Thomas M. (1991) *Find the Director and Other Hitchcock Games*. Athens: University of Georgia Press.

Lightning, Robert K. (1999) 'A Domestic Trilogy', *Cineaction*, 50, 32–42.

Lippe, Richard (1999) 'Kim Novak: Vertigo, Performance and Image', *Cineaction*, 50, 46–52.

Longmate, Norman (2002) *How We Lived Then: A History of Everyday Life during the Second World War*. London: Pimlico.

Lynch, David (1997) *Lynch on Lynch*. Edited by Chris Rodley. London: Faber and Faber.

MacCabe, Colin (2003) *Godard: A Portrait of the Artist at Seventy*. London: Bloomsbury.

Magny, Joël (1987) *Claude Chabrol*. Paris: Cahiers du Cinéma.

Marie, Michel (2003) *The French New Wave: An Artistic School*. Translated by Richard Neupert. Oxford: Blackwell

Marker, Chris (1995) 'A free replay (notes on *Vertigo*)', in John Boorman and Walter Donahue (eds) *Projections: Four and a Half*. London: Faber and Faber, 123–30.

McCann, Graham (1997) *Cary Grant: A Class Apart*. London: Fourth Estate.

McGilligan, Patrick (1997) *Fritz Lang: The Nature of the Beast*. London: Faber and Faber.

_____ (2003) *Alfred Hitchcock: A Life in Darkness and Light*. Chichester: John Wiley.

Meyers, Jeffrey (1990) *Graham Greene: A Revaluation*. London: Macmillan.

Modleski, Tania (1988) *The Women Who Knew Too Much: Hitchcock and Feminist Film Theory*. London: Methuen.

Morgan, Michael (2003) *The Space Between Our Ears: How the Brain Represents Visual Space*. London: Weidenfeld & Nicholson.

Morris, Christopher (2000) '"The Birds" and *The Birds*', *Literature Film Quarterly*, 2, 250–8.

Mulvey, Laura (1996) *Fetishism and Curiosity*. London: British Film Institute.

_____ (2000) 'Death Drives: Hitchcock's *Psycho*', *Film Studies*, 2, Spring, 5–14.

Naremore, James (1988) *Acting in the Cinema*. Berkeley: University of California Press.

_____ (1998) *More Than Night: Film Noir in its Contexts*. Berkeley: University of California Press.

_____ (1999) 'Hitchcock at the Margins of Noir', in Richard Allen and Sam Ishii-Gonzalès (eds) *Alfred Hitchcock: Centenary Essays*. London: British Film Institute, 263–78.

Ness, Richard R. (2003) 'Hitchcock, Bergman and the Divided Self', in Sidney Gottlieb and Richard Allen (eds) *The Hitchcock Annual, 2002–3*. New York: New York University, 181–203.

Nochinson, Linda P. (1997) *The Passion of David Lynch*. Austin: University of Texas Press.

Noel, Justine (1994) 'Space, Time and the Sublime in Hume's *Treatise*', *British Journal of Aesthetics*, 34, 3, 218–25.

Orr, John (1998) *Contemporary Cinema*. Edinburgh: Edinburgh University Press.

Paglia, Camille (1998) *The Birds*. London: British Film Institute.

Parkinson, Norman (ed.) (1993) *Mornings in the Dark: The Graham Greene*

Film Reader. Manchester: Carcanet Press.

Perkins, V. F. (1972) *Film as Film: Understanding and Judging Movies.* Harmondsworth: Penguin.

Pomerance, M. (2004) *An Eye for Hitchcock.* New Brunswick, NJ: Rutgers University Press.

Rohmer, Eric (1986) 'The Old and the New' (interview with Jean-Claude Biette, Jacques Bontemps and Jean-Louis Comolli), in Jim Hillier (ed.) *Cahiers du Cinéma, Volume 2, 1960–1968.* London: Routledge, 84–95.

_____ (1989) *The Taste for Beauty.* Translated by Carol Volk. Cambridge: Cambridge University Press.

Rohmer, Eric and Claude Chabrol (1979 (1957)) *Hitchcock: The First Forty-Four Films.* Translated by Stanley Hochman. New York: Frederick Ungar Publishing.

Rothman, William (1982) *Hitchcock – The Murderous Gaze.* Cambridge, MA: Harvard University Press.

Rousseau, Jean-Jacques (1987) *La Nouvelle Héloïse.* Translated by Judith McDowell. University Park, PA: Pennsylvania State University Press.

Rivette, Jacques (1985) 'The Hand', in Jim Hillier (ed.) *Cahiers du Cinéma Volume 1: The 1950s: Neo-Realism, Hollywood, the New Wave.* London: Routledge, 140–5.

Rodley, Chris (ed.) (1997) *Lynch on Lynch.* London: Faber and Faber.

Ryall, Tom (1986) *Alfred Hitchcock and the British Cinema.* London: Croom Helm.

Sallitt, Daniel (1980) 'Point of View and "Intrarealism" in Hitchcock', *Wide Angle,* 4, 1, 39–43.

Scorsese, Martin (1997) 'A Passion for Film', in John Boorman and Walter Donahue (eds) *Projections 7.* London: Faber and Faber, 93–103.

Shelden, Michael (1994) *Graham Greene: The Man Within.* London: Heinemann.

Sherry, Norman (1994) *The Life of Graham Greene (Volume 2: 1939–55).* London: Jonathan Cape.

Smith, Murray (1995) *Engaging Characters: Fiction, Emotion and Cinema.* Oxford: Clarendon Press.

Smith, Susan (1999) 'The Spatial World of Hitchcock's Films: the point-of-view shot, the camera and "intrarealism"', *Cineaction,* 50, 2–15.

_____ (2000) *Hitchcock: Suspense, Humour and Tone.* London: British Film Institute.

Spicer, Andrew (2002) *Film Noir.* Harlow: Pearson.

Spoto, Donald (1983) *The Dark Side of Genius: The Life of Alfred Hitchcock.* London: Plexus.

_____ (1997) *Notorious: The Life of Ingrid Bergman.* London: HarperCollins.

Sterritt, David (1993) *The Films of Alfred Hitchcock.* Cambridge: Cambridge

University Press.

Thomas, Deborah (1996) 'Hitchcock's *I Confess* as Enigmatic Text', *Cineaction*, 40, 32–7.

Towne, Robert (1996) 'On Writing', in John Boorman and Walter Donahue (eds) *Projections 6*. London: Faber and Faber, 109–23.

Truffaut, François (1986a) 'Evolution of the New Wave', in Jim Hillier (ed.) *Cahiers du Cinéma Volume 2 1960–1968*. London: Routledge, 106–13.

_____ (1986b) *Hitchcock by Truffaut* (revised edition). London: Paladin.

_____ (1994) *The Films in My Life*. Translated by Leonard Mayhew. New York: Da Capo Press.

Weis, Elizabeth (1985) 'The Evolution of Hitchcock's Aural Style and Sound in *The Birds*', in Elizabeth Weis and John Belton (eds) *Film Sound: Theory and Practice*. New York: Columbia University Press, 298–312.

Williams, Tony (1999) '*Vertigo*: Authorship as Transformation', *Cineaction*, 50, 56–60.

Wilson, George (1986) *Narration in Light*. Baltimore: Johns Hopkins University Press.

Wollen, Peter (1982) *Readings and Writings: Semiotic Counter-Strategies*. London: NLB.

_____ (1999) '*Rope*: Three Hypotheses', in Richard Allen and Sam Ishii-Gonzalès (eds) *Alfred Hitchcock: Centenary Essays*. London: British Film Institute, 73–86.

_____ (2002) *Paris, Hollywood: Writings on Film*. London: Verso.

Wood, Robin (1989) *Hitchcock's Films Revisited*. London: Faber and Faber.

Žižek, Slavoj (ed.) (1992) *Everything You Always Wanted to Know about Lacan (But Were Afraid to Ask Hitchcock)*. London: Verso.

INDEX

Names

Adorno, Theodor 162
Ainslie, Sam 1
Akerman, Chantal 136, 185
Allen, Jay Presson 38
Amenábar, Alejandro 174
Anderson, Judith 84–6, 108
Anderson, Kevin 174
Anderson, Maxwell 170
Andersson, Harriet 19
Antonioni, Michelangelo 9, 18–21, 50, 105
Arquette, Patricia 168, 17
Auber, Brigitte 30
Audran, Stéphane 140–6

Bacall, Lauren 94, 158
Baker, Diane 16
Balcon, Michael 61
Balsam, Martin 55
Bankhead, Tallulah 20
Barrault, Marie-Christine 147, 149
Barrie, J. M. 9
Basinger, Kim 3
Baxter, Anne 15, 127, 172, 176–84
Bazin, André 57–9, 130–1,
Béart, Emmanuelle 142
Bel Geddes, Barbara 44
Belton, John 57–9
Bellour, Raymond 63
Bennett, Charles 64, 93
Bergman, Ingmar 3, 10, 18–20, 106
Bergman, Ingrid 2, 5, 14, 32, 37, 42, 46, 62, 98–102, 109–16, 122–3, 126, 138, 146, 168
Bergson, Henri 134
Bernstein, Sidney 116
Black, Karen 9, 35
Blake, Robert 168–9
Bluteau, Lothaire 177

Boehm, Carl 67
Bogart, Humphrey 158, 162
Boileau, Pierre 170
Bonitzer, Pascal 130
Boorman, John 174
Bouquet, Michel 141
Boulting, John 94, 97
Boulting, Roy 94
Boyle, Robert 10, 22, 62
Bradbury, Ray 138
Brando, Marlon 48
Brialy, Jean-Claude 147
Bridges, Jeff 3, 5
Brisseau, Jean-Claude 130
Brisson, Carl 15
Brooks, Louise 74
Buchan, John 8, 65, 80–1, 91–6
Buckley, Betty 4
Buñuel, Luis 7, 96
Burgess, Guy 103
Burks, Robert 10
Burr, Raymond 100, 120

Cain, James M. 153, 156
Caine, Michael 35, 69
Campbell, Steven 1
Camus, Albert 148
Canning, Victor 88
Capra, Frank 66
Carné, Marcel 106, 158
Carpenter, John 2
Carroll, Leo. G. 36, 100–2
Carroll, Madeleine 42, 66
Cartwright, Veronica 18
Cassavetes, John 10
Cassel, Jean-Pierre 143
Cavalcanti, Alberto 7, 95
Chabrol, Claude 2, 7, 9, 32, 38–9, 41, 43–4, 130–4, 136–46

Film titles